D1738208

INTERNATIONAL CRISIS AND
DOMESTIC POLITICS

International Crisis and Domestic Politics

Major Political Conflicts in the 1980s

Edited by

James W. Lamare

New York
Westport, Connecticut
London

Copyright Acknowledgments

The author and publisher are grateful for permission to reprint excerpts from the following:

"The Afghan Conflict and Soviet Domestic Politics," by T. H. Rigby, is from Amin Saikal and William Maley, eds., *The Soviet Withdrawal from Afghanistan* (Cambridge: Cambridge University Press, 1989). Reprinted by permission from Cambridge University Press.

"Jews and Arabs in Israel: Everybody Hates Somebody, Sometime," by Michal Shamir and John L. Sullivan, is from the *Journal of Conflict Resolution*, Vol. 29, No. 2 (June 1985), pp. 283–305. Reprinted by permission from Sage Publications, Inc.

Library of Congress Cataloging-in-Publication Data

International crisis and domestic politics : major political conflicts
  in the 1980s / edited by James W. Lamare.
     p. cm.
  Includes bibliographical references and index.
  ISBN 0–275–93304–0 (alk. paper)
  1. International relations. 2. Politics and war. 3. Internal
security. 4. Public opinion.   I. Lamare, James.
JX1391.I632   1991
327'.09'048—dc20   90–7803

British Library Cataloguing in Publication Data is available.

Library of Congress Catalog Card Number: 90–7803
ISBN: 0–275–93304–0

First published in 1991

Praeger Publishers, One Madison Avenue, New York, NY 10010
An imprint of Greenwood Publishing Group, Inc.

Printed in the United States of America

The paper used in this book complies with the
Permanent Paper Standard issued by the National
Information Standards Organization (Z39.48–1984).

10 9 8 7 6 5 4 3 2 1

Contents

Tables and Figures

TABLES

FIGURES

INTERNATIONAL CRISIS AND DOMESTIC POLITICS

1

Introduction

James W. Lamare

The chapters in this volume explore the impact of international crisis on domestic politics. When countries become politically entangled with each other, it is quite likely—although not inevitable—that the drama that unfolds upon the international stage will have some effect upon the internal politics of at least one of the disputing parties.

Reactions to external threat emanating from such conflicts have been indirectly explored by many scholars from diverse academic backgrounds, including anthropology, sociology, political science, and psychology (see, in review, Stein 1976). There is, for instance, a substantial body of evidence gathered from studies conducted in laboratory settings under experimental conditions showing that members of groups coalesce when they are under external threats to their security and well-being. Generalizing this consolidation effect to the real world of politics seems theoretically sensible, but has, nonetheless, proven empirically difficult (North 1962).

Many thorny methodological problems are involved in trying to track accurately domestic responses to threatening external stimuli. Collecting information in the right time sequence in order to gauge the impact of the crisis is sometimes more the result of fortuity than of planned research, especially given the unpredictability of the occurrence of international incidents. Analyzing the particular domestic effect of international conflict as part of a wider configuration of forces stemming from both international and domestic sources that might influence internal politics is often beyond the capabilities of even the most dedicated (and financially well-endowed) researcher.

Moreover, measuring the precise impact that an exogenous international encounter has upon the endogenous political processes varies according to several factors, the most important of which center around the details of the conflict itself (e.g., its duration, its intensity, its resolution, its casualty toll, and so forth) and the type of political system existing in countries engaged in the conflict (e.g., how responsive the system is to democratic influences).

In a society with a pluralistic political system, events surrounding international conflict are usually fully communicated to the public through the media. Widespread coverage of the controversy sets in motion a scenario that features the interplay of a large number of political actors, including political leaders, political parties and interest groups, and the public. Almost inevitably, a well-publicized international crisis guarantees—usually after the event—some systematic polling of mass opinion, thus allowing both elites and analysts to measure public reactions to the conflict.

Since external conflict—at least at the initial stage—normally produces widespread domestic enthusiasm in democratic societies, elites risk little in mobilizing mass sentiment and, indeed, might be tempted to become embroiled in international disputes in order to shore up their support base on the home front. There can, however, be a domestic downside to international conflict. Unsuccessful and protracted international endeavors can undermine elite support. Since a sense of solidarity occurs in each country participant to the conflict, the animosity created by the dispute is often mutual and rigid, making deescalation of the controversy more difficult.

More centralized states are not immune to the effects of international conflict and pressure. Significant military losses on the international battlefield have led to the demise of autocratic regimes. While, for instance, Margaret Thatcher and her government (see Chapter 3) basked in Britain's military victory in the Falklands, this war precipitated the downfall of the military authorities in Argentina who had initiated the crisis in the first place (see Levy and Vakili 1989).

Even the Soviet Union, where the regime has deliberately attempted to remain in full control of events and outcomes, has had its history shaped by external pressures beyond the management of its government. From the origins of the revolution in 1917 to the withdrawal of troops from Afghanistan (see Chapter 7), the Soviet Union has had to respond to international conflict and pressure. In short, as Jack Snyder notes, "overall the record suggests that the international environment . . . can have a significant impact on both the long-run development of Soviet political institutions and the short-run fate of Soviet political coalitions" (Snyder 1989: 211).

In this volume the effect of international crisis on domestic politics is examined from various angles. It goes without saying that not all international crises are covered in this exercise. Furthermore, the details of each international conflict covered and its domestic consequences are restricted by available information and by the unique perspectives of the author(s) of each article. Finally, pressure coming from an international crisis is but one of many factors that might influence domestic politics. Most assuredly, internal forces mix with external influences in structuring the domestic political scene. Indeed, it is arguable that, on balance, within-system variables are normally more important than external ones in influencing domestic political arrangements and outcomes. Nonetheless, as the chapters in this volume indicate, international conflicts frequently do play an important role in domestic politics.

The events focused upon herein cover many of the major conflicts that gripped relations between nations during the 1980s. Moreover, many of the countries involved in these disputes are among the leading powers in the world. Each article presents a variant of the type of impact that international crisis does (or does not) have on domestic politics.

Chapter 2 examines the effect of military initiatives taken by President Reagan in Grenada and Libya on the political orientations of the American public. These interventionist strikes produced a classic "rally around the flag" response on the part of the American people. President Reagan benefited from the public's approving reaction. There is some sign that systemic attitudes also improved owing to these largely successful military operations. Americans over the course of the Reagan years came to express more pride in their nation, although their sense of political alienation and their loss of interpersonal trust were unabated during the Reagan administration.

Chapter 3 explores the British response to the Falklands War. The emergence of a positive public reaction to this crisis was delayed until hostilities were well underway—a finding that presents a different twist to the "rally around the flag" syndrome. Once favorable opinion crystallized, it improved the personal popularity of Prime Minister Thatcher and the public standing of the Conservative party, probably enhancing the electoral chances of both in the 1983 British general election.

The focus of Chapter 4 is New Zealand, a country whose antinuclear policy crossed swords with the United States. The controversy that ensued between these nations resulted in a massive consolidation of public opinion behind the New Zealand government's stand. Once formed, public sentiment constrained the government's options in dealing with the conflict. The public rally showed signs of disintegration once the events that initially generated it became history. Recent evidence, however, suggests that the antinuclear opinion created by the conflict has become a mainstay of the New Zealand political culture, even though the crisis itself has, by and large, dissipated.

Chapter 5 shifts to the Middle East, a setting in which the protracted conflict between Israel and its neighbors has had a profound effect upon the attitudes that Jews and Israeli Arabs have toward each other. As noted by Sullivan, "the Arab-Israeli conflict is the major issue in Israeli domestic politics. . . . Israel is characterized by a constant, smoldering state of war, which erupts into major wars from time to time. This conflict is part of the Israeli situation and mentality, and it is reflected in all spheres of life" (Sullivan et al. 1985: 60). The inability to resolve the crisis endangers the democratic fabric of the state of Israel since it engenders widespread distrust and intolerance among groups sharing the same political boundaries.

In Northern Ireland, as documented in Chapter 6, a conflict with its roots firmly planted in the international field has so divided groups sharing the same domestic space that rigid intergroup hostility inhibits resolution. The inability of the British to solve this division in 1973 resulted in the continuation of this impasse throughout the 1980s. Mobilization, countermobilization, and demobilization of different segments of the Northern Ireland public by various elites, including ones from outside the country, have characterized the turmoil in Northern Ireland for many years. Chapter 6 views the rich details of this conflict through the prism of a comprehensive model of the mobilization/demobilization process. It also indicates how rigid, intense, and protracted domestic conflict can have an impact on the international community.

On February 15, 1989, General Boris Gromov, according to Soviet sources, was the last Russian soldier to leave Afghanistan after some nine years of war. The Soviet invasion of (and withdrawal from) Afghanistan, as discussed in Chapter 7, had some influence on the domestic Soviet political scene. Recent reports (*Soviet News* 1990) place the burden of the decision to send troops into Afghanistan in the hands of four high-ranking Soviet officials: Leonid Brezhnev and his defense minister, his chairman of the KGB, and his foreign minister. For years, other political institutions and apparatuses of the state, including the media, played a role supportive of the Soviet entry into Afghanistan. Yet, a negative reaction, in particular among Soviet veterans of the war and people living in Muslim Soviet republics, emerged as the conflict dragged on. In late 1989, some ten years after the invasion, Alexander Dzasokhov, the head of the parliamentary foreign affairs committee, wrote in the name of the Soviet Congress that "the decision to send troops to Afghanistan deserves moral and political condemnation" (*Soviet News* 1990: 13).

Finally, Chapter 8 presents a case study in which external pressure appears to have had little bearing upon domestic politics. Economic sanctions invoked by the European Community to dismantle apartheid in South Africa have landed wide of their mark. However, the principal reason for this misfire may very well lie in the external action itself, one that may have been designed in the first place not to reach its self-proclaimed aim.

REFERENCES

Levy, Jack, and Lily Vakili. "External Scapegoating by Authoritarian Regimes: Argentina in the Falklands/Malvinas Case." Paper presented at the Annual

Meeting of the American Political Science Association, Atlanta, Georgia, 1989.

North, Robert C. "International Conflict and Integration: Problems of Research." In M. Sherif, ed., *Intergroup Group Relations and Leadership*. New York: Wiley, 1962.

Snyder, Jack. "International Leverage on Soviet Domestic Change." *World Politics* 62 (1989): 1–30.

Soviet News. February 2, 1990.

Stein, Arthur A. "Conflict and Cohesion." *Journal of Conflict Resolution* 20 (1976): 143–172.

Sullivan, John L., Michal Shamir, Patrick Walsh, and Nigel Roberts. *Political Tolerance in Context: Support for Unpopular Minorities in Israel, New Zealand, and the United States*. Boulder, Colo.: Westview Press, 1985.

2

International Intervention and Public Support: America during the Reagan Years

James W. Lamare

> The way I see it, there were two great triumphs, two things that I'm proudest of. One is the economic recovery. . . . The other is the recovery of our morale: America is respected again in the world, and looked to for leadership. . . . The fact is, from Grenada to the Washington and Moscow Summits, . . . we've made a difference.
>
> Ronald Reagan, 1989

This chapter explores the impact of President Ronald Reagan's interventionist foreign policy on political orientations. More specifically, it examines the effect of the decisions to invade Grenada and to attack Libya on public support for the president and the political system. Did these actions indeed, as suggested in President Reagan's farewell address, improve the "morale" of the American people?

BEFORE PRESIDENT REAGAN

Presidential action impacts upon Americans at two levels. First, it affects the opinion that the public holds of the president. Second, it can have a bearing upon feelings, attitudes, and values that are deeply embedded in the American political culture. On each of these counts, Americans were signaling a widespread loss of support before Ronald Reagan began to exert U.S. military might abroad.

Presidential Popularity

Available evidence suggests that direct U.S. military intervention in other countries generally results in a significant boost in the popular support of U.S. presidents (Bowen 1989; Brody 1984; Kernell 1978; Lee 1977; Mueller 1973). The public usually rallies around the president regardless of the uncertainty, the riskiness, or the success or failure of his decision to intervene. In times of international crisis, public reaction ordinarily tends more toward unction than toward rational assessment, at least for a while.[1]

The Japanese bombing of Pearl Harbor on December 7, 1941, and the United States' subsequent entry into World War II precipitated a 12 percent increase in popularity for President Roosevelt, from 72 percent to 84 percent—the highest rating received by the president during his four terms. President Truman's decision to invade Korea in 1950 and President Eisenhower's landing of troops in Lebanon eight years later resulted in an approximately 7 percent gain in public regard in each case. After the Cuban missile crisis in 1963 President Kennedy's popularity climbed 12 percent, from a 61 percent to a 73 percent approval rating. The initial bombing of Hanoi ordered by President Johnson in 1966 saw an 8 percent rise in his popularity; his earlier decision to send marines into Santo Domingo occasioned a 6 percent jump. President Ford's direct attempt to free the container ship *Mayaguez* from Cambodian control produced an 11 percent increase in his approval score. Finally, the seizure of the American embassy in Teheran in late 1979 was followed by a 20 percent surge in popular support for President Jimmy Carter. A small (4 percent) increase in public regard occurred after his unsuccessful attempt in 1980 to rescue the hostages captured by the Iranians.

Even interventionist decisions that are uniformly recognized after the fact as unwise have been fully endorsed by large segments of the public, at least during their initial stage of implementation. After the Bay of Pigs fiasco in 1961, for example, President Kennedy's popular standing improved from 78 to 83 percent—the peak rating received by Kennedy during his administration.

Presidents seem well aware of the importance of public support for their policy initiatives. As noted by Roll and Cantril, "popularity ratings are a barometer of the extent to which the public perceives the President as taking decisive action with respect to a major problem—particularly on the international scene" (Roll and Cantril 1972: 128). A surfeit of popularity can lead to presidents' taking uncompromising stands in policy discussions with other political actors, such as legislators or international leaders (Kernell 1986).

Granted, a widely popular president is not always successful in policy debates. Moreover, unpopular presidents have been effective leaders and decision makers (Ceaser 1988). Nonetheless, a slip in popular ratings (even a minor one) "can cause the greatest consternation in the White House and send staffers searching for an accounting of the decline" (Roll and Cantril 1972: 127).

A protracted, unresolved international crisis can lead to an undermining of public support. Similarly, a floundering, blundering, or ultimately unsuccessful international conflict can, over time, backfire with a vengeance on the president's standing with the public. Virtually every modern-day president who initially benefited in the popularity polls from a dramatic move on the international front has seen his approval rating quickly dissipate—unless the action, as was the case in the Cuban missile crisis, was concluded swiftly, decisively, and successfully (Gallup Poll 1980b).

President Roosevelt's surge in public approbation upon the U.S. entry into World War II steadily eroded as hostilities led to injuries and fatalities. President Truman's gain in approval after his decision to invade Korea was only a momentary pause in his inexorable fall in popularity. Similarly, the increase in public regard prompted by President Eisenhower's ordering of the marines into Lebanon was short-lived. As the embarrassment of the Bay of Pigs became clearer, public feeling toward President Kennedy forthwith declined. (Conversely, it took nearly six months for the leap in favorable ratings experienced by President Kennedy's successful and dramatic end to the Cuban missile crisis to disappear.) Lyndon Johnson's ascent in the opinion polls after the charge into Santo Domingo and the escalation of the Vietnam War through the first bombing attack on Hanoi lasted only about a month. The rise in support for President Carter after the initial takeover of the U.S. embassy in Iran soon plummeted as efforts to gain the release of the prisoners failed. Carter's modest rise in public acclamation after the attempt to free the hostages lasted only briefly. Within sixty days of this botched effort, his popularity was halved, from 43 percent to 21 percent—"the lowest recorded for any President since the Gallup Poll initiated these measurements in 1938" (Gallup Poll 1980a).

This loss of support occurs as the public absorbs information reflecting the new reality that comes into existence in the aftermath of the president's decision to take action (Shapiro and Page 1988). For example, news reports on the mounting casualty rates in Korea and Vietnam contributed to a weakening of popular support for several presidents (Mueller 1973). The public's perception of incompetence, as with President Carter's handling of the hostage crisis, undermines the initial enthusiasm that ordinarily accompanies an interventionist strike. With public approval on the wane, a quiet sense of despair—often edged with anger—replaces the feeling of pride that surrounded the original act of direct attack.

Public attitudes toward presidential performance in foreign policy frequently have behavioral consequences. Aldrich, Sullivan, and Borgida, for example, found that in both the 1980 and 1984 presidential elections foreign and international issues "were at least as important as domestic issues in their impact on voting behavior" (Aldrich et al. 1989: 132) and that "the joint impact of [foreign and domestic] issues is in each case almost as strong as that of either party identification or candidate evaluations" (Aldrich, et al. 1989: 133).

In the 1980 election, approximately 15 percent of the voters thought that the Iranian hostage crisis was the foremost problem facing the nation; only inflation was mentioned by more people. On balance, President Carter lost support because of his inability to resolve this issue (Abramson, Aldrich, and Rohde 1983). This was particularly the case for those voters, estimated to be about 10 percent of the electorate, who delayed making their vote decision until election day. According to the Gallup Poll, "attitudes toward foreign policy, and specifically Carter's handling of the hostage problem, were an especially important reason why last-minute voters pulled the lever for Reagan" (Gallup Poll 1980c). Hence presidents do not "waltz before a blind audience," as previous scholarship (reviewed in Aldrich, Sullivan, and Borgida 1989) has suggested, when taking highly visible action along the international front.

Cultural Precepts

Interventionist initiatives also structure public sentiment at a deeper, attitudinal level. A successful conclusion to such an action can enhance public confidence not only in the performance of specific political leaders but also in the political system itself. Swift, decisive resolution of an international incident often provides the public with a prime opportunity to celebrate openly and without reserve, rekindling in the process their sense of patriotism and collective ties.

Psychologists, anthropologists, sociologists, and political scientists (reviewed in Stein 1976) resound in a chorus of agreement that conflict involving external sources (e.g., international actors) ordinarily generates solidarity among members of a group (e.g., a nation). As Coser, echoing a point made by Sumner (1906) a half century before, observes: "It seems to be generally accepted . . . that the distinction between 'ourselves, the we-group, or in-group, and everybody else, or the others-group, out groups,' is established in and through conflict" (Coser 1956). A series of such conflicts probably heightens a sense of legitimacy, thus providing officeholders (e.g., presidents) a deep well of public support that may offset the impact of negative factors, such as their personal transgressions or their failures in other policy areas.

To be sure, arousal of a collective national identity during periods of international crisis is possible only if citizens are already favorably disposed toward their country. Without such binding tendencies, conflict might actually lead to disintegration within the public. Variations among the populations of different countries in reaction to World War II illustrate this point.

In France, the war exacerbated existing divisions in the French population, while in Britain (Coser 1956: 95) and the United States (Key 1961) it drew people together, fusing prior rifts in opinion among members of distinct social and political groups. A solid sense of national commitment was already in place among the British and the Americans before the outbreak of hostilities; in France such dispositional ties were missing.

In the United States children at an early age exhibit a very positive outlook toward their country, its political authority structure, and its governing officials (Hess and Torney 1967; Easton and Dennis 1969). The key player in the developmental sequence that results in this sanguine view has been the president. Young American children—at least before the political turmoil of the 1960s and 1970s—by and large are very favorably disposed toward the president (see Jaros, Hirsch, and Fleron 1968 for an exception to the rule). He is perceived by them as benevolent, effective, and trustworthy. These images generalize to the overall governing process, thus leading to an idealized view of government and political authority.

Although this personal, naive, and totally uncritical perspective diminishes as Americans grow older, it never entirely disappears. Rather, it forms a solid bedrock of latent, diffuse psychological support for the American political system as children move through the life cycle. This positivism accounts for a great deal of the persistence and stability of the U.S. system (Easton and Dennis 1969). The knee-jerk favorable public response elicited by a dramatic presidential initiative overseas probably signals a tapping of this deep reservoir of popular legitimacy.

From the mid–1960s throughout the 1970s, public disenchantment with politics steadily increased. A great deal of this disillusionment developed as a reaction to failed policy performance on the part of the government (Dawson 1973; Harris 1973), including—but not limited to—foreign policy initiatives. The government's handling of significant events—Vietnam, riots, demonstrations and protests, Watergate, corruption, the energy crisis, inflation, the Soviet invasion of Afghanistan, and Americans being held hostage in Iran, to name some of the most newsworthy—gave rise to widespread public dissatisfaction with key components of the political system. The perceived inability of officeholders to solve the problems of the day eroded public confidence in political institutions (Lipset and Schneider 1983) and the trustworthiness of the government (Miller 1974; Gilmour and Lamb 1975).

For more than two decades, the Harris Survey has been monitoring the alienation scores of Americans. Alienation on the Harris index is a multidimensional attitude comprising five questions measuring feelings about the concentration of wealth, power relations, efficacy, and anomie. As Figure 2.1 illustrates, in 1966 only 29 percent of the American public placed high

Figure 2.1
Alienation in America, 1966–88

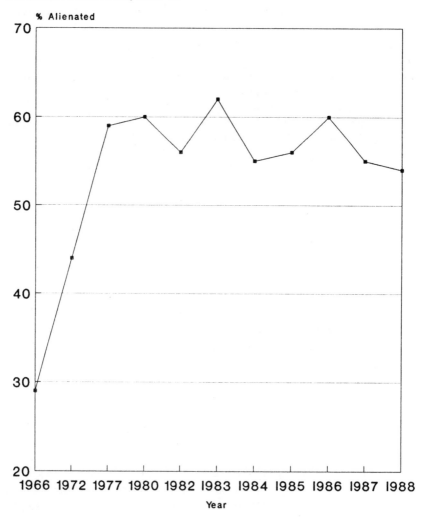

Source: Adapted from the Harris Survey.

on the alienation index. Over the course of the tumultuous events of the next ten years expressions of alienation grew dramatically, reaching a high of 62 percent in August 1976 "in the aftermath of the Watergate episode" (Harris 1983). After a slight drop, alienation climbed back to 62 percent in May 1980 as the Carter administration bumbled in its attempt to free the Americans held prisoner in Iran. During this period the greatest proportional rise in alienation occurred on items measuring efficacy, including the question asking whether "the people running the country don't really care what happens to you."

Americans throughout this era of turmoil and failed policy also began to lose pride in their nation. Since 1979 the Gallup organization has routinely asked members of the public whether, in general, they are "satisfied or dissatisfied with the way things are going in the U.S. at this time." The inaugural year of probing this line of inquiry, as indicated in Figure 2.2, found, on average, only 19 percent of Americans expressing satisfaction with their country. Uneasiness reached its apogee in August 1979 when 84 percent of the public had a negative outlook toward the country and only 12 percent felt any sense of national pride. In January 1981, on the eve of Ronald Reagan's occupancy of the White House, 78 percent of the public were still distraught about conditions in the country.

Children were not immune from this groundswell of public disquietude about political matters. By the late 1960s, young children were becoming critical about the government (Sigel and Brookes 1974). Positive feelings toward authority eroded as some children came to view presidential performance, especially President Johnson's handling of the Vietnam War, in a negative light. The Watergate affair further undermined children's confidence in America's political leaders and the operation of its political system (Rodgers and Lewis 1975; Arterton 1975). The election of Jimmy Carter to the presidency did little to contain this growing political disillusionment among youngsters. The limited socialization data collected during this period (Maddox and Handberg 1979) indicate that young people, even a sample living in the South, had negative feelings about the president.

The United States had shifted a great distance from the halcyon days during which political scientists (such as Almond and Verba 1965) could write confidently of the country's enviable political culture, composed of a strong subjective sense of national identity balanced by a well-developed set of participatory attitudes and behavioral tendencies. The historical period that ushered in this "civic culture" was inextricably tied to the wealth, social opportunity structure, and good spirits that were widely shared among virtually all segments of society after the United States' crowning achievement in bringing World War II to an end and the lofty world position the country held at that moment of history (Lane 1965).

By 1980, the foundation of the civic culture was showing visible signs of stress. The perceived inability of political leaders to formulate and implement strategies and policies capable of coping with the major problems of the 1960s and 1970s—many of which were in the area of foreign affairs— took its toll on popular support for the political system. Stated more bluntly, the lack of forthright and decisive leadership from the White House was undermining popular support, for, as succinctly noted by Greenstein (1982: 4), "the modern president so dominates public attention that he virtually personifies government."

Figure 2.2
Satisfaction with the State of the Nation, 1979–88

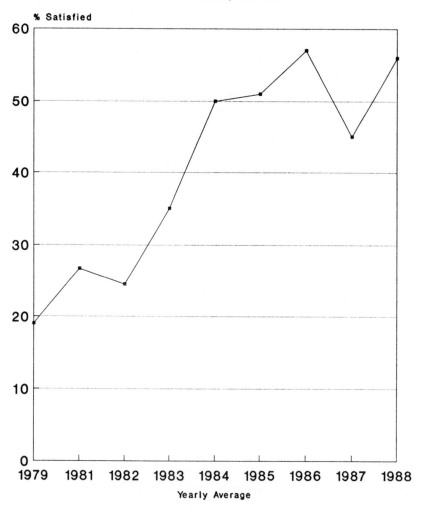

Source: Adapted from the Gallup Poll.

PRESIDENT RONALD REAGAN

President Reagan thus entered the White House at an unprecedented time—at least in modern history—of public disillusionment.[2] The task of assuaging this gloom seemed daunting. The most likely scenario facing President Reagan was ultimate failure. Since 1963, the public's reaction to presidents had become rather predictable.

Upon election, each president would be granted a honeymoon period, a time during which his actions were almost uniformly applauded by an approving public. Fairly quickly, however, the bloom would come off the rose and the president would fall from public favor. During this decline, spurts of growth in public standing might be recorded, but usually they were episodic and short-lived. The glacial flow toward widespread public disapproval would be stemmed only near the end of the presidential term, after the president either had declined to seek reelection or had suffered electoral defeat. The era of one-term presidents seemed indelibly etched upon the American political landscape.

In his first two years in office, Ronald Reagan's presidency appeared to be sinking under the weight of the "failed presidency" syndrome that had already victimized his immediate predecessors (Ceaser 1988). Although he started his first term in office with a lower rate of approval than most contemporary presidents, Reagan soon expanded his popular base of support, reaching a pinnacle of 68 percent public approval of his performance by May 1981. Then the slide began. Slowly but steadily, Reagan's evaluations slipped. The pace quickened throughout 1982, as the public perceived that economic recovery, as promised by the president, appeared unobtainable. With growth in the rate of unemployment seemingly inescapable, public hopes in the president's plan to jump-start the economy waned. By late January 1983, President Reagan registered a public approval rating of only 35 percent. The predicted rot had set in. Another failed presidency seemed in the offing.

However, the Reagan presidency escaped the inevitable (Ostrom and Simon 1989). Rather than a slide, President Reagan's ride with the public resembled a roller coaster. His ups and downs have been grouped by Ceaser (1988) into six distinct movements. The initial rise and fall in Reagan's popularity were followed by periods of restored confidence (summer 1983 to November 1984), anointment (December 1984 to October 1986), debacle (December 1986 to fall 1987), and, in the final months of his presidency, equilibrium—not dismal failure.

The oscillations in President Reagan's approval ratings reflected the public's reaction to his foreign and domestic policy successes and failures, as well as to his style of leadership. Along the foreign policy front Reagan presented the public with ample opportunity to judge his leadership and decision-making capabilities. Lebanon, Libya, and Grenada became bloody battlegrounds delineated by the presence of U.S. military personnel. Nicaragua faced a more oblique U.S. military involvement. A continuous war of hostile words and an enormous military build-up marked the Reagan approach to the Soviet Union, at least in its early stages.

The remainder of this chapter mainly examines the public's response to direct military intervention during the Reagan presidency. President Reagan specifically ordered a military attack in two countries: Grenada and Libya.[3]

To what extent did these acts of militarism enhance the public's feelings about the president? Did they affect more diffuse and fundamental orientations about the American political system?

Grenada and Public Opinion

Grenada, the smallest country in the Western Hemisphere, had by the early 1980s come under the control of a left-leaning government. In its search for overseas investment funds, the government had accepted a joint Soviet and Cuban offer to build an airport runway. Several thousand Cubans came into the country as workers and soldiers. By encouraging these developments, Grenada's regime blatantly ran afoul of the strong anticommunist strain of President Reagan's political philosophy.

In 1983, the Reagan administration clearly signaled its disquietude about Grenada. When internal political conflict and tension mounted in that country, it also proclaimed deep concern about the 2,000 or so Americans in Grenada, most of whom were students attending the St. George University of Medicine. After Prime Minister Maurice Bishop was killed during a successful military-led coup, the administration made very loud noises about a possible invasion of Grenada in order to protect and evacuate American citizens and to stem the tide of Cuban-backed communism. These threats were carried out on October 26, 1983, when President Reagan ordered a military invasion of Grenada.

Nearly 2,000 troops landed in Grenada. Within a very short period of time, the Cubans were routed, the students were liberated, and the United States savored its first clear-cut military victory in many years. All told, out of the 6,000 troops who were mobilized for the Grenada invasion, 18 were killed and 145 wounded. Most of the soldiers were withdrawn by December 15, 1983.

At first, some opinion leaders openly criticized the president's action. Then House Speaker Tip O'Neill (quoted in Kernell 1986: 148) referred to it as "gunboat diplomacy." However, most of the public endorsed President Reagan's decision to intervene. In response to a Gallup poll conducted a month after the event, 59 percent approved "of the way President Reagan is handling . . . the situation in Grenada" (1983). Slightly less than a third (32 percent) disapproved, with the rest expressing no opinion. With the release of these polling results, according to Kernell, "the critics hushed up, and Reagan's previously silent partners became vocal" (Kernell 1986: 145).

The president's direct intervention was most popular among men, people over age 30, whites, Republicans, and those not on the bottom of the occupational, educational, or income ladder. The lower socioeconomic cast to public disapproval was influenced by race. Blacks, in particular, opposed the Reagan initiative in Grenada. Whereas 65 percent of whites and 46

Table 2.1
**Public Approval of President Reagan's Performance before and after
Grenada and Libya**

	Approval Score		
Country:	12-month average before	Immediately after the event	6-month average after
Grenada	41%	53%[1]	54%
Libya	61%	68%[2]	62%

Notes:

1. Poll conducted on November 18-21, 1983.

2. Poll conducted on April 11-14, 1986.

Source: Adapted from *Gallup Report* No. 274, July 1988.

percent of Hispanics sanctioned the president's interposition, only 15 percent of blacks were favorably inclined (Gallup Poll 1983).

The overall effect of the Grenada intervention was to boost the public's evaluation of President Reagan. As indicated in Table 2.1, over the twelve months preceding the landing in Grenada, Reagan's popularity was languishing. In the early part of 1983, as mentioned earlier, it reached its nadir with a 35 percent approval rating. A gradual improvement was recorded as the economic news brightened throughout the year, but until Grenada the president's popular score was stuck, on average, at 44 percent.[4]

Within a month of his decisive action, President Reagan's job performance rating jumped to 53 percent. Moreover, it never fell more than 1 percent below that level until November 1986 (when some of the details about the Iran-Contra affair were first revealed). Even the tragic terrorist truck bombing on October 24, 1983, which killed 240 Marines stationed in Beirut, Lebanon, did not stop the upswing in public regard for the president.[5] Perhaps the Grenada intervention, which occurred within two days of this bombing, offset widespread public dismay at such a loss and rallied Americans behind a decisive, and ultimately victorious, military action.

Libya and Public Opinion

President Reagan ordered the bombing of five different sites in Libya on April 15, 1986, in retaliation for terrorist attacks on American citizens abroad which the administration attributed directly to Libya's Colonel Muammar el-Qaddafi. The air strikes were dramatic and quick, and resulted in a minimum of U.S. casualties. Although roundly criticized by many world leaders, the bombing of Libya was enthusiastically received by the American public.

A Gallup poll (1986) conducted immediately after the attack found 71 percent of the American people condoning the action. Only 21 percent opposed the bombing; the rest had no opinion. Very few significant age, gender, regional, educational, or partisan differences divided the public's endorsement. Whites, by a 26 percent margin, were more supportive of the bombing than non-whites, but even within this latter group a near-majority (49 percent) voiced approval of President Reagan's sorties. Most Americans (68 percent), including a majority (54 percent) of non-whites, expressed approval of the raid, "even if it turns out that the action does not reduce terrorism" (Gallup Poll 1986).

Although many Americans were very worried about the possible consequences of military actions, the Libyan bombing raid nonetheless unleashed a very hostile reaction toward perceived belligerents (Gallup Poll 1986). In the immediate wake of the attack, 52 percent of the public opted for either bombing Libya's oil fields or instigating a military coup as the best means next to deal with the Libyans; only 3 percent preferred no further action. If Syria or Iran were linked to terrorist attacks, nearly two-thirds (64 percent) supported U.S. bombing of these countries. Indeed, after the Libya raid, 62 percent thought that President Reagan made "wide use of military forces to solve foreign-policy problems" (Gallup Poll 1986). Any further terrorist activities by Libya, according to 80 percent of the public, should be met by direct U.S. military intervention.

Interestingly, only 31 percent believed that the bombing would actually decrease terrorism; 40 percent envisioned an increase in such activities, while 23 percent concluded that the rate of terrorist attacks would stay constant. Fully four out of every five Americans were at least a little concerned about the possibility that the Libyan intervention would serve to increase terrorist incidents. A clear majority (56 percent) acknowledged that the bombing made achieving peace in the Middle East more difficult.

Hence, even though the air raid was perceived to be fraught with danger and uncertainty, most Americans endorsed it as a proper means to deal with Libya. A broad spectrum of the public was, by 1986, prepared to support the use of military force against hostile nations. The once pervasive public hesitancy about possible U.S. interventionism abroad—a major legacy of the Vietnam era—was largely gone. Some five years before Libya, pollsters Daniel Yankelovich and Larry Kaagen had already sensed the growing restlessness among the public when they wrote:

By the end of 1980, a series of events had shaken us out of our soul-searching and into a new outward looking state of mind. The public had grown skeptical of detente, and distressed by American impotence in countering the December 1979 Soviet invasion of Afghanistan. It felt bullied by OPEC, humiliated by the Ayatollah Khomeini, . . . out-traded by Japan and out-gunned by the Russians. By the time of the 1980 presidential election, fearing that America was losing control over its foreign affairs, voters were more than ready to exorcise the ghost of Vietnam and replace it with a new posture of American assertiveness. (Yankelovich and Kaagen 1981: 696)

The bombing of Libya categorically catapulted this position to majority status in America.

It also added some bonus points to the overall popularity of Reagan, the commander-in-chief who had ordered the attack. Within a month of the raid, the public's approval of his performance as president climbed to 68 percent, equal to the score achieved five years earlier at the peak of Ronald Reagan's honeymoon period. One should also bear in mind that, as indicated in Table 2.1, Reagan's evaluations had been running fairly high over the course of the twelve months prior to the bombing. The raid resulted in a sharp surge in his already high level of popularity. This jump, however, only lasted a month. By June 1986, the president's approval score settled back to the norm achieved before the Libyan attack. It was to stay at this plateau until the Iran-Contra story broke at the end of 1986.

By the time his presidency was winding down, a majority of Americans— 54 percent in the Gallup poll (1988c) and 58 percent in the Harris poll (1989b)—assessed President Reagan's job performance favorably. Some 52 percent thought that he would go down in American history as an above-average or better president; only 14 percent thought the same of Jimmy Carter at the conclusion of his presidency (Gallup Poll 1988b). Reagan was specifically accorded high marks by the public for his handling of foreign policy, particularly relations with the Soviets. While in July 1988 only 43 percent approved of his managing of the economy, 54 percent saluted his approach to foreign policy—77 percent specifically congratulated the president for his methods of dealing with the Soviet Union (Gallup Poll 1988a).

From his electoral victory in 1980 onward, Ronald Reagan was considered by the public as a strong leader (Citrin and Green 1986). His actions in Grenada and Libya vividly demonstrated a presidential style based upon a firm, no-nonsense approach. Foreign policy making through resolute leadership comported well with what large segments of the American public seemed to want from their leaders.

AFFECT TOWARD SYSTEM

There are mixed signs about the effect of Ronald Reagan's leadership style and policy initiatives on resuscitating public goodwill toward the more diffuse components of the American political system. This ambivalence is uncovered by tracking feelings of confidence and trust among the American people toward authority and the power structure.

Citrin and Green (1986) contend that during Ronald Reagan's first term in office, negative judgments about the responsiveness, efficiency, representativeness, and fairness of government steadily declined. For the first time since the steep erosion of public confidence in politics and politicians that marked the late 1960s and the 1970s, Americans were coming to have more trust in their system of government. To be sure, on balance in 1984 there was still more cynicism than positivism being publicly expressed, but "the substantial size of the increase in political trust is unmistakable and, judged against the movement of recent history, impressive" (Citrin and Green, 1986: 435). Faith in political institutions, such as Congress, the Supreme Court, the executive branch of government, the military, and, most dramatically, the White House, also began to increase at about the midpoint of President Reagan's first term in office (Lipset 1983).

On the other hand, evidence assembled by the Harris alienation index (Harris Poll; 1989a) does not indicate a full return to complete faith and confidence in the U.S. power structure during the Reagan years. As displayed in Figure 2.1, overall alienation scores, though showing some minor defections, remained high between 1981 and 1989. Over the course of the Reagan administration, alienation, on average, gripped 57 percent of the American public. This figure was about equal to the alienation average maintained during the Carter presidency. The lowest level of alienation recorded during President Reagan's two terms in office (54 percent) came as he was preparing to leave the White House.

The most alienated Americans during Ronald Reagan's tenure as president were blacks and the poor (Harris Poll 1989a). At the conclusion of the Reagan administration, 70 percent of the black population scored high in alienation. Black alienation hardly budged during Reagan's eight years in office. In distinction, high-status white Americans manifested much more confidence in their relationships with those in power. For example, only 40 percent of those with a university education were alienated when Reagan left office.

Some of the apparent contradictions in public feelings toward the power structure may be explained by examining the specific questions used in the Harris index of alienation to measure efficacy, trust, and confidence. Table 2.2 details the changes recorded in responses to the items surveyed over the course of the Reagan presidency. Between 1982 and 1988 very little improvement in confidence levels occurred on measures regarding the division of wealth and the public's sense of powerlessness in dealing with diffuse authority figures. Until 1987, Americans were indeed becoming more alienated. It was only during the last two years of the Reagan administration that cynicism declined somewhat.

The sole question that revealed a clear-cut gain in efficacy is one that taps

Table 2.2
Alienation in the United States, 1982–88

Item	1982	1983	1984	1985	1986	1987	1988	net change[1]
The rich get richer and the poor get poorer	72%	79%	74%	76%	81%	73%	72%	---
Most people with power try to take advantage of people like yourself	59%	65%	56%	63%	66%	63%	63%	+ 4%
What you think doesn't count very much anymore	58%	62%	57%	57%	60%	55%	53%	- 5%
You are left out of things going on around you	50%	57%	41%	38%	37%	40%	43%	- 7%
The people running this country don't really care what happens to you	50%	50%	48%	48%	55%	45%	35%	-15%
Index of Alienation[2]	56%	62%	55%	56%	60%	55%	54%	- 2%

Notes:

1. Change between 1982 and 1988. A plus (+) sign indicates an increase in alienation; a minus (-) sign indicates a decrease.

2. This index is calculated on the basis of the average of the percent alienated on each of the five items.

Source: Adapted from the Harris Poll.

relational feelings toward governing officials. Compared with the response pattern found in 1982, by 1988, 15 percent more of the public thought that "people running the country . . . really care what happens to [us]" (Harris 1988). This item is similar in wording to the survey questions investigated by Citrin and Green (1986) in drawing their conclusion that political cynicism and alienation were abating during the Reagan years.

Hence, it appears that political trust increased during the 1980s. A great deal of this rise may well be a direct by-product of President Reagan, for, as noted by Citrin and Green, "after 1980, widespread belief in Reagan's leadership capacities stimulated a resurgence of public confidence in government" (Citrin and Green 1986: 437). Through his determination and strength of resolve, especially evident during times of adversity, Reagan brought many Americans psychologically back into the political system. Dramatic demonstrations of this style, as evidenced in Libya and Grenada, provided highly visible substance to his form of leadership.

At an even deeper level of systemic attachment, the impact of the Reagan presidency is much less ambiguous. As outlined in Figure 2.2, there has been a substantial increase in the number of people satisfied with "the way things are going in the U.S. at this time" (Gallup Poll 1988a). The rise in this feeling was especially evident after 1982.

The inauguration of Ronald Reagan ushered in an immediate doubling of public confidence in the nation. This figure dropped some, however, as the country went through the recession of 1981–82. Between August 1983 and February 1984, the percent satisfied surged 15 points, from 35 percent to 50 percent. During this time frame, economic recovery became a reality and the conquest of Grenada was accomplished.

National pride reached its peak in March 1986 when two-thirds of the American people exuded satisfaction about their country. Incidentally, the Libyan adventure, it may be recalled, occurred within a month of this moment of good feelings. This raises the intriguing possibility that national pride, instead of being a reactive factor, was a supportive—if not a proactive—force accompanying the decision to bomb Libya.

A sharp plunge in satisfaction levels transpired after the disclosure of White House involvement in the Iran-Contra affair. Hints of scandal, duplicity, incompetence, and illegal behavior at the highest level of government resuscitated the ghost of Watergate—at least for a while—and lowered public satisfaction with the nation to 45 percent in September 1987.

At the end of the Reagan administration, public confidence in the country had been somewhat reestablished. By October 1988, 56 percent of Americans voiced content with the nation's state of affairs. A Harris poll (1989b) conducted in early January 1989 revealed that 63 percent of the public rated President Reagan positively for "restoring pride in America among the American people." These findings lend support to the assertion made by Citrin and Green that Ronald Reagan's "presentation of self, whether natural or stage-managed, communicated a sense of pride in the nation and its past" (Citrin and Green 1986: 450). The drama played out through successful invasions and bombings only added to the script.

Again, however, this resurgence in national pride was not spread evenly across the American people (Gallup Poll 1988a). Men, whites, young people (18 to 29 years old), Republicans, and upper-income earners ($40,000 or more annually) were, in 1988, among the most satisfied with the state of the nation. Non-whites, women, people over age 50, Democrats, and the poor were not as content.

To be fair, over the course of the Reagan administration good feelings about the country increased among members of all social groups. For instance, in January 1981 only 18 percent of non-whites were happy about their country; seven years later twice that number were so disposed. However, equally important is the fact that during this time a sense of national pride enveloped members of other social groups more extensively. For instance, there was a 53 percent leap (from 16 percent in 1981 to 69 percent in 1988) in satisfaction among higher-income Americans during the Reagan years.

OTHER FACTORS

To this point, we have examined the effect of President Reagan's military actions on the public's view of his presidency, popular feelings about the nation, and alienation levels among the American people. From the evidence at hand, it appears that, by and large, intervention in Grenada and Libya enhanced the public's image of political matters, especially the performance of the president. Improved public ratings of presidential leadership probably helped restore a measure of pride in the nation and some faith in its system of government.

To be sure, dramatic military victories are not the only reasons accounting for this upswing in public regard. Another important contributory factor is the state of the economy. The effects of macroeconomic factors on political preferences in the United States have been well documented (Feldman 1982; Kiewiet 1983; Monroe 1984; Ostrom and Simon 1985, 1989). The economic recovery experienced during President Reagan's first term in office greatly affected the development of a positive political outlook. When, for instance, unemployment was high, as was the case in 1982, the president's popularity ratings were quite low. As the economy gathered momentum and job opportunities improved, his popularity also increased (Kernell 1986: 203; Ostrom and Simon 1989).

Nonetheless, economic forces do not totally determine political orientations. Even with rates of unemployment taken into account, for instance, the public rally spurred by the landing of marines in Grenada had an independent effect upon President Reagan's rise in popularity (Kernell 1986: 237; see also Ostrom and Simon 1989). Moreover, more direct measures of President Reagan's handling of the economy did not always correspond to heightened popular regard. Throughout 1986, for instance, the Gallup poll showed only a 4 percentage point variation (from 49 to 53 percent) in positive response to the question "Would you tell me whether you approve or disapprove of the way President Reagan is handling [the] problem [of] economic conditions in this country." During that same year, however, his popularity ranged from a high support level of 68 percent—immediately after the Libyan air attack—to a low of 47 percent—as news of the Iran-Contra arms deal spread.

Furthermore, there is evidence showing that public acceptance or rejection of important cultural precepts is not simply reflective of the vagaries of the economy. For example, as noted by Inglehart, "the publics of both Britain and the United States were wealthier in the 1980s than they were in 1959–60, but both experienced an erosion of interpersonal trust from 1960 to 1981" (Inglehart 1988: 1214). Hence, other factors—such as failed leadership, unfulfilled policy promises, and unsuccessful political decisions—might better account for changes in cultural orientations than do macroeconomic performance indicators.

Finally, disentangling the orthogonal effects of several variables (e.g., economic performance, military interventions, and leadership style) on political orientations (e.g., presidential popularity, feelings of trust, and national pride) might well ensure precision in measuring the contribution made by each in a multivariate analysis. However, the political world, as even the most ardent user of such techniques would certainly agree, is not yet totally amenable to such detailed examination. Among many reasons for this situation, the unavailability of crucial data collected in the right sequential time order stands out. Equally important, the theoretical complexity of sorting out the recursive and nonrecursive linkages among key variables that affect political orientations is still proving very taxing (Inglehart 1988). More substantively, it would be theoretically shortsighted to address the intertwining of economic, political, and psychological factors either in zero-sum terms or under simple causal assumptions.

CONCLUSION

President Reagan's decisions to invade Grenada and to bomb Libya did make a difference to the American public. The immediate reaction, as has been the case with most prior military interventions, was a surge of support, a rally around the leader—if not the flag. Presidential popularity spurted upward after these actions, indicating that a collective identity could still be mobilized in times of international crisis.[6]

Although this short-term surge in popularity tended to subside after the dramatic moment of intervention faded, these military actions contributed to the build-up of public goodwill toward the president and toward some basic components of the political system that occurred during the Reagan years. As the 1980s unfolded, Americans started feeling better about their nation and the people and institutions running it. Much of this positivism is attributable to the largely favorable public perception of President Reagan's leadership style, a style highlighted by the decisiveness shown in Grenada and Libya.

Of course, the Grenada and Libyan interventions were short and sweet. High adventure was quickly followed by successful resolution. Protracted conflict with no solution and/or with mounting casualties usually is costly to the president's public persona.

It is also true that this public rally coincided to some extent with economic recovery in America. People became more laudatory about the President as unemployment and inflation went down. Put simply, before Grenada, the public's mood was improving. The continued high marks for Reagan's economic performance probably helped sustain his overall approval ratings after Grenada and Libya, at least until the Iran-Contra affair.

Most assuredly, the shift in public opinion noted during the Reagan years was not all-encompassing, either in social or in psychological terms. Not all social groups were equally caught up in the wave of enthusiasm that swept across America. Blacks, for instance, remained relatively cool toward the president, the power structure, and the state of the nation. To be sure, there was significant improvement in outlook among blacks toward Reagan's performance as president and toward the nation, but the gap between blacks and other racial and ethnic groups remained large.

Some important political orientations were immune from the effects of President Reagan, his leadership style, and his forceful policies such as those demonstrated in Grenada and Libya. Feelings of national pride, presidential popularity, and positivism toward people and institutions running the country recovered substantially from the dark days of the Carter administration. However, general alienation scores did not appreciably improve during the 1980s. Furthermore, only some of the personal and interpersonal dispositions thought crucial to laying the foundation of a civic culture, and thus a democratic society, improved during the decade.

Personal satisfaction, a basic component of a civic culture (Inglehart 1988), grew while Reagan was in office. Public satisfaction "with the way things are going in your personal life" (Gallup Poll 1988b) was on average (76 percent) already relatively high before the 1980 election. Nonetheless, during the Reagan years personal satisfaction improved even more; by 1989, 87 percent of Americans expressed satisfaction with their own lives.

Conversely, feelings of interpersonal trust—perhaps the linchpin of a cooperative, tolerant society—had dipped some 14 percent, from 55 percent in 1959 (Almond and Verba 1965: 213) to about 41 percent in 1986 (Inglehart 1988: 1212). There are virtually no signs that President Reagan's actions, either domestically or internationally, increased mutual trust among Americans. Indeed, a Harris poll (1988) taken at the end of the Reagan years found little optimism that problems dividing Americans would be solved: 87 percent could not see poverty ending in the United States; 82 percent envisioned homelessness as a permanent feature of American life; and slightly over two-thirds concluded that racial discrimination was a staying force. In most cases, these percentages represented an increase in pessimism during the Reagan presidency.

The impact of the Reagan legacy upon political orientations is mixed. There are signs that dramatic actions, such as those in Libya and Grenada, enhanced some basic feelings about the American political system, as well as the president's own standing with the public. However, other fundamental views, especially ones that weave into the fabric of a democratic society, did not improve much during President Reagan's tenure in the White House.

NOTES

1. This information comes from the Gallup organization (Gallup Poll 1980b). Only President Nixon's invasions of Cambodia (in 1970) and Laos (in 1971) went against the trend of popular approval increasing after intervention.

2. It should be pointed out (Harris 1973; Lipset and Schneider 1983) that the public was not just disenchanted with political leaders and offices. Business, professional groups, the press, labor unions—almost every occupational and social functionary in the United States—were suspect in the eyes of most Americans.

3. Marines were also stationed in Beirut as part of the UN peacekeeping force in Lebanon in 1983. Military maneuvers involving substantial numbers of American personnel were also conducted in Honduras and in the Persian Gulf. These instances did not, however, constitute a unilateral direct military intervention into another country.

4. This average is based upon seventeen measures of the president's performance conducted by the Gallup organization between January 28 and 31, 1983, at which time Reagan's popularity was at its lowest ebb, and October 21–24, 1983, the dates of the last poll administered before the Grenada intervention.

5. The public was not enthusiastic about Reagan's handling of the problem in Lebanon (Gallup Poll 1983). Within a month of the terrorist attack on the Marines stationed in Beirut, only 34 percent approved of the president's Lebanese policy; 52 percent disapproved, while 14 percent had no opinion.

6. The rallies mobilized by direct intervention in Lebanon and Grenada had a limited impact upon improving support for Reagan's Nicaraguan policies, including approval of aid to the Contras (Bowen 1989).

REFERENCES

Abramson, Paul R., John H. Aldrich, and David W. Rohde. *Change and Continuity in the 1980 Elections*. Washington, D.C.: Congressional Quarterly Press, 1983.

Aldrich, John, John L. Sullivan, and Eugene Borgida. "Foreign Affairs and Issue Voting: Do Presidential Candidates 'Waltz Before a Blind Audience'?" *American Political Science Review* 83 (1989): 123–142.

Almond, Gabriel, and Sidney Verba. *The Civic Culture*. Boston: Little, Brown, 1965.

Arterton, F. Christopher. "The Impact of Watergate on Children's Attitudes Toward Authority." *Political Science Quarterly* 89 (1975): 269–288.

Bowen, Gordon L. "Presidential Action and Public Opinion about U.S. Nicaraguan Policy: Limits to the 'Rally 'Round the Flag' Syndrome." *P.S.* 12 (1989): 793–799.

Brody, Richard A. "International Crises: A Rallying Point for the President." *Public Opinion* 6 (1984): 41–43.

Ceaser, James. "The Reagan Presidency and American Public Opinion." In Charles O. Jones, ed., *The Reagan Legacy: Promise and Performance*. Chatham, N.J.: Chatham House, 1988.

Citrin, Jack, and Donald Philip Green. "Presidential Leadership and the Resurgence of Trust in Government." *British Journal of Political Science* 16 (1986): 431–453.

Coser, Lewis. *The Functions of Social Conflict*. New York: Free Press, 1956.

Dawson, Richard. *Public Opinion and Contemporary Disarray*. New York: Harper and Row, 1973.

Easton, David, and Jack Dennis. *Children in the Political System*. New York: McGraw-Hill, 1969.

Feldman, Stanley. "Economic Self-interest and Political Behavior." *American Journal of Political Science* 26 (1982): 446–466.

Gallup Poll. *Gallup Opinion Index*, No. 180, 1980a.

———. *Gallup Opinion Index*, No. 182, 1980b.

———. *Gallup Opinion Index*, No. 183, 1980c.

———. *Gallup Report*, No. 218, 1983.

———. *Gallup Report*, No. 246, 1986.

———. "Public More Upbeat about State of Nation." December 25, 1988a.

———. *Gallup Report*, No. 274, 1988b.

———. *Gallup Report*, No. 277, 1988c.

Gilmour, Robert S., and Robert B. Lamb. *Political Alienation in Contemporary America*. New York: St. Martin's Press, 1975.

Greenstein, Fred. *The Hidden-Handed Presidency*. New York: Basic Books, 1982.

Harris, Louis. *The Anguish of Change*. New York: Norton, 1973.

———. *The Harris Survey*, No. 22, 1983.

Harris Poll. No. 103, 1988.

———. No. 1, 1989a.

———. No. 4, 1989b.

Hess, Robert, and Judith Torney. *The Development of Political Attitudes in Children*. Chicago: Aldine, 1967.

Inglehart, Ronald. "The Renaissance of Political Culture." *American Political Science Review* 82 (1988): 1203–1230.

Jaros, Dean, Herbert Hirsch, and Frederick J. Fleron, Jr. "The Malevolent Leader: Political Socialization in an American Subculture." *American Political Science Review* 62 (1968): 564–575.

Kernell, Samuel. "Explaining Presidential Popularity." *American Political Science Review* 72 (1978): 506–522.

———. *Going Public: New Strategies of Presidential Leadership*. Washington, D.C.: Congressional Quarterly Press, 1986.

Key, V. O. *Public Opinion and American Democracy*. New York: Knopf, 1961.

Kiewiet, Roderick D. *Macroeconomics and Macropolitics*. Chicago: University of Chicago Press, 1983.

Lane, Robert E. "The Politics of Consensus in an Age of Affluence." *American Political Science Review* 59 (1965): 874–895.

Lee, Jack. "Rally 'Round the Flag: Foreign Policy Events and Presidential Popularity." *Presidential Studies Quarterly* 7 (1977): 252–255.

Lipset, Seymour M. "Feeling Better: Measuring the Nation's Confidence." *Public Opinion* 6 (1983): 6–9, 56–58.

Lipset, Seymour M., and William Schneider. *The Confidence Gap*. New York: Free Press, 1983.

Maddox, William S., and Roger Handberg. "Presidential Affect and Chauvinism among Children." *American Journal of Political Science* 23 (1979): 426–433.

Miller, Arthur H. "Political Issues and Trust in Government, 1964–1970." *American Political Science Review* 68 (1974): 951–972.

Monroe, Kirsten. *Presidential Popularity and the Economy*. New York: Praeger, 1984.

Mueller, John. *War, Presidents and Public Opinion*. New York: Wiley, 1973.

Ostrom, Charles W., and Dennis M. Simon. "Promise and Performance: A Dynamic Model of Presidential Popularity." *American Political Science Review* 79 (1985): 334–358.

————. "The Man in the Teflon Suit: The Environmental Connection, Political Drama, and Popular Support in the Reagan Presidency." *Public Opinion Quarterly* 53 (1989): 353–387.

Reagan, Ronald. Farewell Address to the Nation, 1989.

Rodgers, Harrell, and Edgar Lewis. "Student Attitudes toward Mr. Nixon: The Consequences of Negative Attitudes toward a President for Political System Support." *American Politics Quarterly* 3 (1975): 423–436.

Roll, Charles W., and Albert H. Cantril. *Polls: Their Use and Misuse in Politics.* New York: Basic Books, 1972.

Shapiro, Robert Y., and Benjamin I, Page. "Foreign Policy and the Rational Public." *Journal of Conflict Resolution* 32 (1988): 211–247.

Sigel, Roberta S., and Marilyn Brookes. "Becoming Critical about Politics." In Richard G. Niemi and Associates, ed., *The Politics of Future Citizens.* San Francisco: Jossey-Bass, 1974.

Stein, Arthur A. "Conflict and Cohesion." *Journal of Conflict Resolution* 20 (1976): 143–172.

Sumner, W. G. *Folkways.* New York: Ginn, 1906.

Yankelovich, Daniel, and Larry Kaagen. "Assertive America." *Foreign Affairs* 59 (1981): 696–713.

3
The Falklands War and British Public Opinion
Helmut Norpoth

The warrior heroes of the past may look down, as Nelson's monument looks down upon us now, without any feeling that the island race has lost its daring.

Winston Churchill, 1940

In the war over the Falklands in 1982, Britain recaptured the remote islands no less convincingly than her government did popular support at home. Foreign war apparently had not lost its wallop to jolt domestic opinion. In the year preceding the Falklands dispute, the popularity of the Thatcher government had sunk to lows rarely seen in the history of such polling. As the economy fell into the deepest recession since the 1930s, with unemployment rising toward a Depression level of three million, the popular stock of the government had crashed. In March 1982, just before the onset of the Falklands War, a Market and Opinion Research International (MORI) poll found that only 36 percent of the British public were satisfied with the performance of Prime Minister Thatcher, while 57 percent expressed dissatisfaction. In June of the same year, right after Argentina's defeat, the numbers were almost exactly reversed in favor of Thatcher: 59 percent to 36 percent.

It is hard to disagree with the conclusion that "Britain rallied 'round the Prime Minister" (Worcester and Jenkins 1982), or that the Falklands "represented a turning point in the fortunes of Margaret Thatcher's Conservative Government" (Freedman 1988; also Crewe 1985; Dunleavy and Husbands 1985; Clarke, Stewart, and Zuk 1986; Mishler, Hoskin, and Fitzgerald

1989). Accepting this view, nonetheless, leaves open several intriguing lines of inquiry.

For one thing, what was it exactly about the Falklands that boosted government popularity in Britain: the provocation by a hostile foreign power or the response of one's own government? In other words, did the Thatcher government simply reap a windfall benefit from the threatening deeds of others or did it earn something for its own performance? Was it simply a matter of instinctively closing ranks, rallying around the flag, and expressing sympathy rather than approval?

Second, did it matter what specific steps the Thatcher government took, so long as it took any? How strongly did the public cry for military action? Did the outcome of the war make a substantial difference in the popularity of the government? Was victory the final judge in this matter?

Third, granted that the Falklands War sparked a boost in government popularity, how soon did the gains disappear? As quickly as they arrived? If so, however striking the case of the Falklands may be, it could be dismissed as a rally without consequence, a testimony more to the whims of public opinion than to the whip of war.

Finally, whatever the gains and losses, did they attach themselves primarily to the person at the head of the government or did they affect support for the governing party as well? Put another way, were any gains just a personal triumph for Prime Minister Thatcher or did the Conservative party share the glory in expressions of party support? Perhaps most important, did party sentiments as measured in the regular polls convert to actual votes at the polls in 1983?

In probing these questions, which can be examined with an abundance of public opinion data on the British side of the conflict, one may begin by pondering the wages of previous wars and international crises for a government's domestic standing.

SOME LESSONS FROM PREVIOUS WARS

If history is a guide, the pattern is not unambiguous. The last major war fought by Britain failed to secure electoral victory for the prime minister's party. No sooner had the papers of surrender been signed by Germany in 1945 than the Conservatives suffered a stunning defeat in the general election. This happened in spite of the immense popularity Churchill had commanded throughout the war, his approval ratings rarely dipping below 80 percent (Gallup 1976: 34–105). Moreover, World War II was a popular one in Britain: Three-quarters of the public, when polled, typically voiced satisfaction with the government's conduct of the war. Yet soundings of party support during the war now and then did not suggest any benefit for the prime minister's party. Near the end of the war, in March–April of 1945, with Churchill's approval at 87 percent, only 24 percent in an opinion poll said they would vote for the Conservatives, as opposed to 40 percent for Labour (Gallup 1976: 105–107). Much glory for the leader, but little for his party.

Churchill, of course, had been leading a coalition government, in which the winner of the 1945 election was a loyal partner. The war was not a partisan issue, and that allowed many voters, without experiencing any dissonance, to hold Churchill in high esteem while casting their vote for Labour. Thus the paradox that a war that unites the country pays little electoral dividend to the leading party. Had World War II been a partisan issue, with Labour being opposed to the war, Churchill would never have enjoyed such high popularity, but his party might have done better given at least some disagreement with Labour's course.

In the United States, likewise, military victory in Europe and Asia did not prevent electoral defeat of the Democrats in House elections in 1946. To put that loss in perspective, note that this was only one of two such losses suffered by the Democrats in the last sixty years. And it came on the heels of what was a popular war. The American public had no regrets for entering it: Three out of four Americans, according to a 1944 survey (cited in Mueller 1973: 63), said entry into the war was no mistake. President Roosevelt's approval ratings stayed high throughout the war years (Gallup 1980: 37). Roosevelt, moreover, sought reelection during the war and, despite his afront against historical precedent, won it easily. A popular, just, victorious war thus assures high esteem for the country's leader; still, his party may lose the election as soon as the guns have fallen silent.

More recent wars, even before the reckoning at the polls, have not enjoyed widespread popular support. To be sure, the American public strongly applauded entry into the war in Korea in 1950 as well as the escalation of the Vietnam War beginning in 1965 (Mueller 1973). But in both cases, popular support soon declined. Furthermore, the Korean War sharply eroded President Truman's popularity. By early 1952, when it was time to prepare for reelection, his approval ratings had sunk to 25 percent. Truman did not seek reelection, and his party lost the presidency that year after a campaign dominated by the three K's: Korea, corruption, and communism. The electorate's disapproval of the Democrats' handling of the Korean War registered in voting studies as a key component of the 1952 presidential election. According to one authoritative source:

As the action in Korea dragged into its third year, it became an increasingly partisan issue, with the Republican leadership arguing either that this country should never have been involved in Korea in the first place or that the Democratic Administration should have brought our involvement there to a successful conclusion. It was an argument of great popular appeal that the Democrats apparently did not effectively answer. (Campbell, Converse, Miller, and Stokes 1960: 527)

History seemed to repeat itself with the next war in Asia. President Johnson himself estimated that the Vietnam War cost him 20 points in approval ratings (as cited in Mueller 1973: 196). He, too, declined to seek reelection; his party also lost the White House. Indeed, from the time of massive American involvement in Vietnam, in early 1965, to Johnson's decision not to seek reelection, in early 1968, his popularity curve dropped from roughly 70 points to barely 40 (Gallup 1980). Studies by Kernell (1978) and Norpoth (1984), among others, have confirmed the damaging effect of Vietnam on Johnson's popularity.

By late 1968, American public opinion was deeply divided over whether getting into the war was the "right thing." Regrets over the Vietnam involvement steadily mounted and today a vast majority expresses the sentiment that the United States should have stayed out: 73 percent, according to a 1985 *New York Times*/CBS News survey (Clymer 1985). It must also be noted that the termination of the war by Johnson's successor played no small role in Nixon's landslide victory in 1972 (Kelley 1983: 108). No doubt, wars like those in Korea and Vietnam are no recipe for shoring up popular support at home. What is less obvious, however, is: Why?

All wars have in common the fact that for the ordinary citizens the costs are tangible, personal, and painful, whereas the benefits are mostly intangible, collective, and vicarious. Seeing one's country go to war may, for a moment, make one's throat feel lumpy and arouse a proud sense of patriotism, but that mood is not easy to sustain. As the sacrifices demanded of people grow more onerous, as the casualties mount and the initial domestic consensus tears, war fosters opposition and protest. In more fragile societies, the discontent may not be limited to the war but may direct its energy against the overall political regime. War, as the saying goes, is the "midwife of revolution." Czarist Russia, Imperial Germany, and the Austro-Hungarian monarchy all fell victims to revolutionary upheaval kindled by World War I.

Victory and defeat seem to be obvious criteria for distinguishing between popular and unpopular wars. Yet even before the outcome is imminent, the popularity of wars often shows signs of fading. For the wars in Korea and Vietnam, Mueller (1973: 61) has shown that the support of the American public declined with rising casualties. What initially appeared to the public as a good cause later drew disapproval—the more so, the more American soldiers died.

How willing the public is to bear the sacrifices required by war certainly depends on the justification of the war. Can the government persuade the public that there is a worthy cause to be achieved by war? This task may not be unreasonably difficult in situations where one's own country is compelled to enter into a war as the result of a clear-cut attack, as was the case in World War II for the United States, or where the threat of occupation by a foreign country is imminent, as was true for Britain then. On the other hand, when war takes place far away from one's own territory without a clear and present danger being felt, the ordinary citizen is not so likely to be persuaded by government claims that the cause of the war is worth the sacrifice.

In sum, war is a chancy ally for a government hoping to boost its domestic standing. At best, it seems to deliver an aura of good feeling, yet without hard electoral benefits; at worst, it may oust the government and perhaps the political regime altogether.

Full-scale wars are not the only international events that may affect domestic opinion. A serious international crisis is commonly thought to influence a government's popularity. The public "rallies 'round the flag" in response to the crisis and the government's popularity usually soars, regardless of the action taken by the government or its wisdom. As documented in Chapter 2, U.S. presidents have ordinarily benefited from such rallies (Mueller 1973; Kernell 1978; Brody 1984). In recent time, there is the example of Jimmy Carter's popularity rising sharply in late 1979 after the seizure of the American embassy in Teheran, his lack of a forceful response notwithstanding. Nearly two decades earlier, Kennedy's rating shot up after the Bay of Pigs operation, even though the planned invasion of Cuba was a calamity (Gallup 1980).

Success or failure of government action thus does not determine the public's willingness to rally around their president, nor does it matter what action a president takes in the face of a dramatic and sharply focused international event. The rally effect, in other words, represents a windfall, not a reward for performance. So, with due justice, it typically evaporates as quickly as it materialized. No government can hope to manage its popularity by capitalizing on rally points.

As for Britain, the Suez crisis of 1956 comes to mind as a candidate for a rally effect (see Epstein 1964). In July of that year Egypt under the leadership of Gamal Nasser had nationalized the Suez canal, prompting a military operation by Britain and France (as well as by Israel) against Egypt after the failure of diplomatic efforts to resolve the dispute. The Anglo-French attack, lasting about a week (October 31 to November 6), proved futile, however, in the face of pressure form both the United States and the Soviet Union to cease military operations.

As suggested by Table 3.1, there is no evidence, however, that Egypt's takeover of the canal sparked a rally 'round the flag in the British public. On the other hand, Prime Minister Eden's popularity did rise in the aftermath of the military operation against Egypt—from 47 percent in October to 57 percent in mid-November of 1956. That the operation had ended disastrously did not seem to matter. The Conservative party also appeared to edge up a notch. Certainly, the popular standing of the prime minister and his party in the wake of the aborted Suez operation was no reason to call for the step that Eden took in January of 1957, namely to resign.

Table 3.1
**Support for Prime Minister and Governing Party among the British
Public during the Suez Crisis, 1956**

Item:	August	September	October	November 10-11
Approving of Eden as Prime Minister	--	51.0%	47.0%	57.0%
Conservative Vote Intention	43.5%	43.0%	42.5%	45.0%

Source: British Gallup.

While some may wonder why the Suez crisis triggered any favorable response in public opinion, others may wonder why it did not spark a stronger one. One important reason for its limited effect was partisanship. From the very beginning the Labour party was openly and staunchly critical of military action, and was united in its opposition to the Eden government when such actions were taken. It was clear to Labour partisans in the British electorate that their party disapproved of military action. Most of them expressed that aversion in opinion polls (cited by Epstein 1964). For a foreign policy question, Suez turned into a usually partisan issue. Labour, in Parliament as well as among the mass public, did not rally 'round the government in the Suez crisis.

It was Conservative partisans who did—around a government, of course, formed by their party. Their backing of military action rose from barely 40 percent in August to over 80 percent in December, according to Gallup polls. "Whatever doubts many of them had earlier about military action appear to have been dissipated, or put to one side, once their leaders took the action. Here, it seems probable, the leaders, particularly the Prime Minister, could effectively lead" (Epstein 1964: 146–147).

What the foregoing discussion of wars and international rallies spells for the likely effects of the Falklands War on the British public depends in large part on what kind of war or international event the episode was.

THE PARAMETERS OF THE FALKLANDS WAR (1982)

Unlike the world wars or the wars in Korea and Vietnam, the Falklands War, if that is even the proper name for the event, was short, swift, and limited—more like a replay of Suez with a happy ending. It unfolded and concluded like "something from the Victorian stage: a simple plot, a small but well-defined cast of characters, a story in three acts with a clear beginning, middle and end, and straightforward conclusion which everybody could understand" (Freedman 1988: 1). To the British audience, it also looked like a morality play in which a villainous regime had committed an outrage. To respond with force was perfectly honorable and justified; it was also feasible. Britain, it turned out, still possessed the military wherewithal to pick up the gauntlet tossed to it by Argentina. The chance of a major escalation of the conflict was remote. Argentina wound up isolated, whereas Britain could count on widespread international support.

To be sure, the enemy posed no threat to British security or economy, nor did the war involve major strategic objectives. Neither side stood to gain a large tangible benefit from the outcome. It was "like two bald men fighting over a comb" (Jorge Luis Borges, as quoted by Theroux 1984: 47). Even so, the emotions ran high, since one of the men claimed the other had stolen his comb. At stake was not a matter of economic or political interest as laboriously set out by government policy, but something more elusive if far more visceral: national pride.

As often in such confrontations, miscalculations bedeviled both sides. (See the accounts of the conflict by Hastings and Jenkins [1983] and the *Sunday Times of London* [1982]). The situation was not meant to end up as a bloody confrontation. Neither of the two governments expected that in the dispute over the Falklands (Malvinas) the other side would continue its diplomacy by that other means called war. In particular, Britain misjudged the salience of the issue for Argentina and that country's determination to seize the islands by military force. Argentina, in turn, misjudged the will of Britain to resist such an act; it did not reckon with the deployment of a British task force. Following that, Britain did not expect that Argentina would actually fight it out militarily in the South Atlantic.

The issue in dispute was British rule over some sparsely populated islands. For roughly 150 years the Falkland Islands, situated about 400 miles off the coast of Argentina, had been settled by British subjects. There was no question of the loyalty of the residents to Britain. Argentina's claim to those islands had a purely geographic rationale, but ran counter to the expressed wishes of the local population. If colonialism was an issue, it would have been a more appropriate term for Argentinian rule over the islands. The determination of the locals to remain under British rule, in fact, was so fervent that the government in London had little or no room to maneuver in dealing with Argentina. Attempts to work out a "lease-back" arrangement Hong Kong–style, whereby Argentina would be given formal sovereignty over the islands while the Falklanders would be able to live as they were accustomed to for the foreseeable future, foundered less on the opposition of the Argentinian side than on the noisy protests in the British House of Commons whenever the slightest hints of such plans were unveiled. Lease-back was sell-out.

Argentina's decision to take the islands by force in 1982 was encouraged by the assumptions that Britain would not or could not resist militarily and that the United States would remain neutral. Each proved mistaken. While the invasion caught the British government by surprise—and exposed weaknesses in its intelligence and flaws in its policy—its reaction to the Argentinian capture of the islands on April 2, 1982, was swift and forceful. The cabinet immediately dispatched a naval task force into the South Atlantic. Meanwhile Britain scored a diplomatic coup at the United Nations, where, to the shock of the unprepared Argentinian government, the Security Council approved a resolution (No. 502) calling for the withdrawal of Argentinian troops. Another bitter disappointment was soon to follow when, after the failure of the Haig mission and other attempts to mediate between the contenders, the United States took Britain's side in the dispute.

The refusal of Argentina to retreat from the Falklands, coupled with the determination of Britain to employ force to achieve such a retreat, led inevitably to a military show-down between the two sides. With the Argentinian capitulation on June 14, 1982, the military clash ended, ten weeks after it had begun. Throughout the conflict, the British press generally supported Thatcher's Falklands policy, although the BBC came under fire for its coverage. Apart from the tabloid press, which sounded as chauvinistic as ever, the *Daily Telegraph* and the *Times* firmly backed Thatcher's policy, while the *Guardian* sounded more critical. In Parliament, Prime Minister Thatcher, unlike Anthony Eden some twenty-five years before, did not encounter open, firm, and savage opposition to her Falklands policy; at worst, Labour abstained. Unlike Suez, the Falklands did not turn into a partisan issue. In that regard, the Falklands resembled World War II, except that Labour was not part of the government in the 1980s. This time the governing party and Prime Minister Thatcher stood to reap whatever glory a just and successful war had to bestow. Let us turn to her first.

THE POPULARITY OF PRIME MINISTER THATCHER

Figure 3.1 charts the percentage answering "satisfied" in response to the question posed in MORI polls: "Are you satisfied or dissatisfied with the wary Mrs. Thatcher is doing her job as Prime Minister?" Since the Falklands War unfolded over a period of three months, and with monthly readings of Thatcher ratings at our disposal, one can estimate the change in those ratings for every month of the war. For sampling reasons alone, of course, measures of such popularity will fluctuate from month to month. Not every observed change suggests a significant impact. Moreover, to isolate the effects to be attributed to an event like the Falklands War, one needs a baseline of government popularity. What rating, in other words, would Thatcher have received in April–June 1982, had there been no Falklands War? Perhaps her popularity was on the upswing anyway? Perhaps other factors and conditions (see Campbell and Ross 1970) occurring simultaneously should receive the credit for any changes in the spring of 1982.

Any baseline of prime minister support carries a large long-term component. For many voters, the question of prime minister approval elicits a partisan reflex. Everything else being equal, most citizens with a Conservative party loyalty will give Prime Minister Thatcher a favorable rating,

Figure 3.1
Satisfaction with Margaret Thatcher as Prime Minister

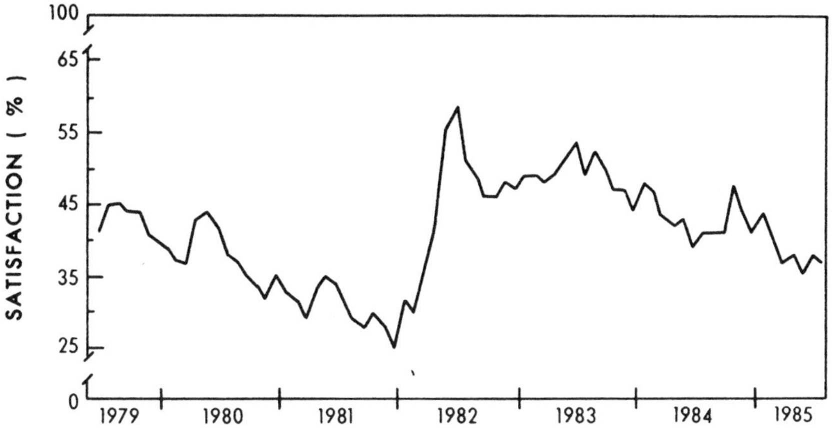

Source: MORI, June 1979–July 1985 (Gallup data used for three missing values).

whereas most Labour partisans will not. The partisan magnet keeps the average rating of the prime minister from hitting either the bottom or the ceiling of the scale. It protects her when things are going badly but denies her the maximum possible benefit when things are going well. At her worst, Thatcher could still count on the support of one in four; at her best, she still missed four in ten.

Within that range Thatcher's ratings are found to fluctuate in the fashion of an autoregressive process (Box and Jenkins 1976). That is to say, they do not wander randomly but exhibit stationary behavior with a considerable memory. Our analysis controls for these features in estimating the impact of the Falklands War. Monthly popularity ratings are adjusted for the long-term component, and an autoregressive parameter, AR (1), is in the popularity equation.

The intervention model for the Falklands specifies a separate effect for each of the three months of the war and allows for the accumulated change to decline in the aftermath. (For details on such models, see Box and Tiao 1975; Hibbs 1977; McCleary and Hay 1980; Norpoth 1987a.) If zero, this "rate"-parameter would tell us that nothing of the change remained even one month after the end of the war; if 1.0, it would indicate that change was permanent. The popularity equation also includes a constant, which indicates whether, prior to the Falklands, Thatcher's ratings had fallen below or risen above the normal support level.

As the estimate for the constant in Table 3.2 suggests, Thatcher's ratings had fallen nearly five points below the normal level prior to the Falklands. The severe recession in 1980–81 as well as the surge in unemployment had

Table 3.2
**The Falklands War and Government Support in Britain: Results of an
Intervention Analysis**

Analysis:	Thatcher's Popularity	Conservative Party Support
Constant	-4.8 (2.4)	-2.7 (3.0)
April 1982	4.5 (2.8)	.8 (2.0)
May 1982	14.7 (2.8)	8.9 (2.0)
June 1982	3.5 (2.9)	4.4 (2.1)
Rate Parameter	.95 (.02)	.94 (.04)
AR(1)	.82 (.06)	.91 (.05)
Q/DF	22/19	13/19

These results were obtained with BMDP2T. The standard errors
of the estimates are provided in parentheses. Estimates more
than twice as large as their standard errors are significant
at the .05 level.

Source: MORI, June 1979–July 1985 (74 monthly observations; for three missing values
British Gallup data used).

taken a toll on her popularity. Thatcher had been losing support even in
her partisan constituency. She was popular only among Conservatives with
intense partisan attachments. During the first month of the war (April 1982),
her standing improved somewhat, enough to bring it back to normal, but
it was not until May that her popularity registered a boom, rising by nearly
15 points. With that, her support expanded beyond the parameters of her
partisan constituency. In the final month of the war (June) her popularity
also recorded a significant, though less dramatic, gain.

These results suggest that, taken by itself, the Argentinian invasion of
the Falklands did not precipitate a massive rally 'round the prime minister.
The affront to Britain by a foreign power did not make the British public
close ranks behind its government. Thatcher was not treated by her public
the way Jimmy Carter was in late 1979 by his public when Americans were
taken hostage in Iran. In fact, in its immediate reaction to the Falklands
invasion the British public was quite unimpressed with its government.
Eight in ten blamed the Thatcher government for the crisis, according to
National Opinion Poll (NOP).

Especially worrisome for the Conservative government was the hint that the party would lose electoral support in its own ranks if it failed to regain the islands (Freedman 1988: 94). Far from rallying behind the government in an act of sympathy with embattled leaders, the British public seemed to demand stern actions and would suspend judgment until they saw the respective deeds. The popular message was unmistakable: Recover the islands or else step aside.

Surveys conducted by MORI for the *Economist* revealed a public taste for military action and little patience with any lease-back scheme. The sending of the task force was greeted with almost unanimous applause, but it was not quite enough. In a mid-April poll, two-thirds expressed support for the landing of troops in the Falklands, a proportion that grew to near-unanimity by late May; the share of those supporting the sinking of ships rose from one in two to eight in ten; and a handful even called for the use of nuclear weapons (Worcester and Jenkins 1982: 54; also *Economist* 1982a, 1982b, 1982c, 1982d).

In mid-April, before the fighting claimed the lives of servicemen, the British public was closely divided over the question of whether retaining sovereignty over the Falklands was worth the loss of British lives. But as the war began to take its toll, the share of those who thought the cause was worth such losses rose to 60 percent, dropping slightly at the time of the sinking of the Argentinian warship *Belgrano* on May 2 and the sinking a few days later of the H.M.S. *Sheffield*.

The government's handling of the conflict received warm applause by mid-April (*Economist* 1982a), with six of ten expressing satisfaction. With Britain's fleet steaming toward a showdown, the gloom of embarrassment and humiliation lifted. As the government pursued its course of retaking the islands, by force if necessary, satisfaction climbed above 80 percent in late May. Along with that, Thatcher's job ratings as prime minister grew more favorable, though never reaching the level at which the Falklands ratings peaked.

These opinions reflect popular satisfaction with actions taken by the government rather than an inclination to give one's government the benefit of the doubt in times of crisis. They express ex-post approval with leadership actions, not misty-eyed rallying 'round the flag. For all her gains in popularity, there were still many who never joined the chorus of approval for Thatcher. One suspects that partisanship kept many Britons from giving a favorable rating to the leader of the partisan opponent, however much they may have applauded the actions taken by the government. Voters without partisan ties in all likelihood formed the bulk of those that boosted Thatcher's standing.

The victorious conclusion of the war did not enhance Thatcher's popularity by a significant dose, according to our results. Was victory not the final judge in this matter? That seems unlikely. More likely, the May gains in popularity left little room for further improvement, given the realities of partisanship in the British electorate. By then, most anticipated victory. When it came, it may not have warranted any additional support. Once the government had committed itself to fight, the British public harbored few doubts that its side would win; only 6 percent of the mid-April MORI poll expected Britain to lose (*Economist* 1982a).

Altogether, over the course of the Falklands War Thatcher's popularity, estimated conservatively, rose roughly 20 points, to a level she had never enjoyed before. In the aftermath of the war, the glow faded, but most reluctantly. Given an estimate of .95 for the rate parameter, her popularity gains eroded at a rate of only .05, or 5 percent each month. One thing is clear: The boost did not evaporate as quickly as it materialized. That, too, dispels the notion that it simply represented a rally effect. The erosion, in fact, was so slow that one might be tempted to conclude that Thatcher achieved a lasting improvement most people with the actions of her government and thus could claim more than fleeting applause for it. She had been put to a crucial test of leadership and, in the eyes of her public, had passed it.

CONSERVATIVE PARTY SUPPORT

The results for Conservative party support, also presented in Table 3.2, indicate that the party shared the leader's Falklands benefit in large measure. The war was not simply a personal triumph for Prime Minister Thatcher. But it seemed to have taken the party a little longer to rise in the popular standings. The first month of the war left its share virtually unaffected, suggesting that the party received no popularity advance whatsoever. As with Thatcher, the middle month raised its stock most substantially. Yet perhaps the ending of the war paid a somewhat larger dividend for the party than for the leader. This may simply be a delay, or the result of a smaller gain in the previous month.

In sheer size, Thatcher's gain certainly edged her party's. In the Falklands conflict, it was Thatcher who led the party rather than the party leading her. Not all of the party elders favored the confrontational course adopted by Thatcher with her brand of "conviction" politics. It is widely believed that "only she among modern British Prime Ministers would have sent that task force not just into the South Atlantic but also into battle in the Falklands" (Newhouse 1986: 75). Many officials expressed the feeling that "it was Mrs. Thatcher's war. She held us to it. She never seemed to flinch from her convictions about its course. She took the risks on her shoulders and she won. She emerged as a remarkable war leader" (Hastings and Jenkins 1983: 355–356).

With the Falklands War, Thatcher stamped the party most visibly with her brand of politics. In the aftermath the party's Falklands gain, like her own, showed remarkable staying power. This was of some consequence since the party question asked about how people would vote in the next general election. It was not simply a question of popularity but of electoral choice. One year after victory in the Falklands, the Conservatives retained, according to our estimate, almost half of the thirteen-point rise in likely voting support accumulated during the war. That put them in a more comfortable position for the next general election than they would have enjoyed without the Falklands. But how comfortable that position was would depend on the ebb and flow of support for the opposition parties.

SUPPORT FOR THE OPPOSITION PARTIES

The Falklands dispute erupted at a moment of great upheaval in the British party system, when Conservative losses (or gains) no longer translated into gains (or losses) for Labour. To be sure, after winning the 1979 general election, the Conservatives lost the electoral contest with Labour in practically every monthly opinion poll until April 1982. While gloomy for Thatcher's party, such poll results did not offer Labour much to cheer about by late 1981. The formation of the Social Democratic party (SDP) and the forging of an alliance with the Liberals had been cutting away Labour's lead over the Conservatives. Moreover, at the helm of the Labour Party was a leader with exceedingly low popularity ratings. Michael Foot, since becoming Labour leader in late 1980, rarely managed to top the twenty-five-point mark of approval, to which even Thatcher, at her worst moments, rarely sank. In March of 1982, just prior to the Falklands, the division of party support almost perfectly approximated a three-way tie.

Measured against that background, as can be seen in Figure 3.2, Labour did not lose much support during the Falklands War. Thus what the Conservative party gained from the Falklands could not have come at Labour's expense. If that is true, logic dictates that the third player of the electoral game, the Liberal/SDP Alliance, must have been the Falklands loser in British politics (Crewe 1982). To be sure, the Alliance had been slipping from its brief position of dominance in January 1982 (Worcester 1983). The Falklands War caught the Alliance in a downward drift. This is not to say that the slide was inevitable and would lead the Alliance to oblivion. Parties typically do not decline (or rise) in linear fashion. The Falklands War cut Alliance support by roughly ten points. What is more, the Alliance failed to regain that ground during the next twelve months. With the Falklands War over, neither the Alliance nor Labour posed a serious threat to a Conservative victory in the short run. In the long run, the standing of the Alliance never recovered from the loss suffered in the spring of 1982.

Public reaction to the Falklands did not prompt an electoral realignment. More likely the war reallocated a highly volatile mass of electoral support. It has been noted before that the "Liberals' support . . . was derived not from

Figure 3.2
Support for British Parties in Opinion Polls, 1982

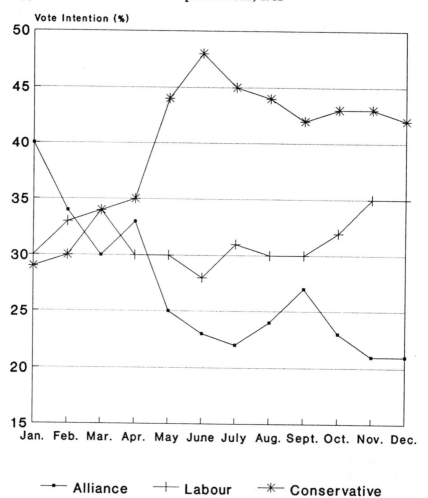

Source: MORI.

a stable and well-defined body of electors but from a constantly changing group. A more realistic analogy would be with a peripheral cloud of particles emitted almost at random from a larger mass, to which most would return after a brief separation" (Butler and Stokes 1969: 315). That image certainly applies no less to the Liberals' partner in the Alliance, the Social Democrats. Since they were barely a year old in early 1982, their support was brand-new. It fed on two streams of discontent, one with Conservative performance in office, the other with Labour's transformation in opposition.

To attach such a pool of voters firmly to a new party is a historic task that is only rarely successful. The last time a party had done so in Britain was when the Labour party displaced the Liberals some sixty years ago. If dissatisfaction with the governing party (and the Labour opposition) was the key motive for Alliance support, then it is extremely likely that a massive demonstration of success by the governing party could undercut support for the new venture. There can be little doubt that the Falklands proved to be the kind of success that can ruin the prospects of a new party. On the other hand, with Labour reduced to its core of partisans the Falklands could not do much damage to its support.

WAS IT REALLY THE FALKLANDS?

That the standing of Prime Minister Thatcher and her party improved sharply in 1982 at the time of the Falklands War is beyond dispute. But as always, the question remains: *post hoc, ergo proper hoc*? Couldn't it have been a coincidence? Some people think so. A recent study, using time series of the sort used above, concludes that "the Falklands factor . . . did not exert a significant influence on the standing of Mrs. Thatcher's government in the polls" (Sanders, Ward, Marsh, and Fletcher 1987: 298–299). Instead that standing recovered as "the result largely of intelligent (or, perhaps, cynical or even fortuitous) macroeconomic management" (Sanders, Ward, Marsh, and Fletcher 1987: 281). The economy, not the war, holds the trump card.

The 1982, the British economy did show signs of recovering from the deepest recession since the 1930s. The gross domestic product grew by more than 4 percent in the first quarter of 1983 as the general election drew near. Meanwhile, inflation, the big issue of the 1970s, was being wrung out of the economy, dropping to 4 percent by early 1983. Unemployment, on the other hand, darkened the economic sky, with the numbers swelling toward the unprecedented three-million mark and then stubbornly settling at that high plateau. Still, it may not be unreasonable to expect to find some brightening of the government's prospects around the time of the Falklands.

Curiously enough, the two key items of good news, namely economic growth and inflation, do not appear in the "best predictive model" reported by Sanders, Ward, Marsh, and Fletcher (1987). Unemployment does, but that would largely tell us why the standing of the Thatcher government was so depressed before it recovered. Instead, the set of predictors of the "best" popularity equation includes, in addition to unemployment: public sector borrowing requirements (PSBR), the exchange rate, and personal economic expectations. Together these four variables account for 87 percent of the variance in government popularity. Adding a Falklands term to that equation raises the explained variance by barely half a percent and suggests that the Falklands increased government popularity by only a slight and statistically insignificant amount.

To be sure, unemployment took a fierce toll on government support, as other studies, including this author's, have shown (Dunleavy and Husbands 1985; Norpoth 1987b). It largely accounts for the collapse of popularity in the period prior to the Falklands. Being a key problem cited by respondents in polls, the effect is understandable. That is less obvious for PSBR and the exchange rate, especially with the lags at which they are introduced: twelve months for the exchange rate and six months for PSBR. How are these two items thought to convert to government popularity? What distinguishes them from the others in the veritable armada of over twenty economic variables considered for use, before lagging?

It is not farfetched to suspect that this kind of study runs a high risk of capitalizing on chance. When the number of cases is small (effectively forty-two here) and the number of independent variables entered in the analysis is large and strongly correlated, the findings are highly volatile and capricious, as the reanalysis of the Sanders data by Clarke, Mishler, and Whiteley (1990) demonstrates. (For additional discussion, see the exchange in *Contemporary Record* 1987; 1988a; 1988b.) Add a case, drop a variable, change a lag, and the equation is likely to shift abruptly. The simple step of allowing for a one-month lag for the Falklands, a highly justified step in light of the findings above and one taken generously with all the economic variables in the Sanders analysis, has the effect of rendering both the exchange rate and the PSBR insignificant, while tripling the size of the Falklands impact and leaving its significance beyond doubt (Clarke, Mishler, and Whiteley 1990).

For all the ingenuity displayed by the Sanders analysis, one predictor serves as the linchpin: personal economic expectations. This is the one item that clearly shines brightly in 1982, perhaps reflecting the good news on prices and growth. It is also an animal of a different color than unemployment, PSBR, and the exchange rate. It is captured through opinion polls, just like government popularity. It would be surprising not to find a substantial correlation between those two kinds of opinions, especially if they are ascertained in the same interview. It is fair to ask whether economic expectations are truly exogenous to the government approval ratings.

Moreover, are those expectations exogenous to political shocks radiating from interventions like the Falklands action? As the curve of economic expectations makes clear, they surged dramatically by fourteen points in April-June of 1982, which happens to be the Falklands period and the time when government popularity shot up roughly fifteen points. What could trigger such a sudden brightening of economic outlook? When has an economic upturn ever generated such a sharp kick in a government's popularity? It is so unreasonable to surmise that the surge in government popularity on the heels of the Falklands also boosted the public's confidence in the economic future—for a moment at least?

There is evidence from opinion polls at the time that the Falklands succeeded in displacing the number-one item of bad economic news, unemployment, from public concern. When asked to name "the most important problem facing Britain today," close to seven in ten had named unemployment in MORI polls throughout 1981 and early 1982. In mid-April of 1982, only 39 percent did so, exactly the same as named the Falklands (*Economist* 1982a). Two weeks later the Falklands occupied the undisputed number-one rank, with a share of 61 percent compared with 25 percent for unemployment (*Economist* 1982c). Can one believe that the surge in government popularity at that very moment correlated only spuriously with the Falklands?

THE FALKLANDS AND THE 1983 GENERAL ELECTION

Recovery of government popularity, be it the prime minister's or the party's standing, in the middle of a term is one thing, victory in the next general election is another. The findings of our time series analysis above suggested that the Conservatives entered the 1983 election with a partisan support approximately six points higher than would have been the case without the Falklands. But that is an aggregate result in need of confirmation through individual opinion. This is not the place to conduct a full-fledged analysis of voting behavior in that election. Nonetheless, some questions can be addressed: Was the Falklands a salient issue in 1983? Was opinion on it skewed in favor of the Conservative party? Did Falklands opinions relate to vote choices, with partisanship held constant?

Admittedly, the Falklands was not the most burning issue in the eyes of British voters in 1983. Only one in ten rated it "extremely important" in deciding how to vote. That was well below the rating for such issues as unemployment, health and social services, inflation, and defense. These were issues that raised concerns. By contrast, the Falklands was a matter settled. In many ways, an issue settled is not an issue anymore. Success does not breed concern but forgetfulness. Still, that does not mean that governments receive no reward for their accomplishments. Most likely, some voters whom the Falklands drove into the arms of the Conservative party had their minds on other things a year later.

Its modest salience notwithstanding, the Falklands ranked as a key accomplishment of the Thatcher government in 1983, a very close second to inflation. Three-quarters of the British public gave the Conservatives a favorable mark for their handling of the Falklands, rating the performance as either very good or fairly good (Table 3.3). Yes, the public's assessments of the Falklands bore a partisan stamp, but partisanship only helped distinguish between shades of approval. While approval was practically unanimous among Conservative partisans, a majority of Labour partisans also

Table 3.3
The Public's View of Party Performance in the Falklands Dispute One Year Later

Item:	
Feel that Conservative Government handled Falklands dispute...	**Percent**
Very well	43
Fairly well	32
Not very well	13
Not at all well	10
Don't know	2
TOTAL PERCENT	100%
Feel that Labour Party would have handled Falklands dispute...	**Percent**
Better	16
Worse	43
Same	31
Mixed views	4
Don't know	6
TOTAL PERCENT	100%

Source: 1983 British Election Study conducted July 5–October 5. (N = 3,955)

gave the Conservative government a favorable score for its handling of the Falklands.

If the Falklands was a partisan issue it was only so in the sense that few Britons believed Labour would have done a better job. One would expect such an opinion from Conservative loyalists, but even among their Labour counterparts fewer than 40 percent thought of their party that way. Among voters without partisan attachments, for every one who thought Labour would have done better there were four who thought it would have done worse. This kind of skewed distribution, decisively favoring one party at the expense of the other, fulfills a key requirement for an issue to influence vote choices.

The Conservative party stood to gain from opinions on the Falklands in the 1983 election. Indeed, within each partisan camp the inclination to vote Conservative in 1983 rose markedly with Falklands approval. As Figure 3.3

Figure 3.3
Conservative Vote by Falklands Opinion and Party Identification

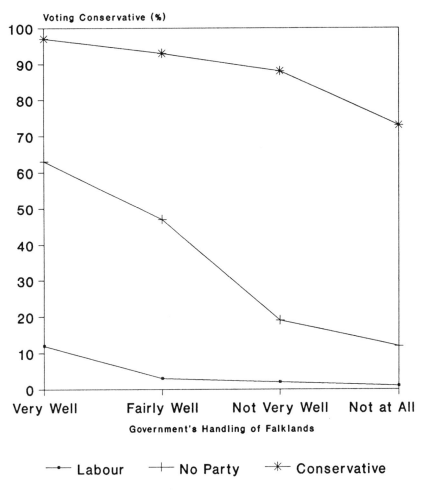

Voting Conservative (%)

Government's Handling of Falklands

—•— Labour   —+— No Party   —*— Conservative

Source: 1983 British Election Study, conducted July 5–October 5. (N = 3,955)

shows, practically every voter with a Conservative party attachment who felt the government had handled the Falklands "very well" voted Conservative, as opposed to just over 70 percent of those—few as they were— who thought the government had handled it "not at all well." Good feelings about the Falklands helped solidify Conservative support in the British electorate. At the same time, good feelings exerted a slight pull on Labour partisans away from their party. One in eight of such voters wound up voting Conservative. Most striking, however, was the gradient of Conservative support among voters professing no party attachment. A solid majority among them voted for Thatcher's party when they strongly approved of her government's handling of the Falklands; just over 10 percent did so when they disapproved strongly.

This, of course, is not to say that all these voters made up their minds solely in light of their Falklands verdict. For many voters, favorable feelings about the Falklands went hand in hand with favorable opinions about the decline of inflation and an unfavorable opinion about the state of the Labour party. When this happens, it is nearly impossible to attribute an exact contribution to a particular issue. Consequently, no claim is made that the Falklands was the most decisive element in the 1983 British election. At the same time, it was not a negligible factor. For whatever it is worth, when asked (in an open-ended question) why they thought the Conservatives beat Labour in 1983, 11 percent volunteered "the Falklands." To be sure, far more referred to the "Labour party divided" (33 percent) or to "Thatcher" (20 percent), but among specific policies mentioned only defense/disarmament (12 percent) surpassed the Falklands.

CONCLUSION

Since Dunkirk no other event, foreign or domestic, appears to have jolted public opinion in Britain like the Falklands War of 1982. Even though Argentina's invasion of the islands posed no threat to Britain's national security or to its vital economic interests, it aroused the general public to a degree that seemed astonishing for the 1980s.

Public reaction to an international crisis like the Argentinian occupation is often seen as a "rally 'round the flag," sparking a popularity boost for the government under fire. It is an almost instinctive response of people to a foreign action before one's own government has decided on countermeasures. In the Falklands case, however, there is no evidence that the Thatcher government received a popularity benefit of that kind. What Argentina did in the Falklands was not enough to make British voters take a more favorable view of their government. On the contrary, they felt let down by their own side. Unlike the American public, the British public does not seem to respond with an outpouring of sympathy for their leader at a moment of crisis.

It is only when the government took forceful steps to recapture the islands that its popularity rose. It may seem remarkable how firmly the British public espoused military actions, how they itched to fight. Was the spirit of Empire still alive? Had the island race, after all, in Churchill's words, not lost its daring? The sharp rise in Thatcher's popularity in May 1982 came clearly on the heels of actions involving the use of military force. It was a reward for having taken action, not the benefit of the doubt given to one's government in difficult and uncertain times. The public liked what it saw and responded with better approval ratings for the prime minister.

In this instance of foreign policy, then, mass opinion did not simply follow the lead of government actions. Instead the *vox populi* may have put the government under considerable pressure to act the way it did. To be sure, Prime Minister Thatcher needed little prodding. She did not hesitate to order the recapture of the islands by force and never wavered in her pursuit of that goal. But there can be little doubt that a half-hearted policy, unwilling to use force, would have met with strong public disapproval. In that event the government might have fallen in public esteem even below the dismal level it had reached in 1981.

Victory did not in the end greatly enhance Thatcher's standing. It certainly did not account for the lion's share of her popularity gain from the Falklands. If the British public was not prepared to extend a popularity advance to their embattled government when Argentina tossed the gauntlet, neither did they wait to make their popularity award until after the battle was won. It is no foregone conclusion that a defeat for Britain would have erased Thatcher's popularity gains. Much would depend on the precise circumstances of defeat. Recall that the failure of the Suez operation in 1956 did not cost the Eden government popular support, his resignation notwithstanding.

A protracted war, on the other hand, might very well have undermined government support, just as it did in the American public during the wars in Korea and Vietnam. A lengthy military engagement would have dramatized the cost side of the war, with mounting casualties and a drain of the domestic economy. It would have raised increasing doubts in the mass public as to whether the fate of the remote islands was worth the sacrifices. The Falklands War ended before such doubts could seep in and corrode the feelings of vicarious pride and joy in seeing Britain great once again.

The popularity boost Prime Minister Thatcher reaped from the war showed a remarkable staying power. Certainly, if it had been a rally effect it should have dissipated in a few months. But it was more than an unearned run. For two years afterward, at least, favorable opinion of her government's handling of the Falklands drowned the effect on Thatcher's popularity deriving from unfavorable opinion about the economic record, especially unemployment. In a more intangible way, the Falklands etched an image of Thatcher as an unflinching leader in the mind of the British public.

Though less dramatic, the gain of Conservative party support largely duplicated the pattern found for the prime minister. Long-term partisan attachments constrain the expressions of short-term party support to a greater extent than is true for prime ministerial popularity. Still, the Falklands helped the Conservative party unify its electoral constituency, reclaiming many of those who had drifted away during the hard times of 1980–81; it also prompted some temporary defections from the Labour ranks, but not many. More critical was the success of capturing the majority of nonpartisan voters. The weakening of party attachments in the age of "dealignment" (Crewe 1982) had spawned a large mass of voters who could be swayed by new issues and parties, like the Social Democrats, but also by the well-received performance of one of the existing parties in a national crisis.

The division of party support established in the wake of the Falklands endured, with slight corrections, until the next general election. This is not to say that the Falklands won it for Thatcher's party in 1983. One issue rarely does. It is true that the economy showed signs of recovery during that time, but the persistence of record unemployment makes it improbable that the economy was a helpful issue for the Conservatives in 1983. The Falklands certainly was such an issue, however much one may quibble over the magnitude of its electoral contribution.

NOTE

The data analyzed in this chapter were made available by Market and Opinion Research International (MORI), British Gallup, and the ESRC Data Archive. I am especially thankful to Bob Worcester, Bob Wybrow, Kathy Sayer, and Eric Roughley. Of course, none of these providers bears any responsibility for the analysis and interpretation of these data. I also thank Simo Virtanen for assisting me with the data analysis, and Frank Myers for helpful suggestions.

REFERENCES

Box, George E. P., and Gwilym M. Jenkins. *Time Series Analysis: Forecasting and Control.* Rev. ed. San Francisco: Holden-Day, 1976.

Box, George E. P., and G. C. Tiao. "Intervention Analysis with Applications to Economic and Environmental Problems." *Journal of the American Statistical Association* 70 (1975): 70–79.

Brody, Richard A. "International Crises: A Rallying Point for the President." *Public Opinion* 6 (1984): 41–43.

Butler, David, and Donald Stokes. *Political Change in Britain.* New York: St. Martin's Press, 1969.

Campbell, Angus, Philip E. Converse, Warren E. Miller, and Donald Stokes. *The American Voter.* New York: Wiley, 1960.

Campbell, Donald T., and H. Laurence Ross. "The Connecticut Crackdown on Speeding." In Edward R. Tufte, ed., *The Quantitative Analysis of Social Problems.* Reading, Mass.: Addison-Wesley, 1970.

Clarke, Harold, William Mishler, and Paul Whiteley. "Recapturing the Falklands— Models of Conservative Popularity, 1979–1983." *British Journal of Political Science* 20 (1990): 63–81.

Clarke, Harold, Marianne Stewart, and Gary Zuk. "Politics, Economics and Party Popularity in Britain, 1979–83." *Electoral Studies* 5 (1986): 123–141.

Clymer, Adam. "Perception of America's World Role Ten Years after Vietnam." Paper presented at the American Political Science Association Annual Meeting, New Orleans, Louisiana, 1985.

Contemporary Record. "Controversy: The Falklands Factor." Autumn 1987.
———. "The Falklands Factor: The Latest Blast." Winter 1988a.
———. "Controversy: The Falklands Factor." Spring 1988b.
Crewe, Ivor. "Is Britain's Two-Party System Really About to Crumble?" *Electoral Studies* 2 (1982): 275–313.
———. "How to Win a Landslide Without Really Trying." In Austin Ranney, ed., *Britain at the Polls 1983.* Durham, N.C.: Duke University Press, 1985.
Dunleavy, Patrick, and Christopher T. Husbands. *British Democracy at the Crossroads.* Boston and London: Allen and Unwin, 1985.
Economist. "How Britons Think." April 17, 1982a.
———. "We Like It so Far." April 24, 1982b.
———. "Satisfaction Peaks." May 8, 1982c.
———. "End of War." June 26, 1982c.
Epstein, Leon. *British Politics in the Suez Crisis.* Urbana, Ill.: Illinois University Press, 1964.
Freedman, Lawrence. *Britain and the Falklands War.* New York and Oxford: Basil Blackwell, 1988.
Gallup, George H. *The Gallup International Public Opinion Polls: Great Britain 1937–1975.* Vol. 1. New York: Random House, 1976.
Gallup Opinion Index, No. 182, 1980.
Hastings, Max, and Simon Jenkins. *The Battle for the Falklands.* New York and London: Norton, 1983.
Hibbs, Douglas A., Jr. "On Analyzing the Effects of Policy Interventions: Box-Jenkins and Box-Tiao vs. Structural Equation Models." In David Heise, ed., *Sociological Methodology 1977.* San Francisco: Jossey-Bass, 1977.
Kelley, Stanley. *Interpreting Elections.* Princeton, N.J.: Princeton University Press, 1983.
Kernell, Samuel. "Explaining Presidential Popularity." *American Political Science Review* 72 (1978): 506–522.
McCleary, Richard, and Richard A. Hay, Jr. *Applied Time Series Analysis.* Beverly Hills, Calif. and London: Sage, 1980.
Mishler, William, Marilyn Hoskin, and Roy Fitzgerald. "British Parties in the Balance: A Time Series Analysis of Long-Term Trends in Labour and Conservative Support." *British Journal of Political Science* 19 (1989): 211–236.
Mueller, John. *War, Presidents and Public Opinion.* New York: Wiley, 1973.
Newhouse, John. "Profiles: Margaret Thatcher." *The New Yorker*, February 10, 1986.
Norpoth, Helmut. "Economics, Politics and the Cycle of Presidential Popularity." *Political Behavior* 6 (1984): 253–273.
———. "The Falklands War and Government Popularity in Britain: Rally without Consequence or Surge without Decline?" *Electoral Studies* 6 (1987a): 3–16.
———. "Guns and Butter and Government Popularity in Britain." *American Political Science Review* 81 (1987b): 949–959.
Sanders, David, Hugh Ward, David Marsh, and Tony Fletcher. "Government Popularity and the Falklands War: A Reassessment." *British Journal of Political Science* 17 (1987): 281–313.
Sunday Times of London Insight Team. *War in the Falklands.* New York and London: Harper and Row, 1982.

Theroux, Paul. *The Kingdom by the Sea.* New York: Washington Square Press, 1984.
Worcester, Robert. "Comment." *Electoral Studies* 2 (1982): 84.
Worcester, Robert, and Simon Jenkins. "Britain Rallies 'Round the Prime Minister."
    Public Opinion 5 (1982): 53–55.

4
The ANZUS Conflict and New Zealand Politics

W. Keith Jackson and James W. Lamare

On July 14, 1984, New Zealanders voted into office a Labour government committed to banning nuclear-capable ships from visiting their country's ports. With that electoral verdict a major conflict between New Zealand and the United States over nuclear ship visits and the meaning of the security arrangement between the two created by the ANZUS treaty would soon erupt. Additionally, a complicated set of interactions involving the public, pressure groups, and political leadership in the policy-making process of New Zealand would become quite evident. As noted upon reflection by New Zealand's former prime minister David Lange, "our scrutiny of the [ANZUS] alliance with the United States caused a great deal of domestic controversy" (Lange 1989). This chapter examines the nature of this international conflict and the effect that it has had on politics within New Zealand.

BACKGROUND TO THE CONFLICT

Before the Labour government's ban on nuclear ship visits, thirteen nuclear-capable vessels—all of them flying the U.S. flag—had berthed in New Zealand waters between the first such stopover in April 1960 and the last in March 1984 (Bercovitch 1988: 250–254). It is the United States' view (Albinski 1988) that the ANZUS Security Treaty, which was signed by Australia, New Zealand, and the United States in San Francisco in September 1951, requires its alliance partners to permit port access to United States warships, whether they are nuclear-capable or not. Before its change in nuclear policy, New Zealand, especially when governed by the National party, essentially endorsed the U.S. (and Australian) position that membership in ANZUS, and the security benefits that it provided, meant allowing all classes of U.S. warships into the country's harbors.

Prior to the recent controversy between New Zealand and the United States, relations between the two countries had been quite amicable. One of the most surprising aspects of the ANZUS controversy lay in the fact that it was so uncharacteristic of New Zealand foreign policy. Apart from a gesture of independence in the League of Nations in 1938 (Wilson 1962: 69–71) under the first Labour government, New Zealand had had an exemplary record as a faithful ally.

Originally a colony of the United Kingdom, New Zealand supported Britain loyally, as a member both of the Empire and of the Commonwealth, whether in the Boer War or in the two world wars. The statement of a Labour prime minister at the beginning of World War II—"where Britain goes, we go, where Britain stands, we stand"—was worn like a badge of honor. When, despite the pleas of the British government, Australia withdrew its troops from the Middle East theater in 1942 to counter the Japanese threat in the Pacific, New Zealand remained steadfast in its commitment, even at the possible risk to its own shores (Reese 1969: 23).

In the 1960s the New Zealand flag flew alongside those of its Australian and American allies in Vietnam. As recently as 1982, New Zealand dispatched a frigate on station in the Indian Ocean in order to support its old ally Britain in the Falklands War. Despite its remoteness, New Zealand is virtually unrivaled for its participation in wars during the course of this century. Until 1984, constancy, reliability, and predictability were the watchwords of the country's external relations. What led to such a radical change in this long-established pattern of behavior?

At the outset there is a need to distinguish between support and deference. For all of its minor differences with what was still widely referred to as the "mother" country, New Zealand's support of Britain in time of need was familial and unquestioning. The relationship with the United States, although close, tended to the deferential.

There is also the danger of being unable to distinguish between the formal ANZUS treaty and New Zealand–U.S. relations in general. For New Zealand, these relations were based upon common cause against Germany and Japan in World War II. Never was it intended for the United States to become the prevailing power in New Zealand's region of the Pacific Ocean. The 1944 Canberra Pact between Australia and New Zealand demonstrated "Australian and New Zealand determination not only to seek a full part in the final campaigns against Japan and in the peace settlement that would follow, but also to resist American domination of the post-war South-west Pacific" (Reese 1969: 44). For the antipodean countries, ANZUS was the price extracted from the United States for its agreement to the Japanese Peace Treaty (Burnett 1988: 5–6).

The secondary role of the ANZUS alliance for New Zealand was clearly illustrated during the 1956 Suez Crisis. Forced to choose between its traditional ally, Britain, and its new, immensely more powerful ally, the United States, New Zealand remained doggedly loyal to Britain, however ill-judged the venture. For its part, the United States initially appeared to have little enthusiasm for the treaty, showing "no eagerness to make AN-ZUS more than a means of exchanging views and information and of fostering a common approach to problems, and suspicions grew in Australia and New Zealand that the Eisenhower administration in Washington was cool towards the alliance" (Reese 1969: 145).

Following the debacle of Suez and the later visit by the British secretary of state for Commonwealth relations in 1961, during which New Zealand was told of Britain's plan to gain entry into the European Common Market, with the consequent threat this action posed to New Zealand's economy, the center of gravity shifted. New Zealand had to recognize its more direct dependence upon the United States, which, as a result of the Korean War and the French collapse in Indochina, was evincing much greater interest in the affairs of the Pacific. For a time, it seemed that this direct dependence might be mitigated by the existence of the South-East Asia Treaty Organization (SEATO), in which Britain was represented. Such hopes were illusory, however. There was considerable controversy, for example, over how much New Zealand's commitment to Vietnam owed to the SEATO pact and how much of it arose out of ANZUS. It was not until the 1970s that ANZUS came to be recognized as the principal treaty that provided an external security blanket for New Zealand.

Even so, New Zealanders envisioned ANZUS as only a party of its overall relationship with the United States. They tended to view the pact more as an alliance than as a binding formal treaty arrangement. It is arguable, for instance, that New Zealand's willingness to send troops to Vietnam was more the product of this alliance sentiment than the result of a specific treaty obligation. Fundamentally, this was the cornerstone upon which in 1984 Prime Minister David Lange built his case for continuation of New Zealand's membership in ANZUS, but without nuclear ship visits by its treaty partners. What the Labour government failed to appreciate, however, was that although it might be possible to develop an alliance without a formal defense treaty, once a treaty was in place it would become virtually impossible to nullify its central provisions (whether specific or implied) without affecting the basic nature of the alliance.

The antinuclear thrust of New Zealand's position was nurtured in the activities of a myriad of pressure groups that dot the country's landscape (Clements 1988). For a country with only three million people, New Zealand is lavishly endowed with an extensive pressure group system. Contrary to the central arguments of Mancur Olson (1971), many of the strongest of these groups are driven by incentives that promote their view of the collective good of the country. Certainly this has been the case with peace

and environmental organizations. Throughout the 1960s and 1970s in particular, environmental and peace groups worked steadily to educate the
public about the dangers of nuclear energy and, especially, nuclear weapons.
Local governing bodies were lobbied, usually effectively, to declare themselves nuclear-free zones—a cost-free exercise. As the various pollution-
related problems of the Northern Hemisphere mounted, the relatively pol-
lution-free environment of New Zealand became more prized.

The testing of nuclear weapons in the South Pacific by France served as
a proximate reminder that nuclear issues were not all that far removed from
New Zealand. In 1971, a public opinion poll found that 82 percent of New
Zealanders opposed French testing. A year later nearly 49 percent supported
a trade ban imposed on the unloading of French ships by New Zealand's
leading labor union organization—the Federation of Labour (FOL)—as a
protest against nuclear testing in the region, even though the FOL was not
very popular among most of the public. In the mid–1970s, 60 percent
approved of the Peace Media Foundation's sending of a flotilla into the
French nuclear test zone.[1]

Visits by nuclear-capable U.S. warships to New Zealand's ports became
a direct target of antinuclear activists. Such forays into the country's waters
were readily seen as an unwanted and unnecessary intrusion into the nuclear-
free environment of New Zealand. In a country that appears to flourish on
protest movements, protestors baiting these monsters on the waters in their
dinghies, rowboats, and surfboards became a highly visible national sport.
A large minority of the public endorsed the message of these protests.
Several polls conducted between 1976 and 1983 show that a fairly constant
40 percent of New Zealanders were opposed to the presence of nuclear-
armed vessels in their country's harbors.

Despite the smallness of the New Zealand contribution, the Vietnam War
too left deep scars on New Zealand society. Although New Zealand troops
in Vietnam were all volunteers and not conscripts as in the United States,
young New Zealanders emulated their peers in the United States in mass
protests and demonstrations on a scale rarely seen in their country. Law
and order itself came to be on trial as the legitimacy of the state was questioned.

The effect was to stimulate anti-Americanism, or, more accurately, strong
opposition to U.S. foreign policy entanglements. For many New Zealanders, especially the young, U.S.–dominated alliance systems began to be
viewed as a source of disharmony. With the advent of the Vietnam War
the pressures upon New Zealand to conform to U.S. policies clearly increased. As the costs of alliance participation mounted, questions were raised
over the overall cost-benefit ratio of the alliance system, both domestically
and internationally. Subsequently, a U.S. examination of attitudes in Australia and New Zealand described such views in detail. The alliance, it
reported, could be seen as "potentially entrapping, pushing the two coun-

tries into unwelcome and yet unavoidable American adventures" (Vasey and Albinski, quoted in McMillan 1985: 92–93).

The questioning of discipline and authority that characterized the younger generation was not limited to internal politics but extended to great-power decisions, which began to be viewed as decidedly fallible. One consequence was that New Zealand's remoteness in the South Pacific, for so long widely considered as a source of weakness and vulnerability, came to be accepted as a source of strength.

Thus, the effects of the Vietnam War served to reinforce powerfully the strains of the nationalism stimulated by Britain's blunt warning in 1961 that New Zealand would have to stand on its own feet and learn to trade elsewhere. By the early 1970s, with the initiation of Labour Prime Minister Norman Kirk's "moral" foreign policy and the protests against French nuclear testing in the Pacific, New Zealanders became growingly conscious of the reality of their position as an isolated, small South Pacific island-nation rather than as a part of the large whole that had once been the British Empire. The seeds of nationalistic independence were firmly planted as the pressures of ANZUS membership reminded New Zealanders of their dependence on the United States.

Translating this uneasiness about alliance relations into public policy became the mission of members of the Labour party of New Zealand. It should be borne in mind that, by and large, party government is live and well in New Zealand. That is, political parties are the principal mechanisms through which ideas are converted into public policy. The election of a party frequently means the transformation of that party's platform into government policy in New Zealand.

At first, it was the left-wing members in the Labour party who questioned the meaning of alliance relations, especially with the United States. However, to attribute the acceptance of New Zealand's current antinuclear policy totally to these activists is unduly flattering, for the process of which they were a part was far more complex. It involved an intricate web of actors, the most important of whom were members of Parliament, pressure groups, and the public, as well as the Labour party. The ban on nuclear ship visits is a classic example of Lindblom's (1959) "muddling through" rather than a clear-cut policy, resolutely pursued. Ineptitude, miscuing, and outright mistakes offer a less dramatic but far more convincing characterization of this policy process than a conspiracy organized by left-wing radicals.

A consistent thread in the process was to be found in the internal organization of the Labour party. Calls at the party's annual conferences to withdraw from great-power alliances, such as SEATO and ANZUS, were regular features on the agenda from at least 1956 onward. Although initially little more than of nuisance value, the Vietnam War, in particular, spurred a steady rise in the curve of support from delegates for these measures. Party leaders and members of Parliament, however, were aware that the opinions of delegates, although well argued, were frequently highly spiced emotional appeals not shared by the bulk of the general public. Nonnuclearism, like pacifism, was generally regarded as an impractical ideal.

Nevertheless, support also grew gradually for remits opposing the establishment or extension of nuclear facilities, whether in the form of ships, submarines, missiles, or navigational aides. In fact, no nuclear ship visits took place between 1965 and 1975, because of doubts relating to legal liability should any of the ships have a nuclear accident while in port. During this interlude ANZUS, however, was not affected by any important precedent in Labour party thinking. When nuclear ship visits resumed in 1976, the issues of ANZUS and such visits were firmly fused in the minds of conference delegates, although important Labour officials, such as shadow defense minister Michael Connelly, remained tightly tethered to the principles of ANZUS—including the propriety of nuclear ship visits.

However, the Labour leadership position on visits by nuclear-capable vessels and ANZUS was steadily being undermined from two directions. On the one hand, the rank and file of the party organization was strengthening its hold on the policy-making machinery (Strachan 1985: 161). On the other, an attack on former Labour prime minister Bill Rowling by his National party successor, Prime Minister Robert Muldoon, was to eventually have the effect of elevating the prohibition of the nuclear ships issue from conference resolution to official party policy.

When David Lange became leader of the Labour party in 1983, he suggested that the party's defense policy should be altered to conform to that of its Australian counterpart, which allowed for the passage of nuclear-propelled, but not nuclear-armed, warships. At that time, Lange made no secret of his belief that Labour's nuclear weapons–free zone could only be achieved realistically if a Labour government accommodated visits by nuclear-powered ships. In Lange's words: "My objective is to get as much assurance of an absence of nuclear weaponry as possible" (*New Zealand Herald* 1983). Lange was bluntly informed by the president of the party, Jim Anderton, however, that the leader had no power to modify party policy. The party thus contested the 1984 election on a policy banning nuclear ship visits in any form.

Ironically, during New Zealand's relatively short campaign period, it was the then-sitting prime minister, Sir Robert Muldoon, who mostly sought to make nuclear ship visits an election issue. Muldoon insisted that banning such visits would lead to an end of the ANZUS alliance. The Labour party countered that New Zealand could adopt an antinuclear policy and still have the protection of ANZUS. Two of the country's more important minor parties supported Labour's ban. Indeed, the espousal of that policy by the New Zealand party—widely regarded as a right-wing or libertarian-oriented party—helped make the call for a ban politically respectable.

Labour's electoral victory in July 1984 did not necessarily guarantee that its antinuclear pledge would become governmental policy. Given the propensity of New Zealand's political parties to make a multitude of election promises, many of which are broad and unspecific, no government ever succeeds in implementing all of them. Promises that may either be too difficult to implement or politically embarrassing may be dropped well down the list of agenda items. Because of the irreconcilable nature of Labour's pledge to be in a nuclear-free ANZUS, banning the visits of nuclear-capable vessels seemed a likely candidate for such treatment. Moreover, Labour's counterpart party in Australia backed off its promise to restrict nuclear-armed warships from its country's waters after Bob Hawke became prime minister.

THE CONFLICT

The night after his victory Prime Minister–elect David Lange met with Secretary of State George Shultz in Wellington. What exactly transpired at this meeting is open to interpretation. Lange contends that he steadfastly reaffirmed his party's intention to implement its "no nukes" promise as soon as the Labour government was in place. U.S. officials claim that Lange refused to either confirm or deny whether his campaign pledge would be honored. This hedge was taken by the Americans as an encouraging sign that an acceptable accommodation could be reached (*New Zealand Times* 1984). Regardless, it was made clear to the New Zealand prime minister–elect that a ban on nuclear ships would be adjudged by Washington as a serious breach of the ANZUS alliance and sanctions would follow such an action.

The situation soon began to clarify. In November 1984, the United States requested and was granted blanket permission for visits of any of its non-nuclear-capable vessels (McMillan 1985). This was in line with the general policy of the New Zealand government which specifically "welcomes visits by naval vessels that are not nuclear armed or powered" (*The Defence Question* 1985: 11). Indeed, between 1958 and 1984 there had been more than 150 visits to New Zealand (not counting multiple port calls by the same vessel) by nonnuclear American ships (Bercovitch 1988: 250–254). With regard to nuclear ship visits, Lange, speaking at the end of 1984, appeared to minimize any potential problems by suggesting that the Americans would not seek port access of such vessels because they would not want to be rebuffed by New Zealand. He believed that Washington officials were intelligent, perceptive, and reluctant to engage in some needless, provocative incident: "We have the utmost co-operation on this matter" (*Christchurch Press* 1984).

This optimism quickly faded. In early 1985, after a series of private meetings between members of the New Zealand and U.S. governments, it was decided that the United States would seek permission to berth the

U.S.S. *Buchanan* in New Zealand. The *Buchanan* was a rather old destroyer with, in all probability, no nuclear capability. New Zealand countered that the visit would be permitted only if the government could be fully assured that the *Buchanan* was not nuclear armed or powered. Given Washington's refusal to divulge such information, it became the responsibility of the prime minister to determine the nuclear properties of the *Buchanan*. Lange's inability to totally rule out a nuclear quality to the *Buchanan* led to a denial of port access and the cancellation by the United States of the proposed visit.

This sequence of events turned out, in retrospect, to be the breaking point in U.S.–New Zealand relations over the nuclear ships issue. As noted by McMillan (1985: 79), "if the United States had not requested access for the *USS Buchanan* and if New Zealand had not refused access, the worst of the dispute between the two countries might have been avoided." Why did the proposed visit of an old non–nuclear-powered ship cause such difficulties?

It seems clear that the request for the *Buchanan* visit represented a genuine attempt by the Americans to accommodate New Zealand's interests. There was considerable speculation at the time of the request that this ship was chosen in order for the United States to test whether New Zealand's new policy could accommodate the strict American code of neither confirming nor denying the presence of nuclear weaponry aboard its ships (*New Zealand Herald* 1985a). There was also reason to believe that Lange had been given an unofficial assurance by Washington that the *Buchanan* would not be nuclear armed and that, accordingly, the Americans expected no difficulty with their request for a visit.

True, the prime minister has emphatically denied any suggestions about a secret assurance, but, curiously, he was also reported as saying: "Had the *USS Buchanan* come to New Zealand...the United States would have moved strenuously to ensure it was not carrying nuclear weapons" (*New Zealand Herald* 1985a). A subsequent statement by the U.S. ambassador to New Zealand, H. Monroe Browne, that the New Zealand government had refused the visit "apparently because it could not satisfy itself that the ship was not nuclear armed" (*New Zealand Herald* 1985b) can also be read as supporting this viewpoint. Certainly in private conversations with U.S. officials both in the State Department and in New Zealand, the overwhelming impression received is that Washington had done everything possible to accommodate Lange's requirements.

Rightly or wrongly, U.S. officials believed that there had been a tacit understanding with the prime minister that the *Buchanan* would be admitted. Consequently there was a deep sense of betrayal when the request was denied. The mistrust of Prime Minister Lange was further exacerbated by the fact that he was absent on a private visit to the Tokelau Islands at a crucial stage of the proceedings. What had hitherto been a policy controversy now became, for the Americans, a matter of duplicity.

On the other side, Lange could well have experienced a disjunction between what he could promise as leader and what he could perform as prime minister. Recall that as the newly elected leader of the Labour party in 1983 Lange had unsuccessfully sought to restrict official party policy to banning only nuclear-armed vessels. The main problem, however, was the nuclear ban itself. Just as the original election manifesto promise to prohibit nuclear ship visits and to retain ANZUS was an improbable combination, so too the evolution of the policy to "trust me" (meaning Lange) to make an independent assessment of the nuclear capability of U.S. ships based upon New Zealand intelligence reflected little more than political naiveté.

Regardless of the justification, as of February 4, 1985, the proposed visit of the U.S.S. *Buchanan* to New Zealand was off. The United States immediately held New Zealand in violation of Article II of the ANZUS treaty, which calls for "the Parties separately and jointly by means of continuous and effective self-help and mutual aid [to] maintain and develop their individual and collective capacity to resist armed attack." Sanctions were swiftly invoked. The United States cancelled an invitation previously extended to New Zealand to participate in scheduled naval exercises. The amount of military intelligence supplied to New Zealand by U.S. sources was substantially reduced. New Zealand was denied the right to purchase equipment for its defense forces at specially discounted prices. Meetings between high-level officials of each country's government were deliberately voided by Washington. Furthermore the Reagan administration moved to hurt New Zealand's economic base by dropping its

opposition to Congressional legislation trying to restrict agricultural imports (upon which New Zealand depends so heavily) into the United States, withdrawing support for New Zealand's butter sales in third countries, reducing the quota of beef imported from New Zealand, and using American influence in Europe or Japan to encourage a reduction in the purchase of New Zealand dairy products. (Bercovitch 1988: 2)

The nuclear ships conflict was at its zenith.

DOMESTIC REACTION

The public reaction to the Labour government's ban on nuclear warships was swift and enthusiastic. In August 1984, less than a month after the government announced its policy, 76 percent of New Zealanders noted their approval of the ban on the entry of nuclear weapons into their country. A year earlier, without such a prohibition in effect, only 46 percent of the public disapproved of visits by nuclear-armed warships. Hence the government's antinuclear policy received a wide round of applause from most of the New Zealand public.

As has been argued elsewhere (Lamare 1987a), this massive swing behind the government's policy suggests a consolidation effect. That is, the New Zealand public appears to have rallied behind their government as the conflict with the United States developed. Cleavages that structured nuclear opinion before the ANZUS controversy erupted disappeared as the public closed ranks in support of their government. In 1983 disapproval of nuclear ship visits was manifested more among women than men, more among the young than the old, more among higher- than lower-status New Zealanders, and more among Labour and third-party supporters than partisans of the National party. After the antinuclear policy was proclaimed, these differences faded.

Across the board, gender, age, socioeconomic status, and party affiliation became less important in differentiating nuclear opinion. For instance, in 1983 when the National government permitted nuclear ship visits, only 23 percent of that party's faithful opposed this policy. A year later, even though their party had just suffered a rather humiliating defeat in the 1984 election, 63 percent of National identifiers supported the Labour government's ban. This 40 percent movement in opinion was the largest shift recorded among political and social groups in New Zealand between 1983 and 1984.

Such public rallies behind government policies in times of international conflict are not uncommon. Foreign policy initiatives in the United States and Britain usually are followed by public consolidation in support of these endeavors (see Chapters 2 and 3). There is an abundance of social, psychological, and anthropological evidence (reviewed in Stein 1976) demonstrating that external threat breeds internal group solidarity. Indeed, Darendorf (quoted in Levine and Campbell 1972: 31) concludes that this asymmetrical effect constitutes a "general law."

As the ANZUS conflict intensified, public consolidation, at least on the surface, remained intact. Immediately after New Zealand rejected the proposed *Buchanan* visit and the United States responded by invoking sanctions, the public stood firm in its support of the ban on nuclear weapons. A poll conducted on February 9, 1985—four days after the *Buchanan* visit was cancelled—found 73 percent of New Zealanders agreeing with the Labour government's prohibition. Some five weeks later, after the U.S. threats and sanctions had been aired, the public approval score had improved to 77 percent. Moreover, a critical, defensive attitude developed among the ban's supporters (for more details about this attitude structure, see Lamare 1987b). For them, New Zealand was being treated unfairly by the United States. Their country had not neglected its treaty responsibilities. If it came to the point of choosing between allowing nuclear ships port access or breaking defense ties with the United States, most of these New Zealanders preferred the latter course of action.

In many ways the public's solidarity limited the Labour government's maneuverability during the ANZUS crisis. Peace groups could legitimately talk of a consensus of antinuclear feeling in New Zealand. Any perceived deviation from Labour's antincuclear policy on the part of government officials, including the prime minister, could be resoundingly criticized by these activists. Moreover, leaders of these groups had direct access to Labour MPs. Indeed, several of these MPs were openly sympathetic, if not politically indebted, to these groups. When, for instance, it was thought that the prime minister might be softening his antinuclear stand in his discussions with the Americans over the request for the *Buchanan* visit, peace activists and a handful of Labour MPs sternly reminded Lange of the widespread public support for his government's ban.

Even its adversaries pressured the government to conform to its antinuclear commitment. In 1985, for instance, the deputy leader of the Democratic party, one of New Zealand's more successful third parties, introduced a bill to enact the "no nukes" policy into law, as promised in Labour's election manifesto. The purpose of this action was, of course, to embarrass the government and to emphasize the lack of progress that had been made in moving toward creating the promised legislative backbone to the nuclear ships ban.

Hence, through a variety of means, the issue was kept before the public. The matter was, after all, official public policy and support for it by members of the parliamentary wing of the party and some ministers meant that the government had scant room even for agenda manipulation. For example, Lange's search for a means by which New Zealanders could be assured that the *Buchanan* (or any other U.S. ship) was not nuclear-capable could not cross a threshold of public acceptability. Evidence, such as a ship's point of departure or the nature of its delivery systems, could have been offered as proof. However, without U.S. confirmation or denial such information could have been held by the public to be suspect. Considering that Washington was resolute in sticking to its "neither confirm nor deny" policy, New Zealand was left to trust that the United States would not send a nuclear vessel. Given the widespread perception among New Zealanders that the Americans had violated its promised embargo on allowing nuclear weapons to enter Japan's water, the Labour government would have been publicly ridiculed if it had accepted a Japanese-style solution based upon trust. The prime minister—particularly a Labour prime minister—whatever his personal inclinations or the pressures brought to bear by a super-power ally, had little alternative but to give priority to domestic considerations.

Moreover, the government found the nuclear ships issue to be very useful in trying to maintain its appeal among its natural constituents. For a myriad of reasons, Labour, once in government, embarked upon a domestic economic program that contravened the preferences of many segments of its coalition base. More specifically, the government launched a market-oriented approach to solve the economic and financial problems plaguing New Zealand. Privatization of state-owned assets, restructuring of government departments, user pays in a wide variety of areas, including tertiary education, and tax packages designed to stimulate business growth were pursued aggressively by the government. Such policies ran counter to the ideological tradition and the thrust of the Labour party, leading to growing uneasiness and restlessness among many of its traditional members and supporters—especially those in trade unions. Thus, the government needed a high-profile, popular policy that would clearly signal that this was in fact a Labour government, standing on Labour principles. Here, the nonnuclear policy provided the obvious, necessary trade-off.

With public support in full swing, the government entered into the post-*Buchanan* phase of the ANZUS conflict without much room to change the direction of its policy. After several failed attempts at negotiation, the United States declared in 1986 that by sticking to its nonnuclear policy New Zealand had, in effect, withdrawn from the ANZUS treaty arrangement. The United States would no longer guarantee the military protection of its once close and faithful ally. For its part, the Labour government in 1987 went further by enacting its policy into legislation, thus requiring any future government to change the law if it wanted to revoke the antinuclear ban.

The Labour government appears to have gained a great deal of electoral mileage out of its nuclear ships ban. The Labour party went into the 1987 national election riding the crest of a wave of widespread popularity. Indicative of this phenomenon is the fact that the National party, hitherto the only party to welcome nuclear ship visits, shifted ground during the 1987 campaign in order to accommodate public sentiment on this issue. National's leadership began to argue in favor of no nuclear weapons in the country, stressing that it would trust Washington not to request port access for vessels carrying such armament into New Zealand. Moreover, there is some evidence (Aimer and Vowles 1989) showing that Labour's nuclear position served, on balance, to constrain wholesale defection by voters who were disenchanted with the market direction of the government's economic and social policies.

Hence the consolidation effect precipitated by the initial conflict that flared over the nuclear ships ban had a great influence over the conduct of domestic policy making and politics in New Zealand. However, the lasting importance of this consolidation remained problematic for two reasons. First, the structural scope of the antinuclear attitude was limited. It only encompassed views toward nuclear weapons and criticism of the U.S. treatment of New Zealand during the height of the controversy. Opinion toward visits by nuclear-powered vessels and the overall public commitment to membership in ANZUS were not fully enveloped within this attitude structure. Second, there were signs that the solidarity that had emerged among all groups of New Zealanders in the initial phase of the conflict was showing signs of disintegration.

On the first point: New Zealanders—both before and after the conflict—

Figure 4.1
The Development of Antinuclear Opinion in New Zealand, 1982–89

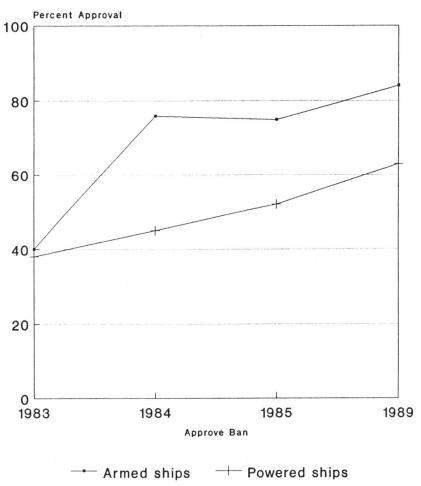

Source: Heylen Research Centre, Auckland, New Zealand.

showed a greater willingness to accept the berthing of nuclear-powered ships than nuclear-armed vessels (see Figure 4.1). In 1982, 38 percent opposed port visits by nuclear-propelled ships. Within a month after the 1984 controversy occurred, that figure had increased only 8 percent (to 46 percent). Public disapproval of visits by nuclear-powered ships increased as the conflict intensified in early 1985. But even after the cancellation of the *Buchanan* visit and the imposition of sanctions by the United States, the public disapproval of nuclear-powered vessels reached only 52 percent, some

25 percent less than the number of New Zealanders rejecting the entry of nuclear weapons into their country.

Moreover, many New Zealanders continued to value ANZUS membership even at the height of the nuclear ships conflict. A nationwide poll (reported in Foreign Affairs Group 1985: 11) conducted in February 1985 uncovered widespread support for continued membership in ANZUS: 78 percent of the public approved of New Zealand's participation in the alliance, while only 12 percent disapproved. In both March and October of that year, New Zealanders were evenly divided when forced to choose between breaking defense ties with the United States and allowing nuclear-armed ships into their country's ports. A year later (Defence Committee of Enquiry 1986), most (44 percent) preferred a nuclear-free ANZUS to being in ANZUS with nuclear ship visits (37 percent), and to no such ships and no ANZUS membership (16 percent). When pushed to choose between a nuclear-free policy and ANZUS membership, a majority (52 percent) stated—albeit, for some, quite reluctantly—that they would prefer being in ANZUS *with* nuclear ship visits to having a nonnuclear policy and withdrawal from the alliance (44 percent).[2]

On the second point: As early as February 1985, some cracks in the foundation of the consolidation effect were becoming evident (Lamare 1987b). Cleavages in opinion toward the ban on nuclear weapons emerged along much the same lines as had existed in 1983 before the ANZUS conflict. Specifically, age, gender, and party identification again came to structure opinion.

By February 1985, nearly 10 percentage points separated the support given to the ban on nuclear weapons by New Zealanders under and those over age 40 (Lamare 1989). Six months earlier (August 1984), this age division did not exist. However, a similar age difference was evidence in 1983, a year before the outbreak of the ANZUS conflict.

A generational gap in opinion on nuclear matters is not uncommon in many capitalistic, industrialized societies (Inglehart 1971, 1981). In New Zealand this age division, by and large, reflects pre- and post-World War II experiences and socialization. Younger New Zealanders have been raised largely free from a major war commitment, the ravages of the great depression, and a dependent orientation toward Britain. They have been urged to be independent-minded and assertive. They had also benefited from the availability of higher education and a beneficent and broad set of social welfare policies. As the post–World War II baby boom came of political age, self-confident, idealistic youth became increasingly effective in its questioning of long-established positions and attitudes. Many young people tended to view an alliance system dominated by the United States as a source of disharmony. Not surprisingly, they were more likely to accept the ban on nuclear weapons. Interestingly, Prime Minister David Lange, in his early forties when the ban went into effect, clearly identified with this generation.

Many in the older generation attributed the stopping of the Japanese occupation of the Pacific before it reached New Zealand's shores during World War II to the United States. For them, the ANZUS alliance provided a guarantee of New Zealand's security, a unique entree into the counsels of greater power, and a continuation of a long tradition of New Zealand internationalism making a contribution to the overall peace of the world.

Gender also reemerged in early 1985 to structure views on the ban on nuclear weapons. By March a 7 percent difference in opinion between men and women had replaced a nil gap in August 1984, when the consolidation effect occurred. This difference was the same as that which had existed prior to the ANZUS conflict. A great deal of research (summarized in Lamare 1989) shows that women are more likely than men to be antinuclear and pacific in outlook. New Zealand women fit this pattern well.

The combined effects of gender and age on nuclear opinion are quite pronounced (Lamare 1989). This is especially the case for young women and older men. In March 1985, there was a 25 percent difference between these two groups in reaction to the Labour government's nuclear ships ban. Young women overwhelmingly approved of the policy, while older men mostly rejected the government's position. This age/gender separation existed in 1983 before the controversy, but it became muted immediately after the initial conflict erupted in July 1984.

Party identification normally plays a major role in structuring opinion about issues in New Zealand politics (Lamare 1984). The previously noted dampening of differences in nuclear opinion between partisans that occurred in the immediate wake of the ANZUS controversy soon began to change. By March 1985, Labour and National loyalists were divided by 37 percent in their views of the ban. In May 1986 this separation had increased to 43 percent (Defence Committee of Enquiry 1986). Studies of voting behavior in the 1987 national election (Aimer and Vowles 1989; Simpson 1989) revealed that support for the government's nuclear policy was strongly associated with party affiliation.

Hence, as the ANZUS conflict wore on, age, gender, and party again exerted influence on nuclear opinion. The consolidation effect was most intact immediately after the initial announcement of the ban on nuclear ships was made in 1984. It began to show signs of slippage as the controversy continued, despite the escalation of the war of words between Wellington and Washington that transpired in early 1985. Moreover, by May 1986 the overall public support for the government's policy had shrunk some 11 percent, from nearly 77 percent in March 1985 to 66 percent a year later. The consolidation effect appeared on the brink of disintegration.

The United States could take some heart in the likelihood that public support for the ban was beginning to soften. This might account for the development of a low-key approach to the problem by Washington as the conflict continued. For instance, the United States terminated New Zealand's involvement in the alliance rather quietly. It limited its punitive sanctions mostly to military and intelligence matters, leaving direct economic embargos largely out of the recrimination program. Furthermore, it maintained and even expanded its commitments and presence in the country along other fronts. Finally, it surely hoped that, if New Zealanders elected a National government in 1990, a more agreeable ships policy would be put into place.

While all official contact with Labour government leaders was routinely shunned, Washington publicly courted members of the opposition. For its part, the National leadership—until early 1990—openly came to advocate a ships policy based on trust. Keeping in mind the Japanese approach to nuclear ship visits, National leaders announced that they would have the utmost confidence in the United States not to send vessels carrying nuclear weapons into New Zealand's waters.

In the meantime, some disturbing counter-evidential events were widely publicized in New Zealand. The Chernobyl explosion in the Soviet Union not only was a vivid reminder of the danger of nuclear accidents, it also economically benefited New Zealand, the home of noncontaminated agricultural products. In 1989, it was revealed that some twenty five years earlier, a U.S. fighter airplane equipped with a nuclear bomb had fallen from an aircraft carrier that had just visited Japan. The news raised questions about whether a Japanese approach to nuclear-free waters would be honored in practice by the Americans. This incident, coupled with reports of a series of fires and faults aboard nuclear vessels throughout the world in the first half of 1989, probably reinforced public concern over the risk of nuclear accidents at sea. Indeed, earlier polling had recorded that fear of accidents was one of the major reasons given by New Zealanders when they were asked why they opposed nuclear ship visits to their country.

New Zealand's nuclear ships policy was thrust back onto the center stage of domestic politics on April 25, 1989, when then–prime minister Lange delivered a lecture at Yale University in which he fully discussed the ANZUS crisis. In his address, Mr. Lange "raise[d] the issue of whether New Zealand should give formal notice of withdrawal from the ANZUS Council" (Lange 1989). The speech was roundly criticized in the New Zealand press as a transparent attempt by Lange to shore up this sagging popular support at home; as inappropriate, coming as it did on ANZAC day, a day of remembrance of New Zealand's participation in past wars; and as a sign that Lange was out of step with his own cabinet, which had not been consulted prior to his announcement of the threat to withdraw New Zealand from the ANZUS Council altogether.

Table 4.1
Public Opinion toward the Nuclear Ships Ban, 1989

Item	Response		
	Approve	Don't Know	Disapprove
Labour government policy to ban nuclear weapons into New Zealand	83.5%	3.5%	13.0%
	Approve	Don't Know	Disapprove
Labour government policy to ban nuclear-powered vessels from New Zealand ports	63.0%	4.6%	32.4%
	Break Ties	Don't Know	Allow Ships to Berth
Choice between breaking ties with the U.S. and allowing ships that could be nuclear armed into New Zealand ports	51.6%	8.7%	39.7%

Total number of cases = 1,000

Source: Heylen Research Centre, Auckland, New Zealand. Poll conducted on June 10, 1989.

Missing from this environment of cross-signals over the nuclear ships controversy was information about the New Zealand public's view of the matter. Had the consolidation effect totally unraveled? Or was there still substantial support for New Zealand's antinuclear stand? Popular sentiment about these matters had not been measured since 1986. To gauge the current state of opinion, we commissioned the Heylen Research Centre, one of the country's foremost polling organizations, to survey a national representative sample.[3] Personal interviews took place on June 10, 1989. The responses to the key questions are presented in Table 4.1.

Support for the "Labour government's policy to ban the entry of nuclear weapons into New Zealand" was at 83.5 percent, the highest approval score yet recorded on this policy. Only 3.5 percent had no opinion of the matter. Moreover, public opposition to visits by nuclear-powered vessels had also strengthened. By 1989, 63 percent of New Zealanders approved of the government's ban on these vessels, an 11 percent increase in approval since the question was last asked in 1985 at the height of the ANZUS dispute. Finally, on balance, New Zealanders—by a margin of 51.6 percent to 39.7 percent—preferred breaking defense ties with the United States to allowing nuclear-armed ships into their ports. When forced to choose between a "no nukes" policy and the military protection of the ANZUS alliance, the public chose the former.

Positive feelings about New Zealand's antinuclear policy have crystallized as time has elapsed. Even though the conflict has come off the international boil and the United States has replaced overt threats with low-key diplomatic inducements, there is still widespread public support for the nuclear ships ban. It is difficult to argue that this outlook is simply a continuation of the consolidation effect that resulted when New Zealanders rallied around their government in response to external pressure.

As indicated in Table 4.2, some variations in nuclear opinion between social and political groups existed in 1989. Party identification divided public sentiment sharply. On average, 85 percent of Labour supporters approved of the ban on nuclear-armed and -powered vessels, as well as leaving the alliance in order to preserve a nuclear-free New Zealand. While consistency prevailed among Labour partisans, such was not the case among their National counterparts. The latter supported the ban on nuclear weapons, but their approval declined in the case of nuclear-powered ships, and it did not extend to abandoning the alliance. As a result of these inconsistencies, the average score on the three nuclear questions for National supporters was 47 percent.

These findings had some clear policy implications. The Labour government would have found it most difficult to retreat from its antinuclear stance. By 1989, this was probably the only policy area widely endorsed by the New Zealand public. Along virtually all other policy fronts, the government had become very unpopular during its second term in office. Specifically, it received low ratings in its handling of economic, educational, health, and race relations issues. Only a small fraction of the public—about one in five—considered the government's overall performance to be satisfactory.[4]

The government's credibility was such that even to hint at a break from its antinuclear policy would have been fatal to its chances for reelection. Thus when a change of leadership took place with the resignation of the prime minister, David Lange, in August 1989, his successor, Deputy Prime Minister Geoffrey Palmer, immediately announced that there would be no alteration in the country's antinuclear policy.

Meanwhile, the National party was receiving mixed signals from the

Table 4.2

Nuclear Opinion by Gender, Age, Socioeconomic Status, and Party, 1989

	Approve Ban on Nuclear Weapons	Approve Ban on Nuclear Powered Ships	Prefer to Break Defense Ties with U.S.
GENDER:			
Men	81.4%	58.9%	52.4%
Women	85.5%	66.8%	50.8%
Difference:	3.9%	7.9%	1.6%
SOCIOECONOMIC STATUS[1]			
High	84.9%	59.1%	57.7%
Medium	82.6%	60.5%	45.6%
Low	84.3%	72.7%	60.9%
Difference[2] :	.6%	13.6%	3.2%
AGE:			
15-24 years	88.9%	77.6%	57.4%
25-39 years	88.0%	70.0%	56.7%
40-54 years	82.4%	54.1%	47.5%
55 years and over	74.2%	48.9%	43.5%
Difference[2] :	14.7%	28.7%	13.9%
AGE/GENDER[3]			
Younger women	92.7%	80.4%	54.7%
Younger men	83.8%	64.3%	59.4%
Older women	77.3%	51.4%	46.5%
Older men	75.9%	49.6%	44.1%
Difference[2] :	16.8%	30.8%	15.3%
PARTY CHOICE[4]			
Labour	94.1%	83.9%	76.7%
Other/Undecided	84.7%	74.1%	53.8%
National	73.0%	40.4%	28.7%
Difference[2] :	21.1%	43.5%	48.0%

Total sample size = 1,000

Notes:

1. Socioeconomic status is a combined measure of income, education, occupation, and family size.

2. Refers to the differences between the extremes.

3. Age was dichotomized at 40 years old. Those above this age are classified as older, while those below are categorized as younger.

4. Party choice is measured by asking respondents the party for which they would vote if the election were held today. New Labour Party supporters were included in the Labour Party totals. Partisans of the Democratic Party were included in the other category along with the undecided and respondents refusing to answer.

Source: Heylen Research Centre, Auckland, New Zealand. Poll conducted on June 10, 1989.

public. The widespread growth in public support for a nuclear-free New Zealand made promising an early return to the alliance (and the possibility of renewed nuclear ship visits if the party became the government) an electoral risk. A strong element of National supporters approved of the ban on nuclear weapons. However, many of these partisans preferred being in the alliance to sticking with the ban, thus putting some interesting cross-pressure on the party leadership.

Men and women across the spectrum of socioeconomic status approved of the prohibition of nuclear-capable ships. Age, however, differentiated nuclear opinion in 1989. The younger the New Zealander, the more the support for a ban on nuclear-armed and -powered vessels, even if such an endorsement meant breaking defense ties with the United States. Conversely, older New Zealanders were the least supportive of these positions.

The age-related patterns become even more interesting when gender is added into the picture. As indicated in Table 4.2, younger (under age 40) women were the most supportive of the government's antinuclear policies, followed in order by younger (under 40) men, older women, and older men. By and large, the younger the gender group, the greater the antinuclear support. For instance, 85 percent of the youngest (age 15 to 24) women in the sample approved of the ban on nuclear-powered vessels, while only 46 percent of men over 55 agreed with this position. This 39 percent difference in opinion indicated a wide gender/age gap on nuclear matters in New Zealand.

CONCLUSION

Antinuclear opinion in New Zealand went from minority status to a widely supported public policy in a very short period of time. The initial ANZUS conflict resulted in a widespread public rally behind its government. Interestingly, apart from some heated political rhetoric, the conflict— as far as international conflicts go—was rather mild in nature. No shots were fired. No invasion occurred. Direct economic sanctions were threatened but not comprehensively carried out. Regardless, the U.S. reaction to New Zealand's ban on nuclear ship visits precipitated a consolidation of public opinion behind the government's position.

The internal dynamism of New Zealand's political system affected this transformation of minority opinion to popular policy. Most of the country's leading parties promoted the antinuclear view. Peace groups tenaciously pursued the acceptance of antinuclear policy, both at the elite and mass levels. Labour members of Parliament kept a watchful eye on the party's leaders to prevent any waver in the implementation of this policy.

The widespread support for the Labour government's stand against berthing nuclear vessels gained it valuable public support at critical junctures as it systematically introduced a controversial market-oriented approach to the country's economic problems. Conversely, the government had limited scope for maneuverability in its attempts to resolve the nuclear conflict with the United States. As a result, the government refused requests for ship visits and the United States withdrew its military support for New Zealand and cut intelligence links. The ANZUS treaty soon became a dead letter for New Zealand although a bilateral connection with Australia remained.

It was not until March 1990 that any sign of a thaw in the frozen relations between the two countries was signaled. At that time, Secretary of State James Baker announced that the United States would welcome talks with high-ranking officials of the New Zealand government, although he reaffirmed Washington's opposition to the nuclear ships ban and its intention not to provide New Zealand with military intelligence and equipment. The Labour government responded favorably to this development, but quickly emphasized its continued commitment to the nuclear ban.

The consolidation in public opinion regarding the nuclear ships ban appeared to weaken as the controversy wore on. By 1986, some slippage in support for the ban on nuclear ships had occurred. Moreover, as early as 1985, social and political points of cleavage among New Zealanders began again to differentiate nuclear opinion. Party identification especially divided the public. The opposition National party—along with the U.S. government—could take hope in the growing number of supporters coming to oppose the ban. However, a subsequent round of opinion testing indicated that approval of the ban and its implications for breaking alliance ties had firmed. Figure 4.1 details the rise in support for a nonnuclear policy in New Zealand from 1982 through 1989.

The firming of widespread and consistent endorsement of this position suggests that antinuclear sentiment was becoming a mainstay of the country's political culture. In many ways, the commitment to antinuclearism appears to have transcended partisan politics and has become a national symbol, one that may have been initially created in response to outside pressure but that now exists as a signature of New Zealand identity. Young New Zealanders are coming to political maturity overwhelmingly socialized into this outlook. Indeed, the last bastion of opposition to antinuclearism resides among their older counterparts.

Not surprisingly, in March 1990 the National Party—the last major political organization to oppose Labour's ban—switched its position on nuclear ships visits and announced that, if it formed the government, it too would not accept such vessels into New Zealand's ports, regardless of ANZUS. With that proclamation all political elites in New Zealand became totally synchronized with popular sentiment. Consequently, it is hard to envision the day when nuclear-capable ships will again come into New Zealand's waters.

NOTES

1. Unless otherwise stated, all public opinion information cited in this chapter comes from surveys conducted by the Heylen Research Centre, Auckland, New Zealand.

2. This information is found in the annex to the report of the Defence Committee of Enquiry (1986: 76). The survey was conducted by the National Research Bureau for the Defence Committee of Enquiry. Fully 1,600 New Zealanders were personally interviewed between April 26, 1986, and May 19, 1986. Cluster techniques were used in obtaining the sample. A unitary response rate was achieved through substituting and callbacks.

3. The costs of the poll were shared with the Heylen Research Centre and the Eyewitness News of Television New Zealand. We are most grateful to these organizations for their support. Heylen employs a multistage, stratified sampling frame to select respondents. A personal interview occurred with the person who had his or her last birthday in the residence chosen in the sample draw. The sample contained 1,000 New Zealanders, 15 years of age or older, living in population centers with more than 2,500 people. Repeated callbacks ensured a response rate in excess of 90 percent. The Heylen Research Centre assumes no responsibility for the data analysis or interpretation presented in this chapter.

4. Several of these evaluations of the government's overall and specific policy performance were measured in the 1989 poll on the nuclear ships ban.

REFERENCES

Aimer, Peter, and Jack Vowles. "Nuclear Free New Zealand and Rogernomics: The Survival of the Labour Government." Paper presented at the New Zealand Political Studies Conference, Wellington, New Zealand, 1989.

Albinski, Henry. "The ANZUS Crisis: U.S. Policy Implications and Responses." In Jacob Bercovitch, ed., *ANZUS in Crisis: Alliance Management in International Affairs*. London: Macmillan, 1988.

Bercovitch, Jacob, ed. *ANZUS in Crisis: Alliance Management in International Affairs*. London: Macmillan, 1988.

Burnett, Alan. *The A–NZ–US Triangle*. Canberra: Strategic and Defence Studies Centre, Australian National University, 1988.

Christchurch Press. Christchurch, New Zealand. December 18, 1984.

Clements, Kevin. "New Zealand's Role in Promoting a Nuclear Free Pacific." *Journal of Peace Research* 25 (1988): 395–410.

Defence Committee of Enquiry. *Public Opinion Poll on Defence and Security: What New Zealanders Want*. Wellington: Government Printer, 1986.

The Defence Question: A Discussion Paper. Wellington: Government Printer, 1985.

Foreign Affairs Group. *New Zealand and Australian Public Opinion on Nuclear Ships and ANZUS*. Report prepared for the Parliament of Australia. Canberra: Legislative Research Service, 1985.

Inglehart, Ronald. "The Silent Revolution in Europe: Intergenerational Change in Post-Industrial Societies." *American Political Science Review* 65 (1971): 991–1017.

————. "Post-materialism in an Environment of Insecurity." *American Political Science Review* 75 (1981): 880–900.

Lamare, James W. "Party Identification and Voting Behaviour in New Zealand." *Political Science* 36 (1984): 1–9.

————. "International Conflict: ANZUS and New Zealand Public Opinion." *Journal of Conflict Resolution* 31 (1987a): 420–437.

————. "International Conflict and Opinion Change in New Zealand." *Public Opinion Quarterly* 51 (1987b): 392–399.

————. "Gender and Public Opinion: Defense and Nuclear Issues in New Zealand." *Journal of Peace Research* 26 (1989): 285–296.

Lange, David. "New Zealand Foreign Policy: The Nuclear Issue and Great Power–Small State Relations." The George Herbert Walker, Jr., Lecture, Yale University, 1989.

Levine, R. A., and D. T. Campbell. *Ethnocentrism: Theories of Conflict, Ethnic Attitudes, and Group Behavior.* New York: Wiley, 1972.

Lindblom, Charles. "The Science of Muddling Through." *Public Administration Review* 19 (1959): 79–88.

McMillan, Stuart. *Neither Confirm nor Deny.* Wellington: Allen and Unwin, 1985.

New Zealand Herald. March 30, 1983.

————. March 22, 1985a.

————. April 3, 1985b.

New Zealand Times. September 23, 1984.

Olson, Mancur. *The Logic of Collective Action.* Cambridge, Mass.: Harvard University Press, 1971.

Reese, Trevor. *Australia, New Zealand and the United States.* London: Oxford University Press, 1969.

Simpson, Alan. "Hamilton Electoral Surveys—1987." Paper presented at the New Zealand Political Studies Conference, Wellington, New Zealand, 1989.

Stein, Arthur A. "Conflict and Cohesion." *Journal of Conflict Resolution* 20 (1976): 143–172.

Strachan, David. "A Party Transformed: Organisational Change in the New Zealand Labour Party." In Hyam Gold, ed., *New Zealand Politics in Perspective.* Wellington: Longman Paul, 1985.

Wilson, J. V. "New Zealand's Participation in International Organisations." In T. C. Larkin, ed., *New Zealand's External Relations.* Wellington: New Zealand Institute of Public Administration, 1962.

5

Jews and Arabs in Israel: Everybody Hates Somebody, Sometime

Michal Shamir and John L. Sullivan

Israelis live very much in the shadow of the Israeli-Arab conflict. It affects all aspects of life, particularly the relationship between the Jewish majority and the Arab minority. The current research examines the patterns of political tolerance and intolerance in each of these groups. These patterns are largely structured by the larger conflict, as the most important sources of political tolerance generally lie in political processes (Sullivan et al. 1982; Shamir and Sullivan 1982, 1983).

Tolerance means indulgence for ideas and groups differing from or conflicting with one's own. Political tolerance requires a willingness to apply political democratic rights, such as freedom of expression, organization, and representation, and equality before the law, to groups or individuals that one finds objectionable. The test of tolerance for an individual as for a society is therefore in the context of a serious objection, often in the context of a perceived threat. The Arab-Israeli conflict, on which the Jews and Arabs in Israel obviously disagree, puts both groups in such a context, which makes the Israeli case a most interesting one for the general study of tolerance.

BACKGROUND

The political context is well known. The Arab-Israeli conflict defines the major issue dimension in Israeli domestic politics. Indeed, it is the dominant feature of Israel's existence, despite the peace agreement with Egypt. It is characterized by a permanent state of war that erupts into major war from time to time. This is part of the Israeli situation and mentality and is reflected in all spheres of life. Demographics are also an important aspect of the conflict. Israel's population at the end of 1982 numbered 4,063,600, of which 3,373,200 were Jews and 690,400 were Arabs.[1] Israeli Arabs constitute a minority of about one-sixth, yet they are part of the Arab majority in the Mideast, where the Jews are a tiny minority.

Given the parameters of the conflict, both groups—the Jewish majority and the Arab minority—find themselves in a threatening situation. In the face of five major wars, numerous terrorist attacks and attempted attacks, and hostile neighbors, the Jewish perceptual consensus is that the conflict is a matter of life or death, that if Israel loses one war "the Jews will be thrown into the sea," as the Arab slogan goes. The mentality is one of "siege" and "no choice." Being the majority in Israel, the Jews define the character of the state. Jewish nationalism—Zionism—is an important attribute (see Shapiro 1977) clearly not shared by the Arab minority. It entails views and policies contrary to the wishes and interests of the Arab minority. Some such policies concern them directly, such as the Law of Return, which encourages Jewish immigration; the expropriation of Arab land; and the imposition of military government over specific zones in the country between 1948 and 1966. More broadly, the Arab minority dissents from Jewish attitudes and policies toward the Arab states, the occupied territories, and the Palestinian problem (Smooha and Peretz 1982). The Israeli Arabs are put in a situation that makes it almost impossible for them to define their identity and their loyalty: "How to be loyal Israelis and remain true Arabs" (Haddad et al. 1977:97; Landau 1969; Peres and Yuval-Davis 1969; Peres 1970, 1971; Tessler 1977; Smooha 1978). In the context of the conflict, they identify to a large extent with the nation's enemy (Smooha and Peretz 1982; Tessler 1977), and they are perceived by the Jews as a hostile minority, even as a fifth column (Tsemah 1980), although there is no support for such a claim. Although they have been incorporated into Israeli society in some ways (Smooha 1980), and despite guaranteed equal protection under the law, asymmetry in Jewish-Arab relations is eminent. Social, economic, and political inequalities, widespread segregation, political control, and cultural differences are still the dominant features of such relationships (Smooha 1978; Lustick 1980). Growing radicalization among the Arabs has been noted by Jewish experts and laypersons (e.g., Rekhess 1976). It is coupled, however, with a factionalism that is less often noticed (Smooha 1980; Smooha and Peretz 1982).

Given the Arab-Israeli conflict and the ensuing majority-minority relations among Jews and Arabs in Israel, it is instructive to investigate the climate of political tolerance within the Jewish majority and the Arab minority in order to further our understanding of Israeli society and of the dynamics of tolerance more generally.

THE ISRAELI-ARAB CONFLICT: IDEOLOGY AND TARGETS FOR INTOLERANCE

The data for our analysis are from a national survey conducted in the fall of 1980. The survey examined a (nonproportional) stratified sample of the

Israeli population, with 913 Jewish and 300 Arab respondents.[2]

We asked our respondents to select, from a list of unpopular groups, the one they liked the least, in order to identify the political targets of intolerance. The list of groups presented to the Arab sample was somewhat different from that presented to the Jews.[3] Several groups that are on the Jewish agenda are not on the Arab agenda, and vice versa. All respondents are also given the option of naming a group not appearing on the list, but very few did so. Table 5.1 lists the groups selected as least-liked (and second-least-liked) and the percentage of respondents choosing each.[4]

Given the preeminent place the Palestine Liberation Organization (PLO) occupies on the Israeli agenda with its terrorist, political, and international roles, we expected a large number of Jewish respondents to choose it as their least-liked group. Yet we attempted to make a clear distinction between the PLO, an outside group with no legal or political standing in Israel, and "groups in Israel that support the PLO." This distinction is important because we are interested in tolerance and intolerance toward groups operating within the system. Thus the PLO as such does not qualify. In the Jewish sample we did not specify these groups (which support the PLO) but left the issue to the respondent's interpretation and understanding.[5] In the Arab questionnaire we specifically named the one best-known such group that outspokenly describes itself as supporting the PLO: Bnei Hakfar, Sons of the Village. Very few Arab respondents selected this group as a target, but 35 percent of the Jews chose the groups in Israel supporting the PLO as their least-liked group, with 22 percent more choosing them as their second-least-liked group.

The next most common target among Jewish respondents is Rakah, the Israeli Communist Party, which has four members in the Eleventh Knesset. Of the respondents, 29 percent chose it as their least-liked group, and 24 percent chose Rakah as their second-least-liked group. Rakah is basically an Arab party in terms of its voters and activists. It is anti-Zionist, its positions are perceived by many Jews as supporting the PLO, and its communist message is much less salient than its Arab nationalistic message (Grielsammer 1978). Among the Arabs only 5 percent selected Rakah as least-liked.

In addition to groups in Israel supporting the PLO and Rakah, several Jewish groups are defined as extreme, unpopular, and left-wing in Israeli politics. We listed four such groups in the Hebrew questionnaire and one (Sheli) in the Arab questionnaire. Mazpen is a small extreme Jewish group, with an anti-Zionist and Trotskyist ideology (Yuval-Davis 1977). It was selected by 5 percent of the Jewish respondents, with an additional 8 percent selecting it as second-least-liked. Sheli is a political party that had two representatives in the Ninth Knesset, but it received less than 1 percent of the vote in the 1981 election and, by 1984, had joined another political party. It is composed of and obtains most of its support from Jews, but is

Table 5.1
Groups Selected as Least Liked by Jews and Arabs

Item:	Jews Least-Liked Group	Jews Second-Least-Liked Group	Arabs Least-Liked Group	Arabs Second-Least-Liked Group
A. Groups				
Groups in Israel supporting the PLO	35%	22%	n.a.	n.a.
Bnei Hakfar	n.a.	n.a.	2%	3%
Rakah (Communists)	29	24	5	3
Mazpen	5	8	n.a.	n.a.
Sheli	1	2	less 1	2
Peace Now	2	2	n.a.	n.a.
Black Panthers	2	3	n.a.	n.a.
Kach (Kahane's Group)	3	3	29	24
Gush Emunim	4	4	29	26
Hatchia	less 1	1	7	13
Neturei Karta (ultra-orthodox)	13	17	n.a.	n.a.
Young Muslims	n.a.	n.a.	7	4
Other Group	1	2	1	1
Don't Know	5	12	20	24
B. Groups defined along the Arab-Israeli conflict dimension	79%	66%	72%	71%
C. Arab group	64%	46%	14%	10%
Jewish group	30%	39%	65%	65%

N = 913   N = 300

also active among Arabs. It was formed out of several leftist splinter groups, including the Jewish members of the Communist Party, which split in 1965 basically along Arab-Jewish lines (Grielsammer 1978). Peace Now is another Jewish leftist group, acting as a pressure group on the issues of the occupied territories, peace with Egypt, and the recent war in Lebanon. The main definition of all these groups is along the Arab-Israeli conflict dimension, although at least the first two have a wider left-wing message. The Black Panthers' most salient definition is ethnic, and their protest has been against injustice and discrimination toward the Sephardic Jews. They also belong to the left wing of the Arab-Israeli conflict and of Israeli politics more generally. Very few respondents selected these last three groups.

Three right-wing groups were mentioned as least-liked: Kach, Gush Emunim, and Hatchia. All three are defined along the Arab-Israeli cleavage. Gush Emunim, the Block of the Faithful, is the group behind many of the settlements in the West Bank. Most of its members are orthodox and religious, believing in the Jewish right to the land of Israel, and in their messianic mission to inhabit and build it. Gush Emunim acts as a pressure group, and its members work through several political parties. Hatchia is a political party with five representatives in the Eleventh Knesset and is closely aligned with Gush Emunim. Kach, Rabbi Kahane's group, is much smaller but has similar views, even calling for forced Arab emigration from Israel and what Kach calls the "liberated territories." Kach ran for Parliament in 1981 but received much less than the minimum 1 percent needed to obtain representation. By 1984, however, it obtained one seat in the Knesset. About 7 percent of the Jews selected one of these groups as their least-liked target, but fully 65 percent of the Arabs did so.

Finally, we listed two religious groups. Neturei Karta, the third most popular target among Jews, is an ultrareligious group that one would be hard put to define as left- or right-wing. It is anti-Zionist and does not recognize the state of Israel, but most references to it relate to its religious extremism and coercion. Thirteen percent chose it as least-liked. Among the Arabs, 7 percent mentioned the Young Muslims, a Muslim orthodox religious as well as nationalistic group that recently gained support in several townships, calling for a return to Islam.

Beyond the details of the targets Jews and Arabs select, the results point to two major conclusions. Arab and Jewish selection patterns are very different, but for both populations, most disliked groups stem from one and the same cleavage dimension, the Arab-Israeli conflict. Fully 79 percent of the Jews select groups belonging to this dimension, and 72 percent of the Arabs do the same. Indeed, if we disregard respondents who did not answer the question, the figures are even more impressive: 83 percent and 90 percent, respectively. But the specific choice of groups is very different, representing a mirror image. Arabs overwhelmingly select Jewish right-wing groups; the ratio is 65 to 7 in the whole sample and 82 to 9 when "no response" is disregarded. Jews select left-wing groups, primarily groups perceived as Arab (PLO supporters and Rakah). The ratio between the left- and right-wing groups is 74 to 7 and between Arab and Jewish groups it is 64 to 30.

The results are very clear: The Jewish-Arab cleavage is dominant with Jews and Arabs on opposite ideological sides. Arabs dislike right-wing (nationalistic) Jewish groups, whereas Jews dislike left-wing (nationalistic) Arab groups. To complete the picture we may look at the ideological self-identification of our respondents. We asked them to define themselves as left-wing or right-wing along a 7-point continuum, from extreme left to extreme right. Of the Arab sample, 50 percent define themselves as left-wingers and only 15 percent as right-wingers. In the Jewish sample 20 percent are left-wingers and 44 percent are right-wingers. The Jews are on the right of the political spectrum; the Arabs are on the left. This spectrum is largely defined in Israel along the Arab-Jewish conflict dimension, more so than on economic matters (Arian and Shamir 1983), and the close identity of the left with compromising views among Jews and Arabs and of the right with Jewish nationalism is clear.

These results reinforce those of Smooha and Peretz (1982), who examined Arab and Jewish attitudes toward the Israeli-Arab conflict. They showed that Israel's Arabs as a whole reject the Jewish national consensus. The Arabs support and the Jews oppose a Palestinian nation, Israeli withdrawal to the pre–1967 borders, recognition of the PLO as a representative of the Palestinians, formation of a Palestinian state on the West Bank and Gaza Strip, repeal of the annexation of East Jerusalem, and the right of repatriation of the Palestinian refugees.

THREAT AND POLITICAL INTOLERANCE

Israeli society is highly polarized on these issues. The spectrum of political groups active in Israeli politics, and the pattern of groups that Jews and Arabs dislike and to which they object, is one manifestation of this polarization. Indeed, when we examine the objections of our respondents to the groups they dislike, they are overwhelmingly political, ideological objections. We asked our respondents in an open-ended question why they disliked the specific group they had selected. Jews often accused their least-liked group of being anti-Israel, anti-Zionist, or pro-Arab (46 percent of the responses). Many Arabs accused their least-liked group of being against the Arabs (24 percent), but 55 percent of them referred to the group's actions, methods, and tactics as the reasons for disliking it (compared to 19 percent in the Jewish sample).[6] Violence, discrimination, settlements, and land expropriations were frequently mentioned.

The objections raised on both sides are highly relevant to the political situation. These are realistic, serious political and ideological objections, most of them revolving around the Arab-Israeli conflict. The opinions (selected more often by Jews) and the action (selected more often by Arabs) of the disliked groups are viewed as threats to one's own rights, particularly national rights.

An objection is a necessary precondition for tolerance. It obviously exists here. But objections are not identical to threat. Logically they are different, although empirically—in particular, in this political context—they are likely to be closely related.[7] We expect Israelis, both Jews and Arabs, to be greatly threatened by the political groups they mentioned. Although it is difficult to assess objectively the degree of actual threat posed to Arabs and to Jews in Israel by their least-liked groups, we expect Arabs to perceive a greater threat than Jews.[8] The source of this expectation is the "hostile minority" status of the Arab community in Israel; their close kinship, socially and ideologically, with the Palestinians in the territories occupied by Israel in the 1967 Six-Day War, and the fact that most of their targets are Jewish right-wing groups that have extreme nationalistic views with regard to those territories, their inhabitants, and Arabs more generally. The fact that the Arabs often mentioned the deeds of their least-liked group as the reason for disliking it may also suggest that Arabs perceive a greater threat than Jews.

This is indeed the case (see Table 5.2). We measured threat in two ways. First we presented to respondents a series of semantic differential items about the group in question. They were asked to rate, on scales ranging from 1 to 7, their least-liked groups on each adjective pair. Table 5.2 presents the percentage of respondents rating their least-liked group toward the undesirable or threatened end of each scale. On all items, Arabs see their disliked group as more threatening than do the Jews. In particular they perceive their targets as more dishonest, violent, and untrustworthy, and as bad. We also asked our respondents to what degree the group posed a personal or regime threat, and on those questions both Arabs and Jews perceive the threat more as a regime threat in political, collective terms than as a personal threat.

Across all these measures of perceived threat, an average of 56 percent of Jews, but fully 68 percent of the Arab sample, were highly threatened. Both percentages are considerably higher if we exclude the important-unimportant adjective pair and the question about personal threat. Clearly, then, both sets of respondents are highly threatened, but the Arabs more so, as one would expect given the fact that the Israeli Jews are the ruling majority in the state of Israel. In fact, on the first five adjectives in Table 5.2a, an average of 88 percent of the Arab respondents feel threatened. We could hardly expect results closer to unanimity.

Table 5.2b emphasizes the differences in threat perception conditional upon whether the respondents select Jewish or Arab groups as their targets. Jews who select Jewish targets and Arabs who select Arab target groups are far less threatened than the Jews who select Arab targets or the Arabs

Table 5.2
Threat Perception of Least-Liked Group among Jews and Arabs

		Jews	Arabs
A.	Perceiving group as:		
	dishonest	62%	91%
	untrustworthy	76	90
	violent	63	87
	bad	72	87
	dangerous	80	84
	important	20	27
	Personal threat is great or very great	23	24
	Regime threat is great or very great	50	55
	Mean percentage threatened	56%	68%
		N=854	N=238

		Jews		Arabs	
B.	Perceiving group as:	Arab Group	Jewish Group	Arab Group	Jewish Group
	dishonest	69%	45%	72%	96%
	untrustworthy	81	65	72	94
	violent	66	65	56	94
	bad	78	62	61	54
	dangerous	85	71	58	90
	important	20	20	49	23
	Personal threat is great or very great	27	15	10	27
	Regime threat is great or very great	54	43	19	62
	Mean percentage threatened	60%	48%	50%	73%
		N=583	N=271	N=43	N=195

selecting Jewish targets. The differences are substantial and are greater for the Arab respondents. These differences are also most pronounced in terms of the adjectives "dishonest," "untrustworthy," "bad," and "dangerous." Still, the Jews who selected Arab targets were more threatened than the Arabs who selected Arab targets, and so being an Arab in Israel does not guarantee a greater level of perceived threat than does being a member of the dominant ethnic group.

Among Arabs the Jewish target groups are perceived as very threatening, particularly in terms of violence, danger, and badness. They are also seen as posing a much greater regime threat, and a somewhat greater personal threat, than the Arab target groups do to those Arabs who chose them as least liked.

This national and ideological polarization is coupled with high levels of perceived threat and leads to an expectation of very low levels of political tolerance in both sectors, which is what we find. We measured tolerance by asking respondents a series of questions about the group they selected as least liked: whether members of the group should be allowed to become prime minister; whether the group ought to be outlawed; whether members should be allowed to hold public rallies; whether members should be allowed to make speeches in public and appear on TV; whether members should be allowed to teach in public schools; whether they should be allowed to study at universities; and whether they ought to have their telephones tapped. Individual respondents are therefore asked questions of tolerance with reference to particular target groups, overcoming the shortcomings of previous measures of tolerance, which ask all respondents about a specific group without inquiring whether an objection toward that group exists at all. Here, objection is ensured by allowing each respondent to choose a least-liked group (Sullivan et al. 1979, 1982). This is particularly important in the current instance, as we cannot expect Israeli Arabs and Jews to dislike the same, or similar, extremist groups.

Table 5.3 presents the percentage of Jewish and Arab respondents who gave tolerant responses to these statements (the percentage agreeing or strongly agreeing with tolerant items and disagreeing or strongly disagreeing with intolerant items). The typical Israeli, whether Jew or Arab, is intolerant, on the average. Arabs are slightly less tolerant than Jews. The average percentage tolerant across seven items is somewhat higher for Jews, and they achieve a tolerant majority on two of the items, while Arabs do so on none. A similar percentage of Jews and Arabs gave tolerant responses on becoming prime minister, holding rallies, and free speech. Arabs were more tolerant on one item, teaching in public schools. This is probably the problem closest to their personal concerns as an Arab minority; the other items are more hypothetical and of less direct relevance to them. Jews were more tolerant on the other three questions: outlawing the least-liked group, phone tapping, and university studies.

Table 5.3
Political Tolerance (Jews and Arabs)

	Percentage tolerant[1]	
A.	Jews	Arabs
Members of the _____ should be banned from being prime minister in Israel.	13	9
Members of the _____ should be allowed to teach in public schools.	26	37
The _____ should be outlawed.	31	8
The _____ should be allowed to hold public rallies.	36	36
Members of the _____ should be allowed to make a speech in public or appear on TV.	38	40
The _____ should have their phones tapped.	53	36
Members of the _____ should not be allowed to study at universities.	57	47
Average	36	30
	N=867	N=242

	Percentage Tolerant			
	Jews		Arabs	
B.	Arab Group	Jewish Group	Arab Group	Jewish Group
Prime minister	11	19	14	8
Teach	21	40	43	35
Outlaw	25	46	17	6
Rallies	28	53	38	36
Speech, TV	31	52	40	41
Phones tapped	45	70	37	37
Study at university	52	70	45	48
Average	30	50	33	30
	N=584	N=271	N=43	N=195

1. Percentage agreeing or strongly agreeing to items measuring tolerance.

The second part of the table differentiates between political tolerance toward Arab and Jewish groups within each sector. Jews who selected Jewish groups as least-liked are more willing to tolerate them than are Jews who picked Arab groups. The average difference in tolerance is 20 percentage points. Indeed, among the Jews who pick some Jewish group as least liked, a tolerant majority obtains for four of the seven items, and on two more items the percentage tolerant is over 40 percent. These relatively high levels of tolerance stand out in comparison to all three other columns. Jews who select an Arab group (Rakah or PLO supporters) as least-liked are much less tolerant, achieving a tolerant majority on only one item. Among Arabs—both those who chose an Arab group and those who chose a Jewish group—the level of tolerance is close to that of Jews who pick Arab groups. They do not achieve a tolerant majority on any item in either category, although tolerance toward Arab groups is somewhat higher than tolerance toward Jewish groups. Among Jews at least, the willingness to apply the democratic rights to a group one opposes is largely a function of whether the target is Jewish or Arab. The two Arab groups come very close in their ideological position to the leftist Jewish groups, yet the Jews' willingness to tolerate them is much lower. Dissent when it is voiced by Arabs is considered less legitimate and is not as likely to be tolerated.

Both Jewish and Arab sectors in Israeli society are characterized by "focused intolerance." Both sectors are in general politically intolerant (Jews mainly toward Arab groups) and the targets for intolerance are highly concentrated. Considering that Jewish public opinion is the one that affects the regime most directly, its characteristics are probably more relevant with regard to system-level manifestations of intolerance. But there is a dynamic feedback relationship between these two publics, and intolerance on either side no doubt breeds intolerance on the other.

ABSTRACT NORMS OF DEMOCRACY AND TOLERANCE

Intolerance often arises from perceptions of threat (Stouffer 1955; Sullivan et al. 1982). Most citizens will be intolerant toward a group if they feel that this group threatens important values or constitutes a danger to the political regime.[9] In an individual-level (multivariate) analysis, we found that perceptions of threat are the most important determinant of political tolerance among Jews and Arabs.

The one factor that has been found to offset threat and to induce tolerance is a strong belief in the abstract norms of democracy. The stronger the belief in these norms, the more people are willing to act on these norms and to apply them in concrete and threatening situations (Sullivan et al. 1982). The fact that tolerance is one value that at times must be weighed against other values that are believed to be at stake finds its expression in various legal doctrines. The "clear and present danger" concept of American liberal legal thought sets one limit on tolerance. Other doctrines, more influential in European political thought and practice, set more severe limits on it easily compromising tolerance in the presence of threat, probably because threat was and is more real in those polities than in the United States. In Israel the most important and often-cited reference to this issue is the High Court of Justice ruling in the Al-Ard case. Al-Ard was an Arab leftist, nationalistic group that operated in the late 1950s and early 1960s. In 1964 it was refused official status as an association, and the Supreme Court, sitting as High Court of Justice, upheld this decision. In its rejection of the group's appeal, the court stated:

It is a very important rule that only extremely weighty considerations may prohibit the registration of an Association. The freedom to organize is one of the mainstays of the democratic regime and one of the basic rights of the citizen. Heaven forbid that we should revoke this right and proscribe as Association simply because one or another of its aims is to aspire toward a change in the legal situation existing in the State. The present situation might be in need of reform from this or another point of view and a movement wishing to organize public opinion in the State in order to bring about reform of the situation may do this within the framework of an Association registered by law, but no free regime can give its hand and conscience to a movement which undermines the regime itself. . . . This restriction is essential. It has often happened in the history of states with democratic regimes that fascist and totalitarian movements of various kinds have arisen against them, and utilized those selfsame rights of the freedom of speech, press and organization granted them by the state in order to conduct their undermining activities under their protection. Whoever saw this during the period of the Weimar Republic will never forget the lesson learned then.

And further:

It is the elementary right of any state to preserve its liberty and very existence in the face of foreign enemies and their collaborators within the camp. As my learned friend has said, no administration should be required to authorize in the name of the freedom of organization, the establishment of a fifth column within the boundaries of its state. On the grounds of the material before us there is a sufficient basis to fear that the Association which the claimant wishes to register has indeed gone on this perilous way, destroying the allegiance which every citizen owes to the state in which he resides. (H. C. 253/64 *Sibri Jiryes v. District Commissioner of Haifa*, 18(4), *Piskei Din*, Reports of the Israel Supreme Court, 673, 6791)

Just as in court decisions the values of political tolerance and other values, such as the constitutional order or national security, are evaluated and counterbalanced, so are they also in individual decisions. In the absence of a strong threat, belief in abstract norms of tolerance will constrain responses to specific instances in which citizens' tolerance is tested. The stronger the

Table 5.4
Support for Abstract Democratic Norms

	Percentage Support	
Item	Jews	Arabs
The people's representatives should represent the majority.	89	71
Every citizen has the right to criticize what the government does.	89	86
Every person is entitled to the same legal rights, no matter what his or her political beliefs.	88	87
I believe in free speech for all no matter what their views might be.	83	89
Groups or people in the minority should be free to try to win majority support for their opinions.	63	72

commitment to these general norms, the more tolerance one expects in specific instances despite the threat they may entail. If the threat is strong enough, however, it may override these abstract beliefs.

It is important, then, to examine the status of democratic norms in Israeli society. Israeli democracy is well established, yet its origins are Eastern European. The early Jewish immigrants were from Eastern Europe, and they left a lasting mark on Israeli political and social organizations, from the political parties and the Histadrut labor union to the moshavim and kibbutzim (e.g., Eisentadt 1967; Shapiro 1976, 1977). Lacking the Anglo-Saxon liberal tradition, Israeli democracy puts more emphasis on majority rule and equality and less on civil liberties and minority rights (Shapiro 1977). One therefore expects differential levels of support for these different aspects of democracy among the Jewish public. If Anglo-Saxon liberal values are not expected to be rooted in Jewish political culture, they surely are not expected to be part of Arab political culture. The Arabs did not have much of a democratic heritage at all before 1948. On the other hand, since they are a minority, the belief in such abstract norms of democracy would be extremely functional for them. Ideals such as free speech and minority rights can only serve to protect the rights and political actions of a minority such as Arabs in Israel.[10]

Table 5.4 shows the percentage of respondents agreeing or strongly agreeing with a series of statements representing abstract democratic principles. The level of support for these principles is generally high and only partly corresponds to our expectations. Almost 90 percent of the Jews support the principles of majority rule (89 percent), the right of criticism (89 percent), and equal legal rights (88 percent). Over 80 percent support free speech. Only on the question of minority rights does this overwhelming majority shrink. It is a considerably reduced majority, down to 63 percent. Among Arabs, we see an overall high level of support for liberal political values of minority rights and free speech. Most important to our concerns is the difference between Jews and Arabs in support for minority rights and for majority rule. Jews have a stronger belief in majority rule than do Arabs (18-point difference), whereas Arabs believe more strongly than Jews (9-point difference) in minority rights.[11]

Recent findings from studies of the citizen orientations of Israeli adolescents show the same pattern. Of an Arab sample, 31 percent rated "being tolerant of others' views" as important for good citizenship, compared to only 5 percent of a Jewish sample (Ichilov and Nave 1981; Ichilov 1983). The abstract norms are not, then, purely abstract, and belief in them is at least in part a function of the group's minority or majority status. We may note that among Arabs the support for these two norms is about equal (about 70 percent), but among the Jews there is a difference of 26 percentage points between support for majority rule and support minority rights.

The discrepancy between the results in Table 5.3 and 5.4—the high level of support for the general norms of democracy and the low level of tolerance when the norms are applied to a specific, disliked group—is very clear. On the issue of free speech, 83 percent of the Jews and 89 percent of the Arabs are supportive, but only 38 percent and 40 percent (a difference of 45 and 49 percentage points, respectively) are willing to allow it to their least-liked group. Such discrepancies are a well-known phenomenon in political research (Prothro and Grigg 1960; McClosky 1964; Lawrence 1976), but their magnitude is greater here.

Furthermore, when we relate support for these abstract democratic norms to the degree of tolerance expressed by respondents, we find that belief in these norms does not predispose Israelis to be more tolerant politically toward unpopular groups (see Table 5.5). Among Jews we find a weak positive impact of general norms on tolerance (a standardized coefficient of .11 in a multivariate model).[12] Belief in these general values makes Jews only slightly more inclined to be tolerant toward a specific unpopular group, much less so than in other societies, such as the United States (Shamir and Sullivan 1983). In the Arab sample there appears to be a negative relationship between the two. On the average, respondents who are more committed to the abstract norms of democracy are less tolerant toward their disliked group, but in a multivariate analysis we find this relationship to be spurious. The direct effect of the general norms of democracy on political tolerance is a statistically nonsignificant − .11. We also find that the more threatened the Arabs are by their least-liked group, most of which are right-wing

Table 5.5
Individual Differences in Tolerance

Item:		N	Mean Tolerance Score	Multivariate Analysis Direct Effect
Democratic Norms[1]				
Arabs	Low	88	15.8	-.11[4]
	High	132	13.7	
Jews	Low	428	14.0	.11
	High	401	16.2	
Threat[2]				
Arabs	Low	34	18.2	-.41
	High	146	14.0	
Jews	Low	365	16.9	-.55
	High	430	13.3	
Ideology[3]				
Arabs	Left	109	13.8	.30[4]
	Center	66	15.1	
	Right	26	16.2	
Jews	Left	145	17.6	-.43
	Center	253	15.6	
	Right	317	13.8	

Notes:

1. Respondents were put into the low group unless they agreed with all five norms in Table 5.4.

2. Threat scores ranged from 7 to 42. Respondents with scores above 29 were classified as high, the rest as low.

3. Ideology was measured on a 7-point continuum, where 1 is self-identification as extreme left and 7 is self-identification as extreme right.

4. Not significant at the .05 level.

Jewish groups, the stronger their belief in these abstract norms. This finding supports our claim that for Arabs, belief in such norms serves an important self-protective function.

It appears that despite the high levels of endorsement of the abstract liberal values of democracy, these values have not been internalized as guides for thought and action among either Jews or Arabs. The weakness of the Anglo-Saxon democratic tradition, combined with the high threat the Jewish majority perceives, makes more Jewish respondents willing to suspend minority rights: They have a weaker belief in those rights in the first place, and their suspension may be deemed necessary to protect the majority. This also explains why the degree of commitment to the general norms has little impact on political tolerance.

INDIVIDUAL DIFFERENCES IN TOLERANCE

The pattern of "focused intolerance" that characterizes the Jewish as well as the Arab public in Israel is structured largely by the Arab-Israeli conflict. We have emphasized the mirror image we obtain, with high intolerance in both sectors, targeted predominantly toward Jewish right-wing groups among Arabs and left-wing Arab groups among Jews. We further examined the perceptions of threat and the degree of commitment to abstract democratic norms in the two publics, and suggested that these too were the by-product of this conflict, as well as of the minority-majority relationships stemming from it. Up to this point the analysis has been mostly on the aggregate level, focusing on the frequency distributions in the two groups. In this section we will present an individual-level analysis, in order to elaborate on the effect of the political context—mainly the Arab-Israeli conflict—on the dynamics of tolerance in Israel.

We have already noted that subjective perceptions of threat are a major determinant of political tolerance. This is true of both Arabs and Jews, as noted in Table 5.5. In both instances, the direct impact of threat on tolerance is the strongest of any independent variable we have examined. This is true of the United States as well as, for example, New Zealand, although in these two societies belief in the general democratic values can, to some extent, offset the effects of perceived threat (Sullivan et al. 1985). In Israel, among both Jews and Arabs, the norms do not serve this protective function.

Ideology also plays a central role in Israeli politics (Eisenstadt 1967; Gutmann 1977; Arian and Shamir 1983). Beyond its importance, the content of the ideological dimension and of the left-right labels is crucial. Zionist nationalism is the major component of ideology, and on it, if on anything, there is widespread consensus among Jews (e.g., Shapiro 1977). Although contributing a major common element to ideology, views and interpretations of nationalism, as they relate to the Arab-Israeli conflict, also provide the major and most salient sources of ideological variance within the Jewish majority and between Jews and Arabs, as we have shown earlier for the patterns of target group selection. The relationship of ideology to political tolerance is therefore immediate. Among Jews, tolerance is explicitly part of left-wing ideology, which is one of relative accommodation of Jewish and Arab nationalism. The right-wing position is nationalistic and less accommodating toward the Arab world, and takes the position that peace can be assured only through military strength. The leftists are more willing to risk concessions for what they believe could be a lasting peace with the Arabs. Thus almost by definition the two competing ideologies should differ in tolerance, as the major cleavage dimension along which target groups are selected is that of the Arab-Israeli conflict.

The same is true for the Arabs, but in the opposite direction. For them the labels are reversed: The left-wing position emphasizes Arab nationalist concerns, whereas the right-wingers are more accommodating in terms of their attitudes toward their minority status, the Jewish state, and the Jews themselves (Smooha 1983, 1980). Among Jews, left-wingers are more tolerant, whereas among Arabs the right-wingers are. Left-wing Jews and right-wing Arabs are the least nationalistic, come closest to each other on the ideological continuum, and are the most accommodating and therefore the most tolerant. But they are minorities in each sector. In their study of Jewish and Arab attitudes on the conflict, Smooha and Peretz report that 72 percent of the Jews scored toward the hawkish end of their index and 60 percent of the Arabs toward the nonhawkish end. "This bimodal distribution leaves only 29 percent of the Arabs and 28 percent of the Jews in the broad middle, sharing compromising views" (Smooha and Peretz 1982: 460–461).

Eliminating a causal model that explains political tolerance (using maximum likelihood confirmatory factor analysis), we found that in the Jewish sample ideology has a direct effect on tolerance (independent of perceptions of threat). In the Arab sample the impact is more indirect, through threat perception, and is of course in the opposite direction. Left-wingers are more threatened by their targets than right-wingers are by theirs, and the more threatened one is, the less tolerant one becomes. (The direct effect of ideology on tolerance is also in the same direction, but this path is statistically nonsignificant.)

CONCLUSION

The degree of political tolerance toward a disliked group can be a largely cognitive, reality-based response to the way one perceives a complex political world (Lane 1969; Elms 1976; Shamir and Sullivan 1982, 1983). The Israeli-Arab conflict is the major factor shaping the political context of Israelis, and as such it is the source of the public climate of intolerance we found in the Jewish majority and in the Arab minority. Similarly, differences in orientations toward the conflict and perceptions of it, as measured by political ideology and perceived threat, are the principal sources of variance in tolerance among individuals in the two groups.

If we might be allowed the luxury of speculation, we suggest that these political sources of intolerances are, in the final analysis, the most critical. We have shown elsewhere that the social and psychological forces that underlie political tolerance and intolerance are largely uniform in democratic societies but that the political context varies greatly in its impact on individual levels of tolerance (Shamir and Sullivan 1983). In examining political tolerance in different societies (Sullivan et al. 1985), the primary differentiating agent is not different personality types in the various societies, but rather the vastly differing political context in which the citizens must live and conduct their political, as well as their everyday, lives. What we suggest is that, should the context change, levels of tolerance among Jews and Arabs could well change, even though their personalities and social characteristics are unaltered. Even more important, in apparently tolerant societies a changing political climate with requisite threats to the values and interests of the citizenry can readily undo such a seemingly solid basis for a democratic regime.

NOTES

This research is part of a broader comprehensive study of tolerance, supported by the United States–Israel Binational Science Foundation (SF), Jerusalem, Israel. It was also supported by the faculty of Social Sciences, the Research Project on Peace, the Institute for Social and Labor Research at Tel Aviv University, and the Office of International Programs at the University of Minnesota.

1. The figures are from the *Statistical Abstract of Israel 1983* (1983: 31, 50). They refer to the pre–1967 boundaries, plus East Jerusalem, which was annexed after the Six-Day War. Our sample, however, does not include East Jerusalem, which has a population of about 120,000. The number of Israeli Arabs, excluding those living in East Jerusalem, is about 570,000.

2. The data were collected by the Israel Institute of Applied Social Research, directed by Louis Guttman. The sample includes only respondents age 20 and up because most Jews enroll in the army at age 18 for two years (women) or three years (men). Both samples were cluster samples, stratified by type of township. A comparison of our samples with population parameters revealed several discrepancies, particularly in the Arab sample. We therefore checked the aggregate results using various weighting schemes. In the Jewish sample the results were identical, so no weighting was needed. In the Arab sample the discrepancies were more pronounced, so the analysis was performed twice, with the original sample and then with a weighted sample. The results were similar (although not identical) and so we report those of the unweighted sample.

The questionnaire for the Jewish sample was in Hebrew, and the interviewers were Jewish. For the Arab sample the questionnaire was in Arabic, and the interviewers were Arabs. The Arabic version of the questionnaire was written by using the technique of double translation—from Hebrew to Arabic, and then by another translator from Arabic back to Hebrew—so as to arrive at similar meaning and substantive, not literal, translation. For more details on sampling and measurement considerations, see Shamir and Sullivan (1982). This analysis is part of a broader comparative study of tolerance, supported by the United Sates–Israel Binational Science Foundation. The results of the comparative analysis of the United States and Israel (Jewish sample) are reported elsewhere (Shamir and Sullivan 1983).

3. The Jewish target groups were selected on the basis of an open-ended question addressed in the ongoing survey of the Institute of Applied Social Research to a sample of the urban Jewish population (constituting about 80 percent of the Jewish population in Israel) in July 1980. The question was worded similarly to the partially closed-ended one in our survey but provided no list of groups from which to choose. The groups on the Arab questionnaire were defined on the basis of consultations with several Arab and Jewish experts (policy-makers and scholars) and a small-scale pretest.

4. Schnall (1979) is a good reference on most of the extreme groups discussed here.

5. In the open-ended question in the pretest, respondents mentioned the PLO and groups supporting the PLO, without naming the specific groups. We therefore did the same in our survey.

6. In the American case, as with the Jews, only 19 percent mentioned methods and tactics as the major reason for disliking a particular target. The most common concern among the U.S. sample was the group's stand against civil liberties (27 percent). This demonstrates nicely the Americans' relatively high concern with democratic norms. Such objections were seldom listed by Israeli respondents (see Sullivan et al. 1982).

7. It is possible for one to object strongly to a particular group because of ideological differences and yet perceive little or no threat from that group on a personal or collective basis.

8. We should note that such expectations are not always borne out. In our comparison of the United States and Jews in Israel, we found Americans to feel more highly threatened by their least-liked groups than Israelis were, contrary to our expectations (Shamir and Sullivan 1982).

9. In previous work we have distinguished and discussed external threat, based on perceived political danger from the least-liked group, and internal threat, based on personality. Both types of threat affect political tolerance (see Sullivan et al. 1982).

10. Rakah's position is a good case in point. As a communist party, Rakah holds an intolerant political ideology, but out of experience it champions the protection of individual and minority rights.

11. The minority rights question is from the Prothro-Grigg (1960) questionnaire, and, like all the questions measuring the abstract norms of democracy, it does not present any particular context for the respondent. But in Israel "minorities" means Arabs, so that the specific connotation of Arabs may be implied. To avoid this as much as possible, we did not use the term "minorities," but instead asked about "groups of people who are in the minority," which we believe expresses the abstract idea divorced from the specific association with Arabs.

12. Degree of tolerance is measured by creating a scale using the first six of the items listed in Table 5.3a. For the Jewish sample the coefficient alpha is .74; for the Arab sample it is .62. We used only the first six items in order to make the scale comparable to that used earlier in the U.S. study (Sullivan et al. 1982). The multivariate model that explains tolerance was estimated by maximum likelihood confirmatory factor analysis. For more details on the measurement and estimation of the model, see Shamir and Sullivan (1982). We may note that the weak impact of the abstract norms on tolerance is not a methodological artifact of lack of variance,

considering that in the American data this variance was even lower, but the relationship was much stronger than in the Israeli samples.

REFERENCES

Arian, A., and M. Shamir. "The Primarily Political Functions of the Left-Right Continuum." *Comparative Politics* 15(1983): 139–158.

Eisenstadt, S. N. *Israel Society*. London: Weidenfeld and Nicolson, 1967.

Elms, Alan C. *Personality in Politics*. New York: Harcourt Brace Jovanovich, 1976.

Grielsammer, A. *Les Communistes Israéliens*. Paris: Presses de la Fondation Nationale des Sciences Politiques, 1978.

Gutmann, E. "Political Parties and Groups: Stability and Change." In M. Lissak and E. Gutmann, eds., *The Israeli Political System* (in Hebrew). Tel-Aviv: Am Oved, 1977.

Haddad, S., R. D. McLaurin, and E. A. Nakhleh. "Minorities in Containment: The Arabs of Israel." In R. D. McLaurin, ed., *The Political Role of Minority Groups in the Middle East*. New York: Praeger, 1979.

Ichilov, O. "Citizenship Orientations of Two Israeli Minority Groups: Israeli-Arab and Eastern-Jewish Youth." Tel-Aviv University (unpublished), 1983.

Ichilov, O., and N. Nave. "The Good Citizen as Viewed by Israeli Adolescents." *Comparative Politics* 13(1981): 361–376.

Landau, J. M. *The Arabs in Israel: A Political Study*. London: Oxford University Press, 1969.

Lane, Robert E. *Political Thinking and Consciousness*. Chicago: Markham, 1969.

Lawrence, D. "Procedural Norms and Tolerance: A Reassessment." *American Political Science Review* 70(1976): 80–100.

Lustick, I. *Arabs in The Jewish State: Israel's Control of a National Minority*. Austin, Tex.: University of Texas Press, 1980.

McClosky, Herbert. "Consensus and Ideology in American Politics." *American Political Science Review* 58(1964): 561–382.

Peres, Y. "Modernization and Nationalism in the Identity of the Israeli Arab." *Middle East Journal* 24(1970): 479–492.

———. "Ethnic Relations in Israel." *American Journal of Sociology* 76(1971): 1021–1047.

Peres, Y., and N. Yuval-Davis. "Some Observations on the National Identity of the Israeli Arab." *Human Relations* 22(1969): 219–233.

Prothro, James W., and C. W. Grigg. "Fundamental Principles of Democracy: Bases of Agreement and Disagreement." *Journal of Politics* 22(1960): 276–294.

Rekhess, E. *The Israeli Arabs since 1967: The Issue of Identity* (in Hebrew). Sekirot No. 1. Tel Aviv: Shiloah Center, Tel Aviv University, 1976.

Schnall, D. *Radical Dissent in Contemporary Israeli Politics: Cracks in the Wall*. New York: Praeger, 1979.

Shamir, Michal, and John L. Sullivan. "Political Tolerance and Intolerance in Israel." Final Report to the United States–Israel Binational Science Foundation, 2297/80, 1982.

———. "The Political Context of Tolerance: The United States and Israel." *American Political Science Review* 77(1983): 911–928.

Shapiro, Y. *The Formative Years of the Israeli Labor Party: The Organization of Power, 1914–1930*. Beverly Hills, Calif.: Sage, 1976.

———. *Israeli Democracy* (in Hebrew). Ramat-Gan, Israel: Massada, 1977.

Smooha, S. *Israel: Pluralism and Conflict*. Berkeley: University of California Press, 1978.

———. *The Orientation and Politicization of the Arab Minority in Israel*. Monographs on the Middle East, 2. Haifa: Jewish-Arab Center, University of Haifa, 1980.

———. "Minority Responses in a Plural Society: A Typology of the Arabs in Israel." *Sociology and Social Research* 67(1983): 436–456.

Smooha, S., and D. Peretz. "The Arabs in Israel." *Journal of Conflict Resolution* 26(1982): 451–484.

Statistical Abstract of Israel 1983. No. 34. Jerusalem: Central Bureau of Statistics, 1983.

Stouffer, Samuel. *Communism, Conformity, and Civil Liberties*. New York: Doubleday, 1955.

Sullivan, John L., G. E. Marcus, S. Feldman, and J. Piereson. "The Sources of Political Tolerance: A Multivariate Analysis." *American Political Science Review* 74(1981): 92–106.

Sullivan, John L., J. Piereson, and G. E. Marcus. "An Alternative Conceptualization of Political Tolerance." *American Political Science Review* 73(1979): 781–794.

———. *Political Tolerance and American Democracy*. Chicago: University of Chicago Press, 1982.

Sullivan, John L., Michal Shamir, Nigel Roberts, and Patrick Walsh. "Political Intolerance and the Structure of Mass Attitudes: A Study of The United States, Israel, and New Zealand." *Comparative Political Studies* 17(1984): 319–344.

Sullivan, John L., Michal Shamir, Patrick Walsh, and Nigel Roberts. *Political Tolerance in Context*. Boulder, Colo.: Westview Press, 1985.

Tessler, M. A. "Israel's Arabs and the Palestinian Problem." *Middle East Journal* 31(1977): 313–329.

Tsemah, M. "The Attitudes of the Jewish Majority in Israel Towards the Arab Minority" (in Hebrew). Research Report. Jerusalem: Van Leer Foundation, 1980.

Yuval-Davis, N. "Mazpen: The Israeli Socialist Organization" (in Hebrew with English abstract). Papers in Sociology. Jerusalem: Eliezer Kaplan School of Economics and Social Sciences, Hebrew University, 1977.

6

Community Conflict Processes: Mobilization and Demobilization in Northern Ireland

Gavan Duffy and Nathalie Frensley

Community conflicts can produce profound international consequences. During successive rounds of mobilization and countermobilization, conflicting parties may appeal for the intervention of their extranational allies. Alternatively, extranational actors may find that conflict trends threaten their interests and intervene of their own accord. In short, as community conflicts become more protracted and intractable, extranational actors more likely find themselves drawn in.

Uncovering knowledge relevant to the prevention and resolution of conflicts, both domestic and international, alone motivates the study of community conflict. Critical reflection on the topic can promote settlement and resolution, and thus inhibit wider conflicts. In this spirit, we present a theoretical model of community conflict processes. We illustrate its heuristic utility by applying it analytically to events culminating in a failed effort to settle the conflict in Northern Ireland.

The Northern Irish conflict neither begins nor ends with the events discussed here. The contemporary conflict arose within a conflict that spans many centuries. It might well be useful to analyze in terms of our pre-understanding the entire conflict history from William of Orange to the present. We have neither the space nor the tenacity to do so here. Instead, the analysis will proceed, rather arbitrarily, from a latent period in the conflict. Likewise, we terminate the discussion arbitrarily at the failure of the Sunningdale Agreement of 1973.[1] Without a thorough examination of the events that unfolded during this time period, it is difficult to understand fully the nature of the conflict that continued to grip Northern Ireland throughout the 1980s.

The present chapter thus serves two purposes. As its theoretical purpose, it seeks to account for events leading to the rejection of Sunningdale in terms of a theory with broader application. Such confrontations of theory with historical fact can simultaneously shed new light on those facts and suggest ways in which to improve the theory. As its practical purpose, the chapter seeks to articulate the historical conditions within which a community conflict was, if not fully resolved, then eased to a degree that reduces the likelihood of spilling over into interstate conflict and increases the likelihood of an eventual comprehensive peace.

A PRE-UNDERSTANDING OF COMMUNITY CONFLICT

Theoretical constructions in the study of conflict must include more than contingent, causal propositions—propositions that predict action consequences from the presence of "objective," structural conditions. They must also include *conceptual* propositions, which represent the choices of the political actors actually engaged in conflict. Practical inferences, grounded in premises that concern the social, cultural, and institutional contexts within which action is embedded, influence those choices (Moon 1975).

We take our theoretical account of community conflict to be more than a theory in the traditional sense of that term. We call it a *pre-understanding*, articulated for the purpose of providing a coherent analytical template for attaining accounts of actual community conflicts that reflect more felicitously those conflicts as experienced by participants. Successive confrontations of the pre-understanding with the data produce a more refined pre-understanding for subsequent analytical use. We believe this approach to be more conducive to the generation of *usable* knowledge—knowledge that is relevant to political practice—than theory-based approaches that fail to incorporate conceptual propositions.

Our pre-understanding draws upon many existing treatments of community conflict and related topics.[2] Though we stand on these and many other shoulders, an important novel element conceptualizes factional conflict as failures by incumbent elites to persuade their constituents to mobilize, demobilize, or maintain group solidarity.

A factional conflict can itself fracture, spawning a subfactional conflict. This, in turn, can spawn a sub-subfactional conflict, which can itself factionalize. Processes of factional conflict follow the patterns laid out in the model. Of course, factional conflicts differ from those that created them with respect to participants and stakes. Nevertheless, we posit that all conflictual sequences, factional or otherwise, follow the same general patterns. Thus, we view factional conflicts as recursions on the processes that produce them.[3]

A MODEL OF CONFLICT

The model in Figure 6.1 depicts the theory in skeletal form. At many points, the text refers to processes that are summarized obliquely in the chart. We use bracketed capital letters to refer to points in the model and hyphenations of these capital letters to refer to pathways through the model.

Conflict Mobilization

Mobilization is the attempt to marshal human and material resources to attain political goals. Mobilization for conflict requires the presence of identifiable groups in the community, and one or more of these groups must share a set of grievances [A]. Elites, who control the leadership positions of their organizations (Rootes 1983: 44), decide whether to mobilize constituents on the basis of a cost-benefit analysis [B]. Benefits may include increased access to material resources, consolidation of elite ascendancy within the group, and/or increased ascendancy within the overall community. Elites set the attainment or denial of these benefits as their stake in the conflict. Costs include the direct monetary costs of mobilization as well as transactions costs, opportunity costs, information costs, and so forth, and the risks of mobilization, such as the possibilities of immediate repression and the failure to mobilize sufficiently (Shefter 1984: 145). If the perceived costs outweigh the benefits, groups elites refrain from mobilization and the conflict remains latent [B-A]. If the benefits outweigh the costs, they mobilize [C].

Elites mobilize constituents by convincing them (1) that the fates of all group members are interdependent (Lewin 1948: 184), (2) that they share a set of grievances which can only be resolved through direct action, and (3) that they must directly confront their real or perceived nemesis (Kriesberg 1973: 72–73, 85). Elites also seek to alter the cost-benefit calculations of their constituents. Exploiting their informational advantage (Lasswell 1966: 211), elites persuade their constituents of the need for direct action by presenting interpretations of the nature and history of group grievances that would seem to warrant such behavior. To the extent that elites can control information (and its interpretation) propagated to their constituents, they can achieve, consolidate, and extend their dominance over the group.

Elites highlight incommensurabilities in modal beliefs across conflict groups, typically painting opponents as irrational, intransigent, devious, and incapable of solving intergroup problems peaceably and/or equitably. They thereby engender and reinforce high levels of affect among their constituents. This rigidifies the cognitive schemata of constituents, which in turn reinforces elite ascendancy and solidarity within the group and demonstrates to rivals the unity and determination of the group. At every

Figure 6.1
Theoretical Model of Conflict Processes

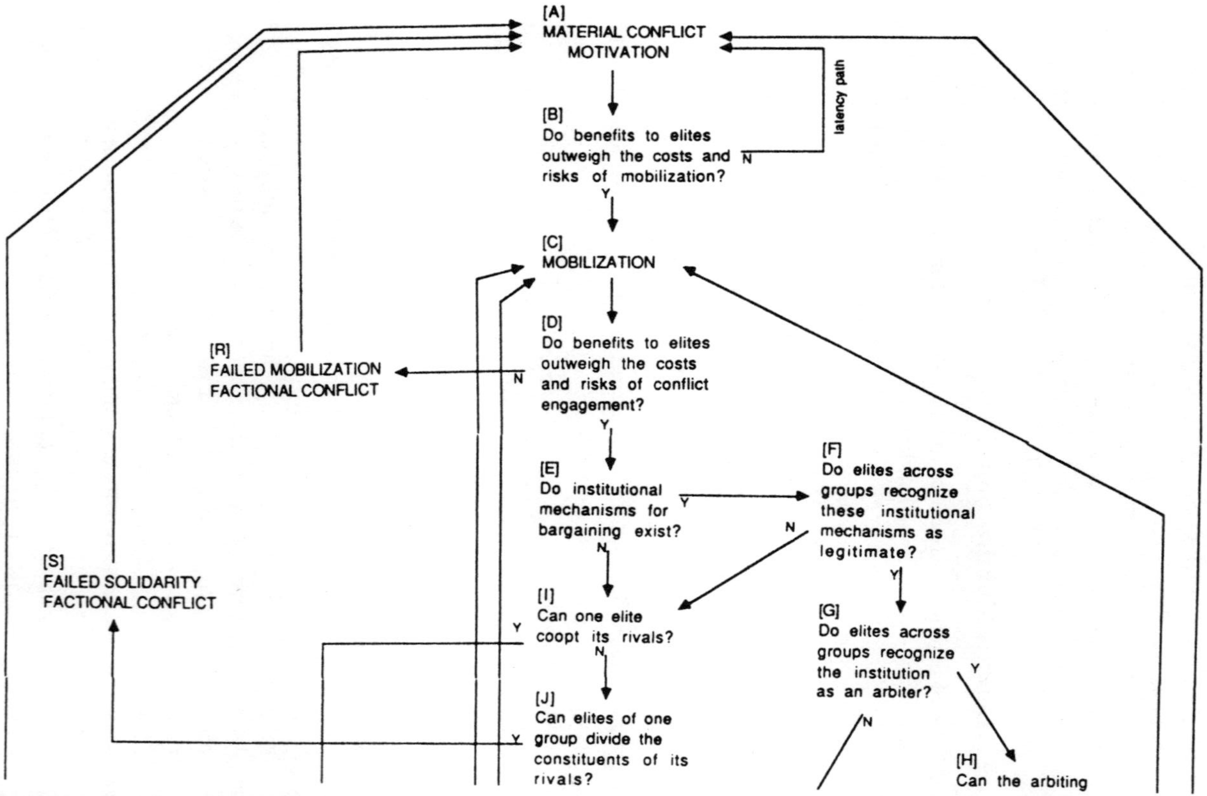

[A]
MATERIAL CONFLICT
MOTIVATION

[B]
Do benefits to elites
outweigh the costs and
risks of mobilization?

latency path

[C]
MOBILIZATION

[D]
Do benefits to elites
outweigh the costs
and risks of conflict
engagement?

[E]
Do institutional
mechanisms for
bargaining exist?

[F]
Do elites across
groups recognize
these institutional
mechanisms as
legitimate?

[G]
Do elites across
groups recognize
the institution
as an arbiter?

[H]
Can the arbiting

[I]
Can one elite
coopt its rivals?

[J]
Can elites of one
group divide the
constituents of its
rivals?

[R]
FAILED MOBILIZATION
FACTIONAL CONFLICT

[S]
FAILED SOLIDARITY
FACTIONAL CONFLICT

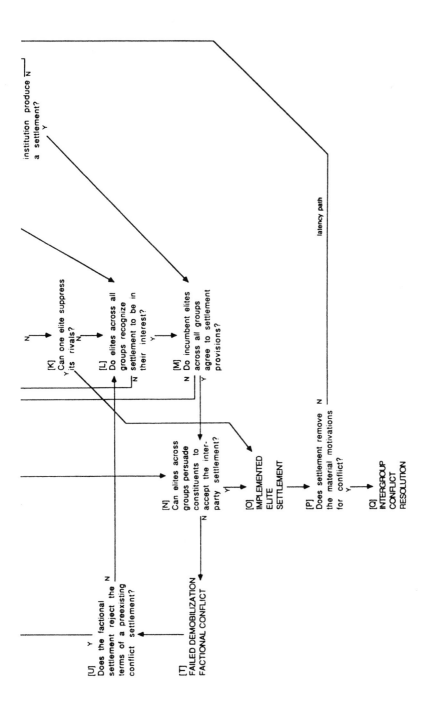

institution produce a settlement?

N

Y

[K] Can one elite suppress its rivals?

N

Y

N

[L] Do elites across all groups recognize settlement to be in their interest?

Y

N

[M] Do incumbent elites across all groups agree to settlement provisions?

N

Y

latency path

[N] Can elites across groups persuade constituents to accept the inter-party settlement?

Y

N

[O] IMPLEMENTED ELITE SETTLEMENT

[P] Does settlement remove the material motivations for conflict?

N

Y

[Q] INTERGROUP CONFLICT RESOLUTION

[U] Does the factional settlement reject the terms of a preexisting conflict settlement?

Y

N

[T] FAILED DEMOBILIZATION FACTIONAL CONFLICT

turn, they attempt to prevent rival elites and any incipient factional elites from subsidizing the information costs of their mass constituents.

To the extent that rival and factional elites can provide constituents with information (and interpretations) that undermine the interests of an incumbent elite, the hegemony of the incumbents is threatened. Incumbent elites thus try to prevent rivals from creating, exacerbating, or exploiting factional cleavages within the group. They try to prevent incipient factional elites from exposing dissonant interests between elites and other constituents.

Factional elites arise from group "cadres" (Rejai 1980: 101) or "opinion leaders"—constituents who mediate elite-mass relations (Katz 1957; De Fleur and Ball-Rokeach 1966: 208–215). The relationship between elites and cadres holds special significance. On the one hand, elites rely on cadres to propagate their political programs and calls for action to the constituency. On the other hand, cadres also represent threats to the ascendency of incumbent elites, should a factional conflict emerge.

Once they have mobilized their constituents, elites assess whether the benefits of conflict outweigh the costs of conflict engagement [D]. This cost-benefit calculation differs qualitatively from the premobilization calculation [B]. This postmobilization calculation exploits information pertaining to the success of mobilization relative to the countermobilization efforts of rival elites. Successful mobilization significantly reduces the risks of conflict engagement, thus lowering the cost calculation and increasing the likelihood that conflict will erupt.

Failed Mobilization Factional Conflict

Unsuccessful mobilization increases the cost calculation. In such cases incumbent elites will be reluctant to confront their rivals. However, cadres may assess the situation differently and challenge the ascendancy of the incumbent elites [R]. This factional conflict, like those at nodes [S] and [T], recurses on the model. In this recursion (i.e., failed mobilization factional conflict [R]), the decision against conflict engagement [D] constitutes the material motivation for conflict. The competing groups are those which support and oppose that decision. As possible outcomes of [R], a challenging cadre may displace incumbent elites or the incumbents may retain their ascendancy. Retention of incumbency may, however, alter the cost calculation of elites at [D] to such a degree that they must either engage in conflict or face displacement by factional elites.

If incumbent elites retain their positions without altering their decision to forgo conflict engagement, the conflict remains latent [R-A] until such time as the situation as perceived by the elite warrants another effort at mobilization and possible conflict engagement. If, however, the challenging cadres displace the incumbent elite, their cost-benefit calculation dominates the group decision at [D] and intergroup conflict engagement proceeds.

Note that the model has two other latency paths, [P-A] and [B-A]. Any factional conflict recursion may traverse these paths. Thus, the model allows factional conflicts to remain latent even while an elite retains its ascendancy.

Institutionalized Conflict

In some conflicts, elites compete within an institutional setting. As a precondition for this possibility, elites across groups must recognize the legitimacy of the institution [F]. If one party does not recognize the legitimacy of the institution, the conflict enters the "hot conflict" pathway, at nodes [I], [J], and [K], discussed below.

Institutions can act as mediators or arbiters [G]. Conflicting parties are more likely to accept mediation when they believe that the intervening institution will treat them fairly. Arbitrating institutions are ordinarily juridical. If an arbitrating institution cannot produce a settlement [H], another phase of mobilization and countermobilization begins [H-C]. If, however, it does produce a settlement, elites across groups must decide [M] whether to accept its terms. Rejection of the terms of such a settlement will promote another cycle of mobilization [H-M-C] (see the discussion below of accepted settlement terms). Additionally, in rejecting an arbitrated or mediated [G-L-M-C] settlement, an elite may also delegitimize the institution as an arbiter (or mediator), effectively foreclosing the institutional settlement path [E-F-G, etc.] in succeeding iterations.

The availability of legitimate institutional mechanisms for bargaining reduces the overall level of hostility between competing groups in two ways. First, such mechanisms afford conflicting parties a pathway to settlement without traversing the "hot conflict" pathway. Second, when groups foresee that the conflict will be conducted institutionally, they direct their mobilization efforts [C] toward gaining increased leverage within the relevant institution. Thus, when legitimate institutional mechanisms for bargaining exist, mobilization tactics will ordinarily be less strident and divisive.

Hot Conflict

If no institutional mechanisms exist [E], or if an elite does not recognize the legitimacy of existing institutions [F], elites attempt to alter the conflict calculations of their rivals. Possible strategies are cooptation of opposing elites [I], divide-and-conquer [J], and intergroup suppression [K]. The order in which elites consider these strategies might vary across conflicts. However, in the abstract, cooptation, division, and suppression reflect a cost ordering. Cooptation is generally least costly to an elite considering these strategies, while suppression is generally most costly. In concrete cases, however, the order in which these strategies are selected depends very much on the interpretations of the relevant decision makers.

In cooptation [I], a coopted elite accepts benefits from a coopting elite, in return for which the former agrees to settlement terms beneficial to the latter. In divide-and-conquer strategies [J], one elite subsidizes the information costs of its rival's constituents, promoting factional conflict [S] by exposing dissonant interests between rival elites and a significant subset of their constituents. Only when the rivals fail to maintain internal solidarity can this strategy succeed.

Successful divide-and-conquer strategies generate a factional conflict that: (1) produces successive iterations of factional conflict, focusing group attention inward and away from the intergroup conflict; (2) alters the group's cost-benefit calculations, facilitating their capitulation; or (3) results in the displacement of group elites by more conciliatory leadership. Even when factional conflict fails to produce elite replacement, it may diminish the ascendant elite's ability to mobilize resources in succeeding phases of the main conflict [S-A-B-C]. With fewer resources to expend on mobilization, these elites may find it too costly. Thus, the conflict becomes latent [S-A-B-A].

In the abstract, the divide-and-conquer strategy is relatively riskier than cooptation. Cooptation can immediately produce an implemented settlement [I-N-O], while the divide-and-conquer strategy must proceed through factional conflict [J-S] before settlement of the intergroup conflict can be considered. Initiating a failed solidarity factional conflict among one's rivals may also backfire. The factional conflict may result in the replacement of the rival's elites with more militant cadres. Also, rivals can enhance group solidarity if they can expose the strategy.

It is possible, of course, that factional conflicts engendered by the divide-and-conquer strategy may become latent. That is, the cost-benefit analyses of factional elites may prevent factional conflict before [S-A-B-A] or after [S-A-B-C-D-R-A] factional mobilization. In this case, the divide-and-conquer strategy of counter-elites in the intergroup conflict fails and other strategies (cooptation [I] or suppression [K]) must be considered.

Suppression is ordinarily the costliest of the three strategies of the hot conflict pathway. Suppressive strategies require elites to allocate extraordinary material and personnel resources over the duration of engagement. Further, suppression invites rivals to engage in counter-suppression and to seek the support of powerful elites outside the conflict arena. If one elite can suppress its rivals, it can impose a settlement [K-O]. If, on the other hand, suppression is not possible, competing elites can opt to settle [K-L-M] or escalate [K-L-C] the conflict.

Settlement and Demobilization

Elite settlements are agreements between the elites of conflicting groups (or factions) aimed at conflict resolution. They may address the (possibly distal) material causes of the conflict, the more proximal effects of the conflict, and/or institutional arrangements designed to mediate (or arbitrate) current and future intergroup grievances. Elite settlements arise from negotiation or from successful coercion. Settlements require that elites recognize their interest in terminating hostilities in favor of possible alternative means of intergroup competition [L] (Burton and Higley 1987). Otherwise, another cycle of mobilization and countermobilization begins [L-C]. If elites do share an interest in settlement, they attempt to specify jointly a set of settlement provisions [M]. However, if they cannot agree to terms, they remobilize [M-C].

To implement a settlement, elites must persuade their constituents to accept its terms [M-N-O]. Thus, we distinguish elite settlements from implemented elite settlements, that is, those which elites across groups have successfully persuaded their constituents to accept. Further, to effect a conflict resolution [Q], settlement terms must address the material disparities that underlie the conflict. Implemented settlements that fail to address these disparities result in latent conflicts [P-A], in which active hostilities cease, but only temporarily. Elite settlements thus constitute a necessary but insufficient precondition for conflict resolutions. The two concepts often are, but should never be, conflated.

Elites attempt to demobilize their constituents—deescalating constituent participation in conflict—in order to implement an intergroup settlement. Demobilization is not the inverse of mobilization. Elites cannot simply shut off a mobilization spigot. They must actively convince their constituents that mobilization is no longer the most effective tactic for attaining group goals. Persuading constituents to accept settlement terms [N] is thus the fundamental requirement for demobilization.

Constituent persuasion is most difficult when elites seek conflict outcomes that serve their own interests, totally irrespective of the interests of their constituents. Moreover, when successful, mobilization strategies in which elites paint their rivals in negative hues may hinder subsequent elite efforts to demobilize constituents. For whatever reasons, demobilization failures can scuttle a preexisting elite settlement, possibly producing a factional conflict [N-T] between those who wish to settle and those who wish to fight on.

Elites most readily persuade constituents to demobilize when settlement terms address the material sources of conflict to the constituents' satisfaction. For this reason, the cooptation pathway to elite settlement [I-N] more likely results in failed demobilization factional conflict [T] than does the pathway from interelite agreement to terms [M-N]. The terms of a cooptation-induced settlement are unlikely to satisfy the material concerns of constituents, who ordinarily do not enjoy the fruits of cooptation.

If interelite settlements proceed not from hot conflict [K-L-M-N] but from institutionalized conflict ([G-L-M-N] or [G-H-M-N]), factional conflict [T] becomes even less likely. Rejections of such settlements would threaten the legitimacy of those institutional arrangements. To the extent that conflicting parties—elites and constituents alike—recognize that the continued legitimacy of these institutional arenas of political conflict is in their interest, they will be reluctant to reject settlements the arena produces.

Failed Demobilization Factional Conflict

Demobilization efforts can succeed even when settlement terms do not address the material sources of the conflict to the satisfaction of constituents. Although elite failure to arrive at settlement terms that attain group goals can surely upset constituents, no factional elite may arise to challenge it at [T]. Alternatively, like other factional conflict recursions, the failed demobilization factional conflict may become latent. In either case, the elite settlement is implemented [O].

Only when factional elites threaten their ascendancy do incumbent elites find intragroup cooptation, divide-and-conquer, and suppression strategies necessary. These strategies differ with respect to cost-benefit calculations when they are considered for factional, rather than intergroup, conflict. Intragroup cooptation dilutes the power of incumbents by admitting factional elites into the group's councils. These new members may reorient group goals against the interests of incumbent elites. Factional divide-and-conquer and suppression strategies to different degrees drain resources from the intergroup conflict. Further, these strategies can highlight interest dissonance within the group.

When failed demobilization factional conflicts occur, their settlement terms can include the rejection of the terms of the settlement of the intergroup conflict [T-U-A]. This does not imply that incumbent elites are displaced, since they may capitulate to more radical factions in order to retain their ascendancy. When the factional settlement does not result in outright rejection of the intergroup settlement [T-U-L], group elites must reassess the efficacy of the intergroup settlement. Node [U] proceeds to nodes [A] or [L] because the factional conflict may have sufficiently altered the conditions of the intergroup conflict to warrant changes in the assessments of the costs and benefits of a nonrejected settlement [L] or of conflict itself [A] if the intergroup settlement is rejected.

Elite anticipations of failed demobilization factional conflict can affect elite behavior at earlier stages of the conflict. Burton (1985) refers to such anticipations as the "reentry problem." Essentially, if parties are to implement a settlement, its terms must be palatable to constituents across groups. Elites at the negotiation table feel reticent to "reenter" their groups with settlement terms they believe a significant portion of their constituency will reject. Elite anticipations of factional threats to their ascendancy can thus prevent settlement, resulting in new rounds of mobilization and counter-mobilization [L-C, M-C].

Conflict Resolution

As noted above, implemented elite settlements [O] do not resolve the intergroup conflict [Q] when the terms of agreement fail to address the original material motivations for the conflict. The conflict may recure [O-P-A] even though the settlement may produce a period of dormancy. This period may even span generations, since the emergence of new group elites not personally bound to the settlement terms may require the full cohort replacement of elites.

If, in settling, competing elites agree to implement mechanisms for community problem solving, they can profoundly alter the future course of the conflict. These mechanisms might include inducements and rewards to establish and maintain norms and institutional parameters within which groups can peacefully compete and within which all parties can view outcomes as nonarbitrary, legitimate, and binding.

Settlements that provide for the elaboration and strengthening of existing institutions and/or for the establishment of new institutions can prevent future conflict iterations from traversing the hot conflict pathway [I-J-K]. Instead, the mediated [F-G-L-M] and arbitrated [F-G-H-M] paths are followed. As new and strengthened institutions gain legitimacy and as elites correct intergroup perceptions fostered during mobilization, settlements are more likely to produce resolutions. That is, the path toward implemented settlement [M-N-O] is more likely to be traversed than is the path toward factional conflict [M-N-T]. Moreover, as institutions become the arena for conflict, elites mobilize [C] more for influence within the halls of institutions and less for influence in the streets.

Sources of Protractedness

Azar characterizes protracted conflicts as those

in which structural behavior (ethnic, religious, linguistic, economic) and affected overt hostile behavior (interaction), creat[e] a complex causal network that makes these conflicts difficult to 'solve'. . . . Because these conflicts involve whole societies, their stakes are very high and the issues become the determining criteria in the definition of national identity and social solidarity. These conflicts are not terminated by explicit decisions, although cessation of overt violence may defuse tensions somewhat. They tend to linger on in time and gradually cool down, become transformed, or wither away. Hence [conflict] management becomes complicated precisely because protracted social conflicts are not specific events at distinct points in time; they are processes. (Azar 1983: 85, 89)

Our pre-understanding coheres well with Azar's account. In particular the propositions identify two distinct classes of protractedness: protractedness from factionalization and protractedness from latency. Above, we identified three subclasses of factional conflict, each of which we linked to a failure on the part of incumbent elites—a failure to mobilize [D-R], a failure to maintain group solidarity [J-S], and a failure to demobilize [N-T].

We also identified three sources of latency. The first arises when elite perceptions of the costs and risks outweigh the potential benefits of mobilization for conflict [B-A]. Even in the absence of overt hostilities, material disparities across identifiable groups may exist. Careful analyses can reveal such disparities before they erupt into live conflict. Policy makers wishing to avoid such internal conflicts can prevent these conflicts by (1) resolving the disparities, and/or (2) ensuring that the costs and risks of mobilization outweigh the potential benefits in the eyes of elites of disadvantaged groups.

The second source of latency passes through the failed mobilization factional conflict recursion [D-R-A]. When the postmobilization costs and risks outweigh the potential benefits of conflict engagement and when no radical faction challenges this assessment, the intergroup conflict remains latent. Policy makers wishing to avoid internal conflicts can promote latency by maintaining an awesome array of repressive apparatuses or by limiting access to the resources insurgents require to challenge advantaged groups.

The third source of latency follows from elite settlements that fail to address the material conflict motivations [O-P-A]. In successive rounds of mobilization and countermobilization, underlying conflict issues can be clouded by the enormous number of ancillary issues that arise subsequently. To the extent that conflict management strategies address these ancillary issues rather than the underlying causes of the conflict, conflicts are not resolved but only "go latent." In this respect, Azar comments that "in a protracted conflict, the conflict becomes an arena for redefining issues rather than a means for resolving them; it is therefore futile to look for any ultimate resolution because the conflict process itself becomes a source rather than the outcome of policy" (Azar 1983:89).

To be sure, issues undergo redefinition in the course of a conflict. Participants often change their focus from the underlying material disparities to the acts (including speech acts) of their rivals in previous rounds of mobilization, countermobilization, and hot conflict. Nevertheless, we find Azar's contention too pessimistic.

To the extent that policy makers can promote settlement terms that address the underlying causes of the conflict as well as the ancillary issues, protracted conflicts can ultimately find resolution. Of course, parties rarely agree immediately to terms regarding the underlying issues. If settlement of these issues were easy, the conflict might never have arisen. If, however, third parties can encourage participants to fashion settlement terms that would construct political institutions for peaceably settling future iterations of the conflict, participants might more readily avoid the hot conflict pathway [I-J-K]. Designers of such institutions must of course take care to ensure that all parties will recognize them as legitimate, thereby avoiding the [E-F-I] pathway. To the extent that policy makers and third parties encourage an attitude of problem solving through the construction of consensually legitimated political institutions, protracted conflicts can be channeled into more peaceful venues.

CONFLICT IN NORTHERN IRELAND

Early Cycles of Mobilization and Countermobilization

Historically, the Catholic minority in Northern Ireland has voiced three main grievances that represent the material motivation [A] of the conflict: (1) underrepresentation in local government; (2) social and employment discrimination; and (3) security measures directed explicitly against them. In the 1950s the lot of Catholics began to improve. State-subsidized access to university education created a larger, well-educated middle class eager to improve its political and economic standing. Late in the decade, however, traditional industries—agriculture, textiles, and engineering—declined and unemployment consequently increased.

In 1963, the moderate Unionist Terence O'Neill became prime minister of Northern Ireland. O'Neill implemented policies that led to greater recognition of trade unions and changed traditional configurations of power. O'Neill's introduction of direct foreign investment and construction of economic growth centers diminished employment discrimination against Catholics and decreased the power of both the traditional Protestant industrial elite and the Protestant working class. In early 1965 O'Neill and his counterpart in the Republic of Ireland, Taoiseach Sean Lemass, held several economic policy discussions. These talks and O'Neill's new economic policies together raised expectations among the Catholic minority.

O'Neill's professed goodwill toward the Catholic community was disingenuous. He implemented no electoral reforms to improve minority political representation. Further, he failed to address Catholic grievances over security policies. The Special Powers Act, which gave the minister for home affairs extraordinary security powers (e.g., arrest without warrant, internment without trial, dispersal of assemblies), remained in force. The Ulster Special Constabulary, or "B Specials," an armed force of Protestants granted police powers, continued to patrol their neighborhoods. Finally, O'Neill's new economic policies actually worsened the economic conditions for Catholics. By creating transport infrastructure favoring Protestant areas and by locating a new university in Coleraine rather than in largely Catholic Derry,[4] O'Neill ensured that any new industrial development would ultimately benefit Protestant more than Catholic labor (Farrell 1976: 240–242).

Illusory or not, O'Neill's policies significantly altered perceptions among Catholic political leaders of the relative costs and benefits of mobilizing mass pressure for Catholic civil rights [B]. The Northern Ireland Civil Rights Association (NICRA), a broad-based, nonsectarian umbrella group, formed in 1967 to press for Catholic civil rights. Its aims included (1) universal suffrage in local elections (at that time, only rate payers could vote),[5] (2) an end to gerrymandered election boundaries and other discriminatory practices in local government, (3) establishment of an office to investigate complaints of discrimination, (4) fair allocations of public housing, (5) repeal of the Special Powers Act, and (6) dissolution of the B Specials.

NICRA initially mobilized [C] for peaceful protest. As its first action, NICRA protested in Armagh and Newry the decision of William Craig (O'Neill's minister for home affairs) to ban a Republican parade through Armagh. Shortly after, a Nationalist Stormont MP squatted in a Caledon house from which a Catholic family had been evicted. This incident became the focal point for the first NICRA march, 2,500 strong, from Coalisland to Dungannon on August 24, 1968.

The paramilitary Ulster Protestant Volunteers (UPV) countermobilized. Minor skirmishes with the UPV hardened the resolve of the NICRA marchers. They planned an October 5 march to "the Diamond," Derry's business district and symbol of Protestant supremacy, which overlooks the Bogside, a Catholic ghetto. Nationalist MPs did not initially support the Derry march, causing NICRA fears, the Apprentice Boys announced they would henceforth hold an annual October 5 parade along the same route.[6]

Derry police intimated to Craig that, if he banned all marches on that day, the Apprentice Boys would conduct a private ceremony (Hastings 1970: 50–51). Craig subsequently announced the ban and readied the Royal Ulster Constabulary (RUC) Reserves. Two cordons of police assaulted the marchers with batons and water cannon. Seventy-seven demonstrators and bystanders were injured. Accounts vary concerning whether the RUC pushed the demonstrators to the Bogside (Farrell 1976: 247) or entered the Bogside only after Catholic youths subsequently vandalized Diamond shops (Hastings 1970: 55–56). When the RUC entered the Bogside, Catholics met them with gasoline bombs.

That evening, Irish and British television viewers were confronted with images of the RUC raising riot shields against peaceful protesters, barraging them with water cannon, and smashing them with nightsticks. A wave of anger swept through the minority community as media coverage stirred liberal opinion in Northern Ireland, the Republic, and Britain.

With events leading up to the Derry confrontation, the conflict had already undergone several cycles of mobilization and countermobilization [C]. Each involved attempts at suppression [K] that heightened Catholic mobilization [K-L-C]. At each cycle, the Protestant majority chose suppressive efforts

[K] over less stringent strategies, such as cooptation [I] and divide-and-conquer [J]. Apparently, the availability of a repressive apparatus under the Special Powers Act made this a less costly alternative than it might have otherwise been.

Northern Irish governmental institutions might have served as bargaining mechanisms, but were not used, since the Catholic minority did not believe them to be legitimate [E-F-I] (or, in this case, since suppression was the least costly hot conflict strategy for the state [E-F-K]). After all, NICRA was protesting actions of Northern Irish political institutions and opposed the political leaders of the state itself. The British government might have served as an institutional bargaining mechanism, but at this point Westminster was reluctant to involve itself directly in Northern Ireland. Westminster did pressure Stormont to implement political and economic reforms during this period, but in no way did it seek to mediate or arbitrate the conflict.

The British-Inspired Cooptation Attempt

O'Neill, Craig, and Brian Faulkner, then–Northern Irish minister for commerce, consulted with British Prime Minister Harold Wilson in early November 1968. Faulkner (1978: 49) commented that "we realized clearly after that meeting that the British Government was anxious to see reforms made to conciliate the Nationalist minority." Wilson in essence urged the Northern Irish government to pursue a less repressive, more cooptive [I] strategy to deal with the opposition movement.

On November 22, the Northern Irish government announced a reform package. It would establish a points system for allocating public housing, create an ombudsman's office for pursuing complaints of discrimination, implement some electoral reforms, and review the Special Powers Act. Nationalist Stormont opposition leaders initially endorsed the package, and Unionist officials accepted it with the understanding that no further concessions would be contemplated.

With the reform package, O'Neill sought to coopt the Catholic minority. Radical Catholics found the package insufficient, however, and signs of a failed demobilization factional conflict began to emerge within the Catholic community [I-N-T]. Unfortunately for O'Neill, elements within the Protestant community also objected to this nascent settlement [I-N-T]. O'Neill would later fail in attempts to divide-and-conquer and then suppress the civil rights movement [I-J-K].

Radical Catholics rejected the reform package because it would not institute the norm of "one man, one vote," which hardliner Protestants viewed as a concession the government must not make (Faulkner 1978: 49). Dilution of their electoral power was a central issue for Catholics. Even in Derry, where Catholics comprised 80 percent of the population, they controlled only 40 percent of the seats in the local governing body. Yet O'Neill's government could not concede the issue. O'Neill produced his reforms despite strenuous opposition within the Unionist party (Hastings 1970: 68). Further electoral concessions might well have split the Unionists (Farrell 1976: 248).

Recognizing that he could not appease the civil rights movement without splitting his own constituency, O'Neill took to the airwaves. In his "Ulster is at a crossroads" speech, O'Neill rallied the support of moderates in both camps, warning of possible British intervention should Catholics and Protestants fail to settle their differences. This trump card initially worked. After the "Crossroads" speech, popular support for O'Neill swelled. He was able to fire his hardline rival, William Craig, for criticizing "this nonsense centered around civil rights" and for suggesting that Northern Ireland counter Westminster's intervention in civil rights matters by declaring its independence from Britain (Buckland 1981: 126; Faulkner 1978: 50).

After the "Crossroads" speech, political activity subsided significantly. The government postponed until May 1969 all summonses related to the protests of late 1968. The government hinted that "one man, one vote" legislation might be forthcoming, through not until 1971 (Hastings 1970: 76). NICRA announced a month-long moratorium on protest activities.

Conditions were ripe for settlement [L-M-N], but NICRA's moderate leadership could not persuade more radical elements to accept the moratorium. Leaders of People's Democracy (PD) announced a march from Belfast to Derry commencing on New Year's Day. The New Left PD leadership, which included Michael Farrell and Bernadette Devlin, pressed for the march in order to prevent other groups in NICRA from accepting what Farrell termed "O'Neill's miserable reforms" (Arthur 1974: 39–40). PD refusal to observe the moratorium (failed demobilization) sparked a factional conflict within NICRA [T] (Arthur 1974: 61; Farrell 1976: 249; Hastings 1970: 78–79).

The PD marchers left Belfast on January 1, 1969. Loyalists harrassed them all along the route, but the major confrontation occurred on January 4 near Burntollet Bridge, about six miles from Derry. When the marchers reached the bridge, a group of 300 Loyalists (including off-duty B Specials) barraged them with rocks, sticks, bottles, crowbars, and nail-studded cudgels. As marchers fled, they were grabbed, beaten, and kicked into unconsciousness. RUC men stood by and watched. Later that day, battles broke out between Catholics from the Bogside and the RUC and Protestants. Violence continued into evening, when Catholics again erected barricades in the Bogside. They complained later that groups of police had assaulted them at random, broken into their homes, and clubbed shoppers in stores (Hastings 1970: 86–87; Farrell 1976: 251).

The Burntollet incident effectively terminated the Catholic factional conflict. Such a conflict would be too risky in the context of hardliner Loyalist suppression [B-A]. O'Neill's cooptation effort thus backfired. Demobilization failed not only within the Catholic community but within the Protestant community as well. The incident at Burntollet eroded the political centers of both communities.

Catholic Remobilization and Protestant Factional Conflict

Once cooptation failed, O'Neill devised a divide-and-conquer strategy [J]. In one statement, he referred to the PD marchers as "mere hooligans ready to attack the police and others." In an interview with the *Washington Post*, he referred to PD members as "anarchists and Trotskyists," and suggested that more moderate Catholics were driving them out of the movement (Arthur 1974: 41). O'Neill's red-baiting could not divide NICRA. The Burntollet incident in fact provided the movement a level of solidarity it had not previously enjoyed.

O'Neill next threatened to mobilize the B Specials to repress the movement [K] (Farrell 1976:252). Given that (1) the B Specials had already been engaged (though not officially) and that (2) government repression would risk British intervention (as O'Neill had himself intimated in his "Crossroads" speech), this threat rang hollow. As activists prepared for another round of mobilization [K-L-C], O'Neill prepared to settle. This settlement also yielded a failed demobilization factional conflict [M-N-T], though this time within the Unionist coalition.

On January 15, O'Neill announced an official inquiry into the civil rights disturbances. The three-member Cameron Commission, composed of a Scottish judge and two academics, one Protestant and one Catholic, would investigate the causes of the disturbances and recommend policy proposals. Faulkner (1978: 50) charged that the cabinet's agreement to introduce legislation to implement "one man, one vote" upon the recommendation of the Cameron Commission represented a gross abrogation of governmental responsibility. Over O'Neill's denials, Faulkner and other ministers resigned. On February 3, twelve Unionist backbenchers demanded O'Neill's resignation. O'Neill countered by calling a general election.

As Unionist politicians factionalized, Protestant militants pressed the schism in the streets. Beginning in late March, the UPV mounted a bombing campaign primarily targeting electric and water plants. By blaming Catholic militants for these acts, they successfully discredited O'Neill's conciliatory efforts (Buckland 1981: 127; O'Neill 1972: 122–123).

Escalating cycles of hot conflict soon wracked the province. On April 19, a Derry riot intensified when the RUC beat a Bogsider unconscious in his home. Rioting spread from Derry to Belfast. Disturbances continued until April 22, when O'Neill publicly accepted the principle of "one man, one vote." The next day, O'Neill's cousin and agriculture minister, Major James Chichester-Clark, resigned in protest (O'Neill 1972: 125).

On April 24, as UPV bombings blamed on the IRA left Belfast without water, O'Neill presented "one man, one vote" to the Unionist party. Although O'Neill won the Unionist vote, he recognized that the bombings and Chichester-Clark's resignation had eroded his support. He expected to lose subsequent votes in the Unionist Standing Committee and the grassroots Unionist Council. O'Neill resigned on April 28 in order to ensure his succession by the moderate Chichester-Clark and not the hardliner Faulkner (Hastings 1970: 113–114; O'Neill 1972: 128–129). Unionists elected Chichester-Clark prime minister by just one vote—O'Neill's.

The British as Institutional Arbiters

Chichester-Clark brought Faulkner into his cabinet, appeasing Unionist hardliners. He granted amnesty for all political protest offenses since October 1968, appeasing militants in both communities. His earlier resignation from O'Neill's cabinet dissociated him from what Unionists saw as capitulation to Catholics. He was thus able to persuade the Unionist Party Standing Committee to accept "one man, one vote." In response, NICRA called a new moratorium on demonstrations.

The honeymoon, however, did not survive the next marching season. As Protestants prepared for the 1969 Apprentice Boys' parade, Derry Catholics established the Bogside Defense Association (BDA) to provide for collective defense (Buckland 1981: 130). A new cycle of mobilization [C] was underway. Chichester-Clark might have refused to sanction marches, thereby increasing increasing the costs of such actions [D]. However, this would once again have factionalized the Unionist party, placing his position as prime minister in jeopardy (Buckland 1981: 130). On August 8, he met in London with British Home Secretary James Callaghan to request the support of British troops if necessary (Farrell 1976: 259). Chichester-Clark believed that Stormont could control deployments of these troops, but Callaghan (1973: 20–21, 26) labored under no such illusion.

When the Apprentice Boys reached the edge of the Bogside on August 12, Catholics pelted them with stones. Their RUC escorts charged the Bogsiders with batons. Bogsiders regrouped behind BDA barricades and threw gasoline bombs. RUC men shot CS gas over the barricades and tried to press through with armored cars. The violence, which lasted two days, quickly spread to other cities and towns.

The BDA requested medical and other nonmilitary aid from British, Irish, and Northern Irish officials. Irish Taoiseach Jack Lynch announced that the Irish Army would establish field hospitals on the border. He also called for the introduction of a UN peacekeeping force and British-Irish negotiations (Farrell 1976: 261; Hastings 1970: 136–137). Chichester-Clark called Lynch's emotional statement "a clumsy and intolerable intrusion into our internal affairs." He announced he would seek "other than police aid" if the situation so demanded (Hastings 1970: 137). Meanwhile, Stormont activated the B Specials to relieve the RUC in the Bogside.

During the riots, British Lieutenant General Ian Freeland discreetly whisked 300 troops from Belfast to Derry. They awaited offshore as Callaghan interrupted Harold Wilson's holiday to discuss the situation. Upon his return, Callaghan received news that Stormont had requested British troops in Derry. Callaghan issued the order, and the first platoons of the Yorkshire regiment came onshore. Freeland immediately opened negotiations with the BDA. They agreed that (1) the B Specials would be withdrawn, (2) the RUC would resume normal police duties, and (3) the BDA would attempt to calm the Catholic crowds (Callaghan 1973: 42). Freeland interposed the British troops between the barricaded Bogsiders and the Northern Irish police, thereby defusing the confrontation (Farrell 1976: 261–262).

While Freeland calmed Derry, Belfast exploded. On August 15, Chichester-Clark requested British troops in Belfast and authorized internment of suspected IRA members. Two British battalions moved to Falls Road. Loyalists threw gasoline bombs at troops who attempted to prevent attacks on Catholic houses. By August 16, the troops had quelled the disturbances, though barricaded Catholic "no go" areas remained. By sending troops, the British government attempted to establish itself as institutional arbiter of the conflict. In so doing, it hoped to prevent immediate revival of hot conflict and to redress the grievances that underlay the conflict [H-M-N-O-P-Q]. In quick succession, British officials announced that the B Specials would be phased out, a tribunal would be established to investigate the riots, and a committee would be established to study the reorganization of the RUC (Bew and Patterson 1985: 21; Farrell 1976: 264; Hastings 1970: 159). On August 28, Callaghan informed Stormont of three Westminster decisions with respect to Northern Ireland: (1) Britain would station a permanent representation at Stormont; (2) three joint British/Northern Irish groups would study ways to address housing and job discrimination and improve community relations; and (3) authorities would release all internees (Farrell 1976: 264).

At this time, elites across all groups recognized the British government as a legitimate [F] and arbitrating [G] institution. Although they enjoyed benefits from home rule, most Protestant elites recognized that their ascendancy depended on continued allegiance to Westminster. For their part, Catholic elites believed Westminster's promise of civil rights in the August 19 Downing Street Declaration (reprinted in Callaghan 1973: 191–192). Most Catholic constituents welcomed the British intervention (Callaghan 1973: 42; Farrell 1976: 265; Hastings 1970: 149).

Some, however, opposed the British actions. Among Protestant extremists, Reverend Ian Paisley recoiled at the prospect of the disbandment of the B Specials—whom he termed "the teeth of the Northern Ireland government" (Hastings 1970: 161). Paisley implied that the British policy would eventually unify Northern Ireland with the Republic (Callaghan 1973: 66). Catholic hardliners feared that the British would ultimately turn their guns on anti-Unionists. Militant Republicans and People's Democracy called for the complete withdrawal of all British forces (Arthur and Jeffrey 1988; Farrell 1976: 265).

Institutional Inaction and the Militant Response

On the surface, matters remained relatively calm through the spring of 1970. The Cameron Commission reported in mid-September. For the most part it vindicated the civil rights movement. The joint commissions also reported, suggesting reforms in housing, employment, and security policy. However, the British failed to produce a settlement, and as a result the political situation remained open for fresh cycles of conflict mobilization [H-C].

Militant Republicans criticized the Official IRA's armchair Marxism and electoral dabbling. In September of 1969, the Belfast Brigade, later the Provisional IRA (Provos), split from the Official IRA. Sinn Fein, the IRA political arm, split in January 1970. The IRA cleavage centered around strategy and tactics, not ideology (Buckland 1981: 143–144; Farrell 1976: 268, 270). It was a failed mobilization factional conflict [R]. The Provos found the Officials' mobilization efforts insufficient to meet the Loyalist challenge and decided to strike out on their own, militantly, in succeeding iterations of the conflict.

Protestant militants also organized for direct action during the period of British inaction. Unionist hardliners increasingly insisted that Catholic rioters sought to overthrow what they considered a democratically elected government (Buckland 1981: 135; Farrell 1976: 261). For his part, Chichester-Clark attempted to maintain Unionist unity. He added hardliner John Brooke to his cabinet and introduced the tough Public Order Bill on February 5. Many hardliners found this insufficient. On March 19, five hardliners, including William Craig, failed to support a vote of confidence on Stormont security policy and were subsequently expelled from the Unionist Parliamentary Party (Farrell 1976: 271–272). Hardliner intransigence foiled British hopes for a reform-minded Stormont. As Paisley's April by-election capture of O'Neill's former constituency indicated, hardliners also gained political momentum.

With the Unionists, as with the IRA, British failure to produce a settlement sparked increased militancy and raised expectations of further conflict. Since previous policies were insufficiently severe to suppress opponents [K-O], arguments for increased militancy naturally gained constituent support. As the centers of both communities moved toward their extremes, the cross-sectarian Alliance party emerged, committed to Northern Irish reforms and the link with Britain.

The militancy of the 1970 marching season reflected the hardliner drift. On June 2, Protestants in Belfast rioted for two nights after an army officer refused to allow them to march through a Catholic neighborhood. Stormont responded by refusing to ban further Orange parades. On June 27, an Orange parade became a riot as it passed through a Catholic area of Belfast. Loyalists attempted to bomb a church in the Short Strand—an isolated Catholic area in predominantly Protestant East Belfast. The British army refused to intervene on grounds that it had insufficient troops. The army instead sealed the bridges leading to Catholic West Belfast, which effectively marooned the Short Strand (Hamill 1984: 35). This created a vacuum that the Provisionals were quite ready to fill. In a major gun battle, Provos repelled the Loyalist attack (Farrell 1976: 273; Hamill 1984: 35).

On July 3, the army raided a house in the Catholic Lower Falls area of Belfast, finding a small arms cache. A riot ensued, and the army and the Official IRA fought an intense gun battle. Three civilians were killed. The army occupied the entire area, imposed a thirty-six-hour curfew, and searched houses, smashing doors and furniture. The search outraged the entire ghetto. Combined with their inaction in the Short Strand, the army now seemed to Catholics less a guarantor of civil rights and more an instrument of repression and terror (Farrell 1976: 273–274).

Available accounts fail to explain the change in the behavior of the British army between the summers of 1969 and 1970. One can surmise, however, that the Tories may have effected a change in Northern Ireland security policy after their electoral victory in May 1970. Whatever the motive for this policy shift, any legitimacy the British government had had as an arbitrating institution vanished. In the eyes of the Catholic minority, Westminster became as illegitimate as Stormont.

Responding to the growing popularity of the Provisional IRA, moderate Catholic politicians coalesced to meet the factional threat. On August 21, 1970, the NILP, NICRA, and minor Nationalist parties formed the new Social Democratic and Labour party (SDLP). The new party enjoyed the support of the government and business community of the Irish Republic (Farrell 1976: 274–275).

Factional division persisted among the Unionists. Hardliners continued to gain political power and mobilized against both the Catholics and moderate Unionist. In August, Paisley and Craig called for rearming the RUC, reintroducing B Specials, and reinstituting internment. On August 26, Robert Porter, moderate minister of home affairs, resigned. John Taylor, a leading hardliner, replaced him. An alliance of Unionist hardliners, the West Ulster Unionist Council (WUUC), formed in September. In October, Chichester-Clark's own South Derry Constituency joined the WUUC. In November, the Belfast Grand County Orange Lodge voted no confidence in the government.[7] In January 1971, 170 delegates to the Ulster Unionist Council called for Chichester-Clark's resignation.

Chichester-Clark attempted to coopt [I] the hardliners. Twice in the spring of 1971 he met with the Tory prime minister, Edward Heath, to request British support of stronger security measures. Each time Heath refused. Between refusals, 4,000 Loyalists marched on Unionist party headquarters demanding reintroduction of internment. Two days after the second refusal, Loyalists marched again, this time to Stormont. Chichester-Clark could neither accede to Loyalist demands nor ignore them. He resigned.

Brian Faulkner, more an ambitious political pragmatist than a rigid hardliner, was elected prime minister. Given the tenor of Unionist politics and increased numbers of Provo bombings, Faulkner's pragmatism led him to adopt a hardline posture. Shortly after his election, he announced that troops could "fire to warn or with effect" upon anyone acting suspiciously (Hamill 1984: 53).

During the 1971 marching season, authorities would no longer react to strife if and when it occurred. They would instead suppress preemptively. On June 7, the army shot an unarmed youth in the Bogside. Three days of rioting followed. On June 8, the army shot and killed another youth. The army claimed both were gunmen or bombers. Riots intensified. A week later, SDLP MPs walked out of Stormont protesting Westminster's refusal to investigate the shootings. John Taylor, minister for home affairs, responded that "it may be necessary to shoot even more in the forthcoming months" (Dillon and Lehane 1973: 286).

On July 19, Faulkner requested the reintroduction of internment. The British army knew, however, of the woeful inadequacy of police records. Even if Westminster approved internment, they would not know who to intern (Hamill 1984: 52–53). Consequently, at dawn on July 23, about 2,000 British soldiers raided Republican homes to gather information on suspects. On August 5, Faulkner and Heath met to discuss internment plans. On August 9, internment began and Stormont simultaneously banned all parades, marches, and demonstrations. Subsequent protests against internment left twenty-two dead. Catholics called rent and tax strikes as well as work stoppages. On August 19, elected Catholic officials in Derry resigned, and on August 23, 130 anti-Unionist officials followed suit.

PD and the Provisional IRA established the Northern Resistance Movement (NRM) to coordinate resistance and organize demonstrations. Unlike the more moderate NICRA, the NRM called for the abolition of Stormont (Farrell 1976: 285). Throughout the early winter, Catholics continued mass mobilizations. The NRM held a Christmas Day march from Belfast to Long Kesh, where over 200 prisoners were interned. In January, the NRM carried out several other marches with NICRA and SDLP participation (Farrell 1976: 285–288).

The NICRA march in Derry and Bloody Sunday—January 30, 1972—was the most portentous of these protests. The government, intent on a display of force, stationed crack paratroopers to block the marchers. The troops opened fire into the crowd, killing thirteen. Although the troops claimed they were under fire, eyewitnesses, including several priests, denied any demonstrators were armed. Subsequent forensic tests proved inconclusive (Hamill 1984: 91–93).

Reaction was swift. On February 1, a one-day protest strike was held throughout Ulster and a three-day strike began at Derry. In the Republic, Taoiseach Lynch declared February 2 a national day of mourning and Dubliners burned the British embassy. Massive throngs attended the funerals. Protesters marched throughout the province. Despite internment, violent action increased after Bloody Sunday. On February 22, the Official IRA bombed the paratroopers' home base in England. Before the end of the month, the town hall at Strabane was blown up and John Taylor, who only seven months earlier had intimated future army shootings, was himself shot and badly wounded. On March 4, militants bombed a crowded Belfast restaurant. Both IRAs disclaimed responsibility. On March 9, three Provos died setting a bomb in Belfast, and a Provo bomb killed two RUC officers and four Belfast civilians.

Direct Rule: The Failure of Imposed Settlement

On March 22, Heath told Faulkner that Westminster would strip Stormont of all security powers. Faulkner threatened to resign. Heath countered by threatening the suspension of Stormont and direct rule from London. Two days later, Faulkner and his cabinet resigned. Heath then announced the suspension of Stormont and appointed William Whitelaw secretary of state for Northern Ireland.[8]

Direct rule again placed the British government in the role of institutional arbitrator. By this time, however, British security actions and political inactions had denied Westminster any legitimacy to perform this role in the eyes of hardliners in both communities. Thus, direct rule could not produce a settlement. In fact, direct rule became a focus for two new conflicts—one between the Catholics and the British, and one between the Protestants and the British.

Catholics versus the British. Many ghetto Catholics deeply suspected the British, who had failed to prevent Loyalist attacks on the Short Strand and other Catholic communities, implemented internment, and perpetrated Bloody Sunday. They vowed to fight on. But because Protestants lost the state apparatus that had guaranteed their ascendancy, Catholics did not universally abhor direct rule. The SDLP, the Catholic Church, and the government in Dublin all welcomed Westminster's rule and called for a cease-fire. Whitelaw's initial policies also provided Catholics with reasons for optimism. He called an amnesty for persons arrested for marching illegally and released a significant number of internees (Farrell 1976: 293–294).

Nonetheless, IRA bombs exploded throughout the province in April. In response to the shooting death of a prominent member of the Official IRA, the IRA wings announced joint reprisals and shot three British soldiers. On May 19, British soldiers killed a 15-year-old boy in the Bogside. In response, the Official IRA blundered. They killed a soldier in the British army on leave from Germany. He also happened to be a Derry Catholic. Incensed, local Bogside women occupied the local Official IRA headquarters for nine days and formed a movement for peace. The Official IRA acceded to the demands of the Bogside women, declaring an unconditional cease-fire on May 29.

The Derry blunder undercut constituent support for the Official IRA. The costs of continued conflict engagement with the British began to exceed the potential benefits [D]. Pressure mounted on the Provisionals to agree to a cease-fire (White 1984: 128). These were the conditions of a failed mobilization factional conflict [R]. However, in the recursion, the Provos apparently believed factional conflict mobilization counter to their interests [B-A]. As a result, the subconflict between the IRA and British followed the [D-R-A] latency path.

Through the SDLP, Provisionals in June negotiated a cease-fire with Whitelaw. At this point, no institutional bargaining mechanism [E] existed. Neither could the Provisionals coopt, divide, or repress the British. They did, however, seek a broader truce [D-E-I-J-K-L]. Whitelaw provided safe-conduct passes to six Provisional IRA leaders, who flew to London for talks on July 7. The IRA peace plan called for British acknowledgment of the right to self-determination, commitment to an early troop withdrawal, and a declaration of general amnesty (White 1984: 130).

Before they could reach any agreement, the British arrested two IRA men in a July 9 Lenadoon housing dispute. The Provos instantly broke off the talks and the cease-fire. The British-IRA conflict escalated [L-C]. Within a week, Provos killed eight soldiers and an RUC officer (White 1984: 131). On July 21, "Bloody Friday," Provisionals launched a major bombing campaign. In twenty-six bombings, two soldiers and nine civilians were killed; 130 more were wounded. Whitelaw suspended the release of internees.

The British countermobilization, Operation Motorman, brought heavy equipment and 4,000 extra troops to Northern Ireland on July 27. At 4:30 A.M. on July 31 the army moved into "no go" areas, destroying the barricades (Farrell 1976: 299; Hamill 1984: 115).

Protestants versus the British. Direct rule outraged extreme Protestants. Responding to direct rule, Vanguard, a Loyalist umbrella organized by William Craig in February, called a two-day strike. The strike shut down electrical power, halted public transportation, and closed major plants throughout the province.

On March 28, Vanguard rallied outside Stormont. At the rally Faulkner strongly attacked direct rule but warned against precipitate action. He agreed with Vanguard that direct rule amounted to British betrayal, but argued that Unionists retained tremendous power—the power of numbers. He advocated mass noncooperation with Whitelaw but discouraged further industrial action, which Vanguard leaders had advocated as a means for making governance of Northern Ireland impossible. Vanguard later disassociated itself from Faulkner's remarks (Boyd 1972: 117).

Protestants believed they had much to fear from direct rule, particularly if Labour regained its majority. Harold Wilson had some months earlier advocated a Fifteen-Point Plan that called for eventual Irish reunification. As the plan also called for Irish membership in the British Commonwealth, it stood no chance of acceptance in Dublin. Nevertheless, because reunification would abolish Stormont and place them in the minority, Protestants understandably felt insecure. They concentrated on forcing the British to suppress the Catholics.

The well-armed, paramilitary Ulster Defence Association (UDA), founded in August 1971 and closely associated with Vanguard, demanded in early May 1972 that the British take down barricades in all Catholic "no go" areas of Belfast and Derry. On May 13, the UDA barricaded the Protestant Woodvale district of Belfast. They threatened to set up "no go" areas in different Protestant districts for five consecutive weekends unless the army acted against the Catholics. On May 20, the army attempted to bulldoze Protestant barricades, but rioting forced their withdrawal. In early June, Whitelaw met with UDA leaders, who agreed to postpone permanent Loyalist "no go" areas. However, the British-IRA truce enraged the UDA, and on June 30 they established concrete barricades intended to be permanent (Farrell 1976: 297–298). The army destroyed these barricades in Operation Motorman.

Street fighting between Protestant extremists and the British raged that fall and winter. Protestants, including the UDA, clashed with British soldiers on September 7 and October 16. During the September 7 disturbances, the army shot two Protestants, including a UDA member. On October 16, troops in armored vehicles ran down and killed two Protestant civilians. The UDA declared itself at war with the British army. The Protestant community responded to the UDA as the Catholic community had responded to the IRA. They pressured the UDA to rescind the declaration. The UDA called off the "war" two days later (Farrell 1976: 304).

Movement toward Settlement

Although the British never intended permanent direct rule (Buckland 1981: 165), international pressures for settlement made that option impossible. Both Ireland and the United Kingdom would soon enter the European Economic Community, making Britain sensitive to the dim European and Irish views of British Northern Ireland policies (Farrell 1976: 300). Additionally, U.S. Senate hearings on Northern Ireland after Bloody Sunday reflected the pressure Britain felt from her U.S. allies (Faulkner 1978: 140).

In August 1972, Whitelaw invited representatives of the Nationalist, Republican Labour, Social Democratic and Labour, Democratic Unionist, Official Unionist, Alliance, and Northern Ireland Labour parties to Darlington, England for discussions on the future of Northern Ireland. Only the Official Unionist, Alliance, and Northern Ireland Labour parties agreed to attend the September 24 "all-party" conference. The Catholic parties refused to participate, citing the continued internment of prisoners. However, the SDLP met informally with Heath on September 11 and issued *Towards a New Ireland*, a document that detailed the party's proposals for constructing new political institutions in the vacuum left by the suspension of Stormont (White 1984: 131–33).

Among Protestants, Ian Paisley also refused to attend, citing the lack of official inquiry into army shootings of Protestants (Faulkner 1978: 177). Brian Faulkner, attempting to heal the Unionist Party rift, asked William Craig to join the delegation. Craig declined, calling the conference an effort to circumvent "constitutional and democratic processes," meaning Stormont (Faulkner 1978: 177–178). The conspicuous absence of Paisley and Craig from initial discussions and planning meetings of the conflict settlement allowed both to mobilize Protestant constituencies against moderate Unionists nearly eighteen months later.

In the interim, the British, Liberal Unionists, and (behind the scenes) moderate Catholics began to hammer out a settlement. Initiative for settlement came from the British government. The Darlington Conference produced the British green paper on October 30. This discussion document reviewed alternatives to direct rule and discussed the social, economic, cultural, and historical factors that affected the likely success or failure of each alternative. It also specified conditions that any solution must address: (1) any new government must include minority participation in the Northern Irish Executive; (2) any new government must be acceptable to the Republic of Ireland; and (3) security policy must remain under Westminster's control (Buckland 1981: 165; Farrell 1976: 300).

Whitelaw further announced the early 1973 Northern Irish referendum on whether to join the Irish Republic or remain within the British Union. This would be followed by local elections with proportional representation and "one man, one vote." Despite continued internment, the SDLP voted to negotiate with the British. Likewise, the Irish government voiced its approval of the green paper and took decisive steps to control IRA activities in the South.

The Protestant mass movement began to divide. In early February, the

British arrested and interned two Loyalists—the first Loyalist internments in over fifty years. In response the UDA clashed with the army in a pitched gun battle in East Belfast. The UDA, Vanguard, and the Loyalist Association of Workers (LAW) called a one-day protest strike, after which two more Loyalists were arrested. Most Protestants opposed confrontation with the British and supported internment even if it might extend to some Protestant militants. Sensing the rise of this attitude among his constituency, Craig began to disassociate himself from the Protestant paramilitary (Farrell 1976: 306).

On March 20, a Westminster white paper outlined new arrangements for Northern Irish governance. It proposed a plan for terminating direct rule and establishing limited regional autonomy. Among its provisions, the white paper proposed replacement of Stormont with a unicameral assembly, elected on the basis of proportional representation, and an executive. The executive, to be drawn from the assembly, could no longer be constituted of members of a single party if that party's support came from only one section of the divided community. Westminster would retain all powers with respect to security, judicial appointment and removal, and electoral districting. A standing advisory commission would prevent political and religious discrimination. The white paper recognized the "Irish dimension" by calling for periodic plebiscites in which voters would declare their opinion with respect to unification with Ireland. It would establish a Council of Ireland for consultation and cooperation between Northern Ireland and the Republic. The council would secure acceptance of the divided status of the island and provide a basis for concerted security policies.

Reaction to the white paper was predictable. The Provisional IRA rejected it immediately, as it would erode their support. The SDLP accepted it "in principle," but demanded an end to internment and early establishment of the Council of Ireland. The moderate, nonsectarian Alliance party welcomed the white paper with enthusiasm. The Official Unionist party neither accepted nor rejected the document *in toto*. It called for renegotiations of its terms. The Grand Orange Lodge condemned the document. Craig rejected the white paper entirely and announced the formation of the Vanguard Unionist Progressive Party (VUPP). In alliance with Paisley's Democratic Unionists, the VUPP would compete in assembly elections despite their opposition to the British plan (Farrell 1976: 306–307).

The Provisional IRA and People's Democracy called a boycott of May 30 local elections, held under proportional representation rules. The boycott failed in all but the hard-core Republican areas. While the SDLP managed to gain control of only one district council, they eliminated their anti-Unionist rivals as serious electoral contenders.

In the June 28 assembly elections, Faulkner's Official Unionists won a plurality of seats. However, hardliners opposed to the white paper comprised a majority of the Protestant forces. The SDLP won a significant minority share. Alliance won a small share, and the NILP won a single seat. To ward off an electoral threat from hardliners, Official Unionists had promised not to share power with "anyone whose primary object is to break the Union with Great Britain," though they carefully avoided counting the SDLP on the Unionist roster of political pariahs (Buckland 1981: 167; Farrell 1976: 309).

Behind the scenes, the British pressed for establishment of the power-sharing executive. In late August, Heath traveled to Belfast to warn party leaders that they must do so quickly. In early September, Whitelaw held talks with the Alliance, SDLP, and Faulkner Unionists. Later that month, Heath urged Irish Taoiseach Liam Cosgrave to pressure the SDLP to come to an agreement on the executive (Buckland 1981: 168; Farrell 1976: 309–310). The SDLP had initially refused to consider the executive until some resolution on internment had been achieved, until the Council of Ireland was established, and until changes were effected that would make the police acceptable in nonpoliced areas. However, fearing a return to direct rule and increased violence, the SDLP decided to break the deadlock (Devlin 1975: 42).

On October 5, the SDLP, Faulkner Unionists, and Alliance agreed to form an executive. Whitelaw announced its formation on November 22. Composed of eleven members (six Unionist, four SDLP, and one Alliance), Faulkner was named chief executive and Gerry Fitt of the SDLP his deputy. Once the executive formed, Whitelaw resigned as British Secretary of State for Northern Ireland to take another position within the Home Office.

Settlement Fails

The coalition was shaky from the start. Unionist and SDLP constituents both suspected the arrangement did not serve their interests. Unionists experienced the greatest difficulties. The successful formation of an executive represented a defeat for Loyalists. Taking action, Paisley and fellow hardliners persuaded two pro-Faulkner assembly members to defect. Faulkner barely defeated an anti-power-sharing motion by only ten votes out of 750 in the Ulster Unionist Council. On December 6, anti-power-sharing Official Unionists, Democratic Unionists, and Vanguard Unionists combined to create the United Ulster Unionist Council (UUUC) (Farrell 1976: 310). As its founding purpose, the UUUC sought to bring down both the executive and the assembly.

As Loyalist opposition mounted, parties to the settlement addressed the most controversial point of the white paper—the Council of Ireland. Also on December 6, a London-Dublin-Belfast Conference began at Sunningdale, England. After four days, the parties agreed on the council's form. It would be bicameral, with a fourteen-member council of ministers and a sixty-member consultative assembly. Membership in both bodies would be divided evenly between the North and the Republic.

The Republic officially confirmed that Northern Ireland would remain part of the United Kingdom until a majority of its electorate declared otherwise. The Republic additionally stepped up its offensive against the IRA and increased its cooperation with the RUC. Irish law prohibited extradition to the North for political offenses, but the Sunningdale delegates agreed to establish a commission to address the problem of "fugitive offenders" (Faulkner 1978: 233; Farrell 1976: 311).

The power-sharing executive assumed office on January 1, 1974, but its future came immediately into doubt. In a major victory for Unionist hardliners, the Ulster Unionist Council passed a motion on January 4 rejecting the Sunningdale package. Faulkner consequently resigned as leader of the Official Unionists, though he remained both head of the pro-assembly Unionists and chief executive. Hardliners thus gained control of the Unionist electoral machinery. Faulkner moved to new offices and established a new party—the Unionist Party of Northern Ireland (UPNI).

Opposition to Sunningdale emerged also in the Republic. On January 11, Irish legislator Kevin Boland challenged Sunningdale in the courts. He charged the agreement violated the Irish Constitution, which claimed the Northern counties for Ireland. The Irish government argued they had not actually agreed to place the North out of their jurisdiction. The courts dismissed Boland's charge, but the Irish defense encouraged Unionist opposition to Sunningdale (Buckland 1981: 170; Faulkner 1978: 246–248).

On February 7, Heath announced a British general election for February 28. Across the Irish Sea, the main issue was economic policy, but in Northern Ireland the Sunningdale issue dominated the election. Labour won the election, returning Harold Wilson as prime minister. He appointed Merlyn Rees Secretary of State for Northern Ireland. Anti-Sunningdale Unionists won 51 percent of the vote and eleven of the twelve Northern Irish seats in the House of Commons.

In light of these results, the Faulknerites bowed to the Unionist opposition to Sunningdale, announcing on March 4 that there could be no Council of Ireland until the Irish Republic repealed sections of their constitution that claim the North (Farrell 1976: 316). On March 13, Cosgrave reaffirmed in the Irish Dail that the North could only be unified with the Republic peacefully, by means of a Northern Irish plebiscite (Deutsch and Magowan 1975: 27). Given political realities in the South, Faulkner (1978: 247–248) and his followers understood that this was the best Cosgrave could do.

The anti-Sunningdale Unionists meanwhile consolidated. The UWC held a three-day strategy conference at Portrush in Antrim, with members of the paramilitary UDA in attendance. The conference produced a six-page document that called for the rejection of Sunningdale and the Council of

Table 6.1
Approval of Sunningdale Proposal (by religion)

	Protestant	Catholic
Good Idea	25.7%	72.4%
Bad Idea	52.2	3.7
Not Heard of It	3.1	6.1
Don't Know	18.9	17.7
Total percent	99.9[1]	99.9[1]
Total number	676	294

X^2 = 245.16   p ≥.001   Cramer's V = .503

1. Does not add to 100 percent because of rounding error.

Source: NOP Market Research, mimeo, NOP/7513, April 1974.

Ireland, a regional Northern Irish parliament in a federal United Kingdom, return of security policy to Northern Ireland, and abolition of the power-sharing executive (Deutsch and Magowan 1975: 46; Farrell 1976: 316–317).

A public opinion survey conducted for BBC Television Ulster (NOP Market Research 1974), administered to a random sample of Northern Irish electors between March 31 and April 7, vividly illustrates the depth of the cleavage in the Protestant community. The pollsters asked respondents, "Do you think the Sunningdale proposal for a Council of Ireland is a good idea or a bad idea in principle?" As Table 6.1 indicates, the vast majority (72.4 percent) of Catholics supported the idea while Protestants split, opposing it two to one. Of all those expressing an opinion, a bare majority thought the proposal a good idea.

The pollsters also presented respondents seven substantive alternative futures (listed in Table 6.2) for Northern Ireland. Respondents were asked, "of those alternatives you have said are acceptable, which *one* do you prefer?" Table 6.2 breaks down the results by religion. Note that 57.8 percent of Catholics but only 18.5 percent of Protestants supported the alternatives of a power-sharing executive. There was some Catholic support (15.1 percent) for a united Ireland, but nowhere near the support that Protestants expressed for full integration into the United Kingdom (35 percent) or a return to one-party rule (33.7 percent).

The Provisional IRA prepared their own rejection of Sunningdale. Wilson announced that Provo documents captured in an RUC raid revealed a plan to occupy sections of Belfast, including facilities of the BBC, Ulster Tele-

Table 6.2
Preferred Option for Settling Northern Ireland Conflict (by religion)

Option Preferred:	Protestant	Catholic
Continuing power-sharing with executive	18.5%	57.8%
Direct rule from Westminster	7.7	7.3
Independent Northern Ireland, outside United Kingdom	1.6	.1
United Ireland outside of United Kingdom	---	15.1
Federal parliament in Ireland with provincial parliaments in Northern Ireland and in the Republic	.1	6.2
Northern Ireland Parliament with one-party rule	33.7	1.0
Full integration of Northern Ireland with United Kingdom	35.9	5.8
Don't Know	1.2	3.5
None of them	2.1	3.1
Total percent	99.9[1]	100.0
Total number	651	293

X^2 = 387.62   p ≥.001   Cramer's V = .641

1. Does not add to 100 percent because of rounding error.

Source: NOR Market Research, mimeo, NOP/7513, April 1974.

vision, the Telephone House, and the Gas Works. Provisional IRA denials notwithstanding, Wilson's announcement plus ongoing Provo attacks fueled anti-Sunningdale sentiment in the Protestant community.

On May 13, the Ulster Workers' Council (UWC), a Protestant working-class group established in late 1973 as successor to the Loyalist Association of Workers, threatened a province-wide blackout and general strike if the executive parties continued to support Sunningdale (Deutsch and Magowan

1975: 55). The UWC claimed the full backing of the Ulster Army Council, which issued the following threat: "If Westminster is not prepared to restore democracy, i.e., the will of the people made clear in an election, then the only other way it can be restored is by a *coup d'état*. Such a *coup d'état* can only mean a civil war" (Deutsch and Magowan 1975: 55).

In the next edition of the *Newsletter*, a Belfast daily, the UWC assured its constituents that they would be provided benefits in the event of a general strike:

If Brian Faulkner and his colleagues vote in the Assembly on Tuesday 14 to support Sunningdale then there will be a general stoppage. Workers' dependents are advised, in such an event, to apply for Supplementary Benefit immediately. Advice Centres will be available in all areas. After 6 P.M. (Tuesday 14th) all essential services will be maintained, and only action by Mr. John Hume [SDLP leader and minister for commerce] will rob the housewife, the farmer, and essential service industries of power. (Quoted in Deutsch and Magowan 1975: 55)

By establishing advice centers and assuring the population access to essential services, the UWC strengthened solidarity among its constituents. They now stood ready to engage moderate Unionists in failed demobilization factional conflict.

At 6:00 P.M. on May 14, the assembly voted for the Sunningdale package. Moments after members emerged from Stormont, a UWC man told journalists that electricity workers would reduce the power supply in the city that evening, forcing industry to shut down. The UUUC issued a statement that evening blaming the strike on the Faulkner Unionists who voted, "without a mandate, for the all-Ireland institutions which evolve from the Sunningdale Agreement." They announced that sufficient electrical power would be available for private homes and essential services unless Hume diverted power for industrial usage (Deutsch and Magowan 1975: 56).

At their insistence, Rees offered to meet Loyalist leaders on May 17. Citing broken British pledges, the UWC refused to attend (Deutsch and Magowan 1975: 60–61; Rees 1985: 55–66). Following the meeting, which produced no agreements, the UWC announced it would withdraw all power reserves from the grid. The next day, however, the UWC announced that unless electricity was used industrially or the British brought in troops they would refrain from cutting all power (Deutsch and Magowan 1975: 62). On May 19, Rees declared a state of emergency (Rees 1985: 68) and Protestants threw up barricades throughout Ulster the next morning.

On May 21, the UWC called a petrol embargo in response to the Northern Ireland Office decision to allow industrial uses of electrical reserves. This ostensibly reduced supplies available for homes and essential services. On May 22, 3,000 British troops moved into Belfast overnight to take down barricades. Most main roads were clear by morning.

Also May 22, Faulkner attempted to coopt the Loyalists. He presented a proposal, to which the executive had already agreed, for revising the Council of Ireland. It would make the council purely consultative until 1977–1978, allowing anti-Sunningdale forces four years to press for further limits on the council. Rees welcomed the proposal, as did Cosgrave. The UWC, however, proclaimed its rejection of Sunningdale, "whatever modifications it might assume" (Deutsch and Magowan 1975: 68).

On May 24, Faulkner, Fitt, and Alliance party leader Oliver Napier met in London with Wilson, Rees, and other top British officials. The Northern Irish leaders proposed a contingency plan to use security forces to control the supply and allocation of electricity and fuel. Faulkner emerged from the meeting with "the clear impression that the Prime Minister was firm in his desire to do whatever was necessary and within his power to stand by the Executive" (Faulkner 1978: 275).

In his national broadcast on May 25, Wilson failed to propose any new concrete measures to address the UWC strike. Instead, he emphasized the costs of Northern Irish dependence on the rest of the United Kingdom. He accused the strikers of "sponging on British democracy" (Faulkner 1978: 275–276). On May 27, Rees authorized army control of fuel distribution (Deutsch and Magowan 1975: 75).[9] The UWC responded with new sanctions. Its coordinating committee announced that from midnight on May 28, provisions of essential services would become the army's responsibility. On May 28, the Department of the Environment warned of low water supply and imminent sewerage problems. Electricity supply had dwindled and some power cuts lasted eighteen hours (Deutsch and Magowan 1975: 77–78).

The Northern Irish government began to capitulate to the hardliners. On May 27, senior civil servants told Faulkner that that they could no longer support the government if it did not negotiate with the UWC. The executive voted on the issue of negotiations. SDLP members abstained while the Alliance and the Unionists voted to negotiate (Deutsch and Magowan 1975: 78; Devlin 1975: 27–28). Faulkner reported the vote to Rees, who told him the British would not negotiate (Deutsch and Magowan 1975: 78; Rees 1985: 86). The Unionist members of the executive resigned, and Rees dissolved the executive, returning Northern Ireland to Westminster's direct rule.

CONCLUSION

We believe our pre-understanding coheres rather well with the historical events recounted here. This exercise underscores the importance of the political environment within which conflict occurs. In particular, events more or less external to the Ulster conflict, such as, the British elections of 1970, appear to have conditioned its course. Likewise, entirely exogenous events, such as the entrance of the United Kingdom and Ireland into the European Economic Community and U.S. political pressures, profoundly affected British policies that shaped the Northern Irish conflict.

Of course, no degree of correspondence to the historical facts of a particular conflict can validate our pre-understanding. Analyses of additional conflicts may well produce anomalies that can fruitfully be applied in extending the pre-understanding, thereby extending its explanatory scope.

With respect to the Northern Irish conflict, the British lost an excellent opportunity for settlement in 1969–1970. Interposing troops between the warring communities calmed the situation enormously. Serious efforts to construct a comprehensive political settlement might have succeeded over the objections of marginalized extremists in both communities. Whether due to the change in British government or some other reason, British failure to facilitate a settlement resulted in new cycles of intense mobilization and countermobilization [H-C].

In failing to defend the Short Strand, the British allowed the Provisional IRA to gain support within the Catholic community. The British response to IRA militancy—army searches of Catholic homes and ultimately interment—served only to delegitimize the British and enhance the prestige of the IRA in the eyes of Catholics (Morgan 1989).

Increased IRA activity in turn provided militant and hardliner Protestants a focal point around which to mobilize. Hardliners could thus effectively oppose concessions to Catholic interests during the period of direct rule. Moreover, by conducting and winning a failed demobilization factional conflict after Sunningdale, the hardliners scuttled any immediate chance for comprehensive political settlement. The die was cast for protracted conflict in Northern Ireland throughout the 1980s.

Though the forces of conciliation hardly need to be told, their task is the construction of consensually legitimate political institutions for governing Northern Ireland. Two barriers stand in the way—the extremist elements of each community.

Protestant hardliners enjoy the sympathies of a mass Loyalist constituency that reacts strongly to any perceived threat to the union with Britain. For Loyalists, union implies loyalty to the British Crown, not necessarily recognition of the authority of British political institutions (Bell 1987: 8–11). Hardliners portray employment competition, civil rights demands, and IRA violence as a zero–sum conflict instigated by a monolithic enemy hostile to the Union, not common problems that citizens can tackle cooperatively.

Republican militants enjoy the sympathies of a significant segment of an economically and socially deprived Catholic constituency. This constituency looks beyond Northern Ireland to the Republic for its group identity. Pride in Gaelic culture and Irish nationalism, as well as respect for the Catholic Church, clash with major tenets of Ulster loyalism (Buckland 1981: 9).

Catholics, particularly in the ghettos, perceive their oppression and suppression of their protests as denials of Catholic values. They perceive repression of the IRA, whose name evokes the Irish fight for independence from Britain, as a zero-sum conflict in which Britain and Ulster Loyalists conspire to perpetuate colonial domination.

Moderates can surmount extremist intransigence only by altering constituent sympathies. Historical patterns of cultural, economic, and social domination ground these sympathies, while educational and religious segregation in the identity-formation stages of childhood reproduce them. Concerted social and economic change can erase the structural conditions that breed intransigence, but only deliberate efforts to free the community from false, sterotypical, jingoistic interpretations of one another can create the necessary environment for concerted political change.

NOTES

Discussions with a great number of people contributed significantly to this work. In particular, we would like to express our gratitude to Hayward R. Alker, Jr., Walter Dean Burnham, Erik A. Devereux, Timothy I. M. Fackler, James S. Fishkin, Renee Gannon, Victoria Hammond, Matthew Harbison, James W. Lamare, L. Huan-Ming Ling, David Pringle, Neil Richardson, Sheryl Shirley, and Robert E. Smith. Professor Richard Rose of the University of Strathclyde, Scotland, graciously provided the survey data analyzed in this paper. These data were collected by NOP Market Research Ltd. of London for the British Broadcasting Corporation. The authors retain all responsibility for any errors.

1. In future work, we plan to compare the Sunningdale failure with a more recent, relatively successful settlement effort.

2. Important inspirations have been Deutsch's (1953) focus on the role of communication in nation-building, Azar's (1983) presentation of protracted social conflict, Shefter's (1984) discussion of party mobilization and demobilization in American politics, and the Burton and Higley (1987) work on elite settlements that introduce democratic institutions. Louis Kriesberg's (1973) synthetic account of conflict theory has undoubtedly served as our most important source. However, as Kriesberg himself states, his account does not generate refutable hypotheses (Kriesberg 1973: 317). We hope our work will help remedy this.

3. The mathematical concept of "recursion" refers to a procedure that invokes itself, though with different arguments. Understanding conflict as a procedure and taking conflict participants, stakes, and issues as the arguments to that procedure, we view factional conflict as a recursive application of the conflict procedure with different arguments.

4. We call this town "Derry" rather than "Londonderry" because most of its inhabitants call it "Derry."

5. "Rate payers" were direct property tax contributors. Corporations, which paid relatively large amounts of such taxes, received large numbers of votes. Renters, who paid such taxes indirectly through rents, were disenfranchised.

6. The Apprentice Boys are an Ulster Protestant organization founded in Derry

to commemorate the actions of the legendary youth apprentices who locked the gates of the walled city against the armies of James II in 1688. The group's traditional annual parade is held on August 12.

7. The Orange Lodges form the Orange Order, a politically important Protestant social organization.

8. Reginald Maulding (1978: 186), Heath's home minister, recounts that the army's situation in Northern Ireland necessitated direct rule by Westminster. The British army could not indefinitely enforce laws made by a parliament to which it was not responsible. Bew and Patterson (1985: 43), however, regard adverse European opinion of British policy in Northern Ireland as the primary determinant.

9. Rees could not use troops to operate the electrical plants without the assistance of middle management (Faulkner 1978: 277).

REFERENCES

Arthur, Paul. *The People's Democracy: 1968–1973*. Belfast: Blackstaff Press, 1974.

Arthur, Paul, and Keith Jeffrey. *Northern Ireland since 1968*. Oxford: Basil Blackwell, 1988.

Azar, Edward E. *The Theory of Protracted Social Conflict and the Challenge of Transforming Conflict Situations*. Merriam Seminar Series on Research Frontiers. Vol. 20, bk. 2. Denver, Colo.: University of Denver Graduate School of International Studies, 1983.

Bell, Geoffrey. *The Protestants of Ulster*. London: Pluto Press, 1987.

Bew, Paul, and Henry Patterson. *The British State and the Ulster Crisis: From Wilson to Thatcher*. London: Verso, 1985.

Boyd, Andrew. *Brian Faulkner and the Crisis of Ulster Unionism*. Tralee, Ireland: Anvil Books, 1972.

Buckland, Patrick. *A History of Northern Ireland*. New York: Holmes and Meier, 1981.

Burton, John W. "About Winning." *International Interactions* 12(1985): 71–91.

Burton, Michael G., and John Higley. "Elite Settlements." *American Sociological Review* 52(1987): 295–307.

Callaghan, James. *A House Divided: The Dilemma of Northern Ireland*. London: William Collins Sons, 1973.

De Fleur, Melvin L., and Sandra Ball-Rokeach. *Theories of Mass Communication*. New York: Longman, 1966.

Deutsch, Karl W. *Nationalism and Social Communication*. Cambridge, Mass.: MIT Press, 1953.

Deutsch, Richard, and Vivien Magowan. *Northern Ireland 1968–74: A Chronology of Events*. Vol. 3. Belfast: Blackstaff Press, 1975.

Devlin, Paddy. *The Fall of the N.I. Executive*. Belfast: Paddy Devlin, 1975.

Dillon, Martin, and Denis Lehane. *Political Murder in Northern Ireland*. Harmondsworth, England: Penguin, 1973.

Farrell, Michael. *Northern Ireland: The Orange State*. London: Pluto Press, 1976.

Faulkner, Brian. *Memoirs of a Statesman*. London: Weidenfeld and Nicolson, 1978.

Hamill, Desmond. *Pig in the Middle: The Army in Northern Ireland 1969–1984*. London: Methuen, 1984.

Hastings, Max. *Ulster 1969: The Fight for Civil Rights in Northern Ireland*. London: Victor Gollancz, 1970.

Katz, Elihu. "The Two-Step Flow of Communication: An Up-to-Date Report on an Hypothesis." *Public Opinion Quarterly* 21(1957): 61–78.

Kriesberg, Louis. *Social Conflicts*. 2nd ed. Englewood Cliffs, N.J.: Prentice-Hall, 1973.

Lasswell, Harold D. "Conflict and Leadership: The Process of Decision and the Nature of Authority." In Anthony de Reuck and Julie Knight, eds., *Conflict and Society*. London: J. and A. Churchill, 1966.

Lewin, Kurt. *Resolving Social Conflicts*. New York: Harper and Row, 1948.

Maulding, Reginald. *Memoirs*. London: Sidgwick and Jackson, 1978.

Moon, J. Donald. "The Logic of Political Inquiry: A Synthesis of Opposed Perspectives." In Fred I. Greenstein and Nelson W. Polsby, eds., *Handbook of Political Science*. Vol. 1. Reading, Mass.: Addison-Wesley, 1975.

Morgan, Michael. "How the British Created the Provos." *Fortnight* 275 (1989): 12–13.

NOP Market Research, Ltd. "Public Opinion in Northern Ireland." NOP/7513. London: NOP Market Research, 1974.

O'Neill, Terence. *The Autobiography of Terence O'Neill*. London: Rupert Hart-Davis, 1972.

Rees, Merlyn. *Northern Ireland: A Personal Perspective*. London: Methuen, 1985.

Rejai, Mostafa. "Theory and Research in the Study of Revolutionary Personnel." In Ted Robert Gurr, ed., *The Handbook of Political Conflict*. New York: Free Press, 1980.

Rootes, C. A. "On the Social Structural Sources of Political Conflict: An Approach from the Sociology of Knowledge." In Louis Kriesberg, ed. *Research in Social Movements, Conflicts and Change*. Vol. 5. Greenwich, Conn.: JAI Press, 1983.

Shefter, Martin. "Political Parties, Political Mobilization, and Political Demobilization." In Thomas Ferguson and Joel Rogers, eds., *The Political Economy*. Armonk, N.Y.: M. E. Sharpe, 1984.

White, Barry. *John Hume: Statesman of the Troubles*. Belfast: Blackstaff Press, 1984.

7

The Afghan Conflict and Soviet Domestic Politics

T. H. Rigby

After nine years of active combat, Soviet troops have withdrawn from Afghanistan without having achieved the political and military objectives for which they were sent there. Their primary objectives may be summarized as defeating the anticommunist insurgency and firmly installing a communist regime under effective Soviet control. Secondary objectives included advancing the Soviet military frontier 1,000 kilometers to the south and to within 500 kilometers of the Arabian Sea, and demonstrating, as in Hungary in 1956 and Czechoslovakia in 1968, that the Soviet Union will not tolerate satellite regimes in neighboring states being overthrown and the transition to "socialism" being reversed. The cost of the Afghanistan enterprise was a major one on several counts. Its purely military costs were kept to a relatively modest level, and there was doubtless some useful learning. Its costs for Soviet foreign relations, however, vis-à-vis both the Western alliance and the Third World, were profoundly and almost unrelievedly negative. Against this background, withdrawal without having achieved the initial objectives must be counted as a major political and military defeat for the Soviet Union.

Such defeats may have an enormous political impact at home. One has only to recall the role of Russia's failures in the Crimean War as a catalyst for the great reforms of the 1860s, including the abolition of serfdom, or in the Russo-Japanese War, which led via the 1905 revolution to the (sadly aborted) beginnings of a liberal constitutional order. Even the cataclysmic impact of World War I—although this seems to be attenuating the analogy egregiously—has a certain relevance which will not have been lost on the more nervous conservatives within the Soviet bureaucracy. The Soviet Union, of course, is hardly peculiar in suffering domestic political consequences from military-political failures abroad, but the autocratic character of its regimes has historically exerted a multiplying effect on these consequences. The French withdrawal from Algeria and the American withdrawal from Vietnam, perhaps the closest foreign analogies in recent decades, certainly had a substantial domestic impact, in the former case at least one of lasting significance. Yet these had nothing like the consequences for the sociopolitical order of the Russian and Soviet cases cited.

Nevertheless, the withdrawal from Afghanistan is unlikely to have persistent and profound domestic political implications in the Soviet Union itself. The most obvious reason for this is that the war has affected the Soviet population far less massively and obviously than did the Algerian and Vietnam wars the French and American populations, respectively, not to mention the effect of the Crimean and Japanese wars on the ordinary people of Russia. This is due as much to the media monopoly enjoyed by the Soviet regime and to the organizational and coercive resources at its disposal to protect it and its policies from serious public criticism, as it is to the relatively modest scale and the geographical and psychological remoteness of its involvement. That said, one must immediately add that the withdrawal will undoubtedly have, is indeed already having, significant consequences within the Soviet Union on a number of levels.

In the short to middle term it will bring a number of substantial benefits. Most obviously, there will be the savings to the Soviet economy. Although the cost of waging the war has not, perhaps, been all that large in relation to the total military budget, it has been escalating and would have had to escalate further if there were to be any chance of a decisive victory over the Mujahideen. The Gorbachev leadership clearly aims at curbing military expenditure during the difficult period of restructuring the economic system, and getting out of Afghanistan, like scrapping intermediate-range missiles, will contribute to this.

If the Soviet withdrawal has implications for *perestroika*, so it does for *glasnost'* too. If they had decided to soldier on in Afghanistan, the freer flow of information to which they are committed, particularly in the press and electronic media, would inevitably have amplified negative public awareness of the war more and more, unless of course it had been treated as a special case calling for old-style distortion and censorship—which is, by the way, largely how it is treated even now—in which case the whole *glasnost'* operation would be discredited.

A more basic reason why withdrawal is politically advantageous is that the war was becoming increasingly unpopular as the casualties mounted and victory seemed no closer (see Nahaylo 1987; Wise 1988). Eastern Europe provides a poor analogy here, since it is from that direction that Russians see the primary threat to their security, and most would probably want their government to hold fast in any combat situation there. Nor, despite China's support for the Afghan resistance, is their relationship such as to touch off the anti-China paranoia widespread among the Russian population. No doubt some ideological conservatives, for whom the "Brezhnev doctrine" is a direct corollary of the sacrosanct principle of "proletarian internationalism," find the desertion of an embattled "fraternal" regime hard to stomach, but such dogmatic notions cut little ice with the general public. Among the right-wing nationalists some must certainly see the withdrawal as a betrayal of Russia's imperial destiny, but others will welcome it, because they resent Russian lives and treasure being squandered on unworthy and ungrateful Third World elites.[1] As for the non–Russian half of the Soviet population, they can only welcome the cessation of sacrifices exacted from them in furtherance of Moscow's imperial ambitions. It was, then, a predominantly unpopular war, and governments that disengage from unpopular wars usually gain political credit, at least in the short run.

THEORY AND IDEOLOGY

The middle-to-long run will be covered later in this chapter. First, however, the implications of the withdrawal for another level of Soviet political life, namely the theoretical or ideological level will be considered.

All rulers operate in the context of clusters of ideas that justify their power and inform their policies. What is peculiar about the Soviet Union and other communist-ruled states is the comprehensive and systematic character of the legitimating world view and its claim to give the only truly scientific account of all aspects of human affairs. All policy, including foreign policy, is supposed to be scientifically based (*nauchno obosnovana*), and there is a literature relating to every policy field that purports to demonstrate this scientific basis, a literature emanating from groups of specialist scholars and "ideological workers." Now, it is quite true that in practice the proclaimed theoretical basis of policy often amounts to little more than *ex post facto* justification of decisions made on entirely pragmatic grounds, and that, arguably, is one respect in which Soviet politics is not so different from anyone else's politics. It is also true that Soviet policy-oriented theory, especially in the Stalin era, but not only then, is often intellectually primitive, giving the impression of a pompously dogmatic and vacuous pseudo-science. Nevertheless it would be a mistake to dismiss it as irrelevant to political action. Marxism-Leninism provides leaders and scholar-ideologists alike with their essential vocabulary for describing social realities, and thereby substantially governs their perceptions of these realities. To sum up: much emphasis is placed on the scientific basis of Soviet policy, groups of specialists are engaged in policy-related studies articulated in terms of Marxist-Leninist concepts, and these studies are relevant to policy development.

It is important to make these points, as they are pertinent both to the decision to commit Soviet troops to Afghanistan and to the decision to withdraw them, while at the same time the Afghanistan experience is clearly having a feedback effect on the theoretical understandings associated with these decisions.

Soviet policy toward the Third World since World War II has undergone a number of sharp twists and turns. Under Stalin its key determinants were a "two-camp" ("socialist" versus "imperialist"), zero-sum view of world politics, combined with marked caution as to direct Soviet involvement in "anti-imperialist" struggles. The rise to power of the ebullient Khrushchev coincided with a phase of economic and military-technological dynamism (Sputnik and the like) in the Soviet Union and an acceleration of the de-colonization process in the world at large. In this context a more active and optimistic Third World policy emerged. The nuclear "balance of terror" between the Soviet and "imperialist" camps was seen as calling for a shift to peaceful (though competitive) coexistence between East and West, while at the same time sharply reducing the risks attending direct Soviet involve-ment with the newly independent countries, with the aim of coopting them into a single Soviet-led "anti-imperialist" movement and encouraging their gradual transition to "socialism."

The Khrushchevian hubris evaporated in the wake of the Cuban missile crisis, the break with China, and the collapse of Soviet influence in a number of newly independent countries. Without discarding the commitment to competitive peaceful coexistence and to the belief that in the long haul the ex-colonial countries would gravitate to "socialism," the Soviet leadership became alarmed at the dangers of unintended nuclear war while at the same time suffering a sharp drop in confidence in their capacity to control the in-ternational communist movement, let alone developments in the nonaligned countries. Khrushchev now placed prime emphasis on improving East-West re-lations and curbed Soviet activities in the Third World (see Zimmerman 1969).

Despite some changes of rhetoric, Khrushchev's successors did not at first depart substantially from these positions, and it was not till the early 1970s that a new upsurge of optimism and activism emerged. The United States was now seen as a declining power, the correlation of forces as moving decisively in favor of "socialism," and the Third World as entering a new era of revolutionary change. In this context the Brezhnev regime sought with a measure of success to combine a policy of superpower détente with an escalation of Soviet involvement, often including military involvement, in radical Third World states with a view to drawing them decisively into the Soviet orbit (see Katz 1982; Hosner and Wolfe 1983; MacFarlane 1985). This new adventurism, however, proved even more short-lived than the Khrushchevian equivalent of two decades earlier. Soviet economic decline, the revival of Western economic and technological dynamism, the resto-ration of American confidence and firmness, and the failure of the Soviet Union's new "socialist" clients in the Third World, despite massive military aid, to consolidate their power and defeat Western-backed insurgents, all contributed to a new pessimism, a reluctance to undertake new involvements, and a concentration of effort on holding the line, on preventing the demise of their "socialist" and "socialist-oriented" clients at the hands of the "counterrevolutionaries" (see Breslauer 1987: 438–441). This orientation was already apparent in Brezhnev's last years and persisted throughout the 1980s. A version of it has become an integral part of Gorbachev's "new political thinking."

All these shifts in policy toward the Third World reflect decisions made at the highest political level, but they were decisions adopted in a context of information and ideas largely created by the leaders' foreign affairs advisers, scholars, and ideologists. These "foreign affairs influentials" are to be found on leaders' personal staffs, in the Central Committee apparatus, in the Foreign Affairs Ministry, among political journalists, and in Academy of Sciences think tanks. Their character and role have greatly changed over the years. Under Stalin they were few in number and limited in influence. Since then there has been a virtually uninterrupted process of expanding numbers, widening access to information (particularly from Western sources), greater diversity of views and freedom of specialist debate and public discussion, and the growing influence of well-trained and intellectually sophisticated area specialists, most of them working in such think tanks as the Institute of World Economy and International Relations (IMEMO), the Institute of the USA and Canada, the Institute on the Economics of the World Socialist System, and the Institute of Oriental Studies.

AFGHANISTAN IN SOVIET THIRD WORLD POLICY

All this is background, but it is very important background for estimating the likely impact of the Afghanistan experience on Soviet Third World policy and its intellectual underpinnings. Without going into detail, the history of Soviet relations with Afghanistan can be seen as following fairly closely the periodization of Soviet Third World policy just outlined. Stalin avoided direct involvement and was satisfied with Afghan neutrality. Khrushchev took advantage of shared hostility toward Pakistan and other overlapping foreign policy interests to foster cooperation with the Afghan government during Mohammad Daoud's premiership, and in 1955 began the provision of military aid. However, it was not till the Brezhnev phase of Third World activism in the early to mid–1970s that substantial Soviet involvement in Afghanistan's internal affairs emerged, following the success of Daoud's coup in 1973, with some help from pro-Soviet leftists. The seizure of power by the Marxist-Leninist People's Democratic party of Afghanistan in April 1978, regardless of whether the Soviet Union had a direct hand in it, was the culmination of this process of growing Soviet influence in Afghan political life, especially in the military.

There are other respects, too, in which Afghanistan fits the general pattern of Soviet Third World policy during the 1970s. The Brezhnev regime, following a long series of disappointments in Soviet relations with "bourgeois nationalist" regimes, now concentrated its main attention on states of "socialist orientation," with revolutionary leaders prepared (as the Cuban Castro regime had been) to set up and rule through Soviet-type vanguard parties, in which the Communist Party of the Soviet Union (CPSU) sought to establish a strong influence. For the most part these turned out to be less developed countries (Ethiopia, Angola, South Yemen) rather than those ruled by the Soviet Union's actual or former "bourgeois nationalist" friends (Egypt, Indonesia, India, Syria) (Fukuyama 1987: 24–45). This policy shift evolved in the context of wide-ranging discussions among Soviet Third World specialists. However, some specialists probably had misgivings about it from the start, and these were soon finding expression in scholarly publications. They suggested that quite specific conditions might be necessary for a country to jump successfully from a feudal or prefeudal society to socialism, bypassing capitalism. They argued the importance of the cultural and structural peculiarities of particular countries, and they warned against "leftist" miscalculations that could lead to debacles. Developments on the ground lent force to these arguments. The revolutionary leaders and their vanguard parties turned out in most cases to enjoy a very narrow basis of support and found themselves confronted with large-scale revolts, assisted, to be sure, from outside but possessing a strong indigenous support which the revolutionaries were unable to crush. In the late 1970s and through the 1980s there was wide-ranging discussion of these issues in the specialist literature (see Hough 1986; Valkenier 1983), and it was in this context that the Soviet leadership shifted to a far more cautious policy of helping its existing clients in the Third World to stay afloat, but avoiding getting embroiled with new ones.

The one major difference between the course of Soviet policy toward Afghanistan and Moscow's other recently acquired clients was obviously the direct involvement of the Soviet armed forces. In the other countries Soviet backing was limited to providing advisers, military supplies, economic aid, and training. Cuban troops were used against clients' rivals, but never Soviet ones. Nevertheless, the introduction of combat troops into Afghanistan probably should not been seen as contradicting the more cautious approach toward Third World involvements, which was already emerging in the late 1970s. It is sufficiently explained by the imminent danger of Afghanistan falling into the hands of political forces actively hostile to Moscow, for the first time in Soviet history, and the lack of other means to prevent this.

The withdrawal of Soviet forces from Afghanistan without their having achieved their objective of eliminating this danger will obviously have large implications for the Soviet Union's Third World alliance system generally. It should be noted that there are important theoretical implications as well. Those scholars who warned against close Soviet involvement with self-proclaimed Marxist regimes in poorly developed countries now see their arguments as vindicated by events. The recriminations have already begun. Academician Oleg Bogomolov (1988) recently declared that his Institute on the Economics of the World Socialist System had considered at the time that the intervention was mistaken, and had said as much in an unsolicited brief to the Brezhnev leadership. Nodari Simoniia of the Institute of Oriental Studies, recalling his twelve-year struggle to draw attention to the erroneous assumptions underlying the upbeat Third World policies of the 1970s against the too-powerful opposition of a group of policy advisers and specialists led by R. A. Ul'ianovskii, Deputy Head of the Central Committee's International Development Department, acidly remarked that if Ul'ianovskii had spent less time attacking his (Simoniia's) theoretical position, but instead "had directed his efforts to comprehending its applicability to, for example, the situation that developed in Afghanistan after 1978, then possibly neither the Afghan nor the Soviet people would have undergone all they have" (Simoniia 1988: 17).[2] Major-General K. M. Tsagolov stated with admirable frankness in an interview in July 1988, "To put it briefly, I was convinced that on 27 April 1978 a military coup [perevorot] had occurred which had the potential possibilities of developing into a national-democratic revolution. Unfortunately, this did not happen. We became the victims of our own illusions" (Tsagolov 1988: 25).

Soviet scholars and ideologists are now faced with the task of defining the precise lessons to be drawn from the Afghanistan experience. Was it only the military intervention that was wrong, or did the chief error lie in the April 1978 revolution? Or were the roots of the problem further back still, in the 1973 coup of Mohammad Daoud? Should Third World countries avoid forced marches to socialism and develop instead a largely free-enterprise market economy, and, if so, should this be more analogous to Lenin's NEP, with a Marxist vanguard party in charge and a strong state sector, or to such "newly industrializing countries" as Thailand, Taiwan, or even South Korea? Or is there some further alternative?

Some Soviet specialists no doubt see wider theoretical implications as well. One may or may not agree with Daniel Papp's (1985: 136) contention that progressive revisions of Soviet theory relating to Third World development could undermine major elements in Soviet Marxist-Leninist ideology generally. However, such revisions are likely to resonate with and reinforce current challenges to the established dogma on social and political development in the Soviet Union itself, including the historical necessity of the bureaucratic command economy, forced collectivization, and the bureaucratization of the party itself.

THE POLITICAL IMPACT OF THE AFGHANISTAN EXPERIENCE

Afghanistan has been a painful learning experience for the Soviet leadership no less than for its specialist advisers and ideologists. Gorbachev and his colleagues have sought to distance themselves from the decision to intervene, implying it resulted from the pernicious conditions and atmosphere of Brezhnev's "period of stagnation." Soviet Foreign Minister Shevardnadze, speaking in Madrid in January 1988, said that "the pain of Afghanistan is our pain too," and he added, "Not having chosen this legacy for ourselves [but] accepting it for what it is, we are also obliged to take decisions as to how to deal with it from here on" (*Pravda* 1988). Failure in Afghanistan, as well as the record of Soviet-supported radical regimes in Africa and elsewhere, will perhaps encourage Soviet leaders to take notice in the future of those specialists who point out the obstacles and uncertainties attending any attempt to effect radical political and social change in Third World countries.

But will it have any direct impact on the power and prestige of individual Soviet leaders? So far Gorbachev and his supporters have avoided laying any personal blame for the unrequested legacy, at least publicly. It is sometimes suggested that Afghanistan may be yet another nail in the political coffins of those older Politburo members who had a hand in the decision to send in Soviet troops, but who knows? Even Gorbachev may have good reason not to want too much exposure of just what was said and done by individual leaders at the end of the Brezhnev era. On the other hand, the decision to withdraw could well become a subject of recrimination if things come badly unstuck in Afghanistan. In this case it would probably figure as just one issue among many, and probably not the most important one, so its impact on Gorbachev's position would doubtless depend largely on how well or badly his policies generally were faring. All the same, the withdrawal obviously involves not only international but also domestic political risks for Gorbachev and his supporters.

Finally, some brief observations are offered on possible middle- to longer-term effects of the Afghanistan experience on political attitudes among the Soviet population. Here one may identify two factors, at least, that could assume some importance.

The first is the Afghan veteran, the *voin-internatsionalist* (soldier-internationalist), to use the official euphemism, or, as the ordinary Russian would call him, the *afganets*. There are now some hundreds of thousands of *afgantsy*, and there has been much in their experience to bind them together and set them apart from their fellow citizens. Combat against Muslim freedom-fighters among a largely hostile population turned out to be utterly different from the war their fathers had fought against the Germans and the war for which their whole education and conditioning had prepared them. Furthermore, for many years they had felt forgotten and neglected by their country; they were rarely mentioned in the official media because the Soviet leaders wanted to play down the role of the Soviet Union's so-called "limited contingent" for political reasons, both domestic and international. This even applied to the military press, although the military publishing house published some rousing tales of derring-do against the treacherous *dushmany* (enemies).[3] It was only with the flowering of *glasnost'* in 1986 that the virtual news blackout was breached and there were increasingly frequent reports of their steadfastness and heroism and their generosity and humanity toward the Afghan population. All the same, there was still no realistic press account of the course of hostilities and the conditions under which the Soviet troops lived and fought, and no official casualty figures were revealed until after the decision to withdraw was announced. When Soviet conscripts who had served in Afghanistan were demobilized, they often had difficulties with jobs, housing, and medical care, and their efforts to secure redress were commonly met with indifference or hostility by the local authorities.[4] The attitude of the general public toward them was also at best ambivalent, and they often felt embittered by the contrast between what had been demanded of them and the cynical materialism and corruption of life back home. Small wonder that they tended to band together for mutual solace and protection, that they were sharply antagonistic toward the predominant semi-westernized youth culture, and that they sometimes formed themselves into vigilante groups that took the law into their own hands (see Tsagolova 1987; Shuster 1986).

Can the *afgantsy* be seen as a "new force" in Soviet society, as some (see *Radio Liberty Research* 1986) have suggested? Surely not a major force, but one that could, perhaps, exert a significant political influence under certain circumstances. We cannot be sure in what direction that influence would point, or what circumstances would activate it. However, the subculture of the *afgantsy*, to judge by their reported behavior and the songs that most clearly articulate their shared attitudes and values, is strong on mutual loyalty and comradeship and on love of Russia; is congenial to the firm hand but not to bureaucracy; has little time for liberal and intellectual niceties; is unimpressed by the West; and is marked by a rather crude romanticism that sometimes contains a distinct strain of the "white man's burden" (see Konovalov 1988 and sources cited therein). One thing is obvious: Should Afghanistan come under the complete dominance of those at whose hands their comrades died, many of them would feel betrayed.

Much in the subculture of the *afgantsy* resonates with the views and attitudes found in the more radical Russian nationalist circles, like those of the *Pamiat'* society. Up to now no organizational links have been reported, but a total triumph for the Mujahideen could provide the catalyst that would bring these two forces together and align them behind any possible challenge to Gorbachev's leadership.

The second important factor is the Islamic question, or, to be more precise, the political attitudes of the historically Muslim peoples of Soviet Central Asia. Two recent developments in this area are clearly worrying Moscow. One is the rise of ethnic nationalism, which these peoples share with those in other non-Russian areas such as the Baltic and the Caucasus. The second is a certain resurgence of Islamic belief and practice—how strong it is hard to estimate, but certainly enough to activate official countermeasures. As a Turkoman university lecturer recently wrote, "In present circumstances the necessity of stepping up atheistic propaganda is becoming obvious" (Akmuradov 1988; see also Petrash 1988; Alimov 1988). Further, there is ample evidence that intensified anti-religious propaganda is being accompanied, as always, by intensified harassment of active Muslims by the police and local authorities.

The upsurge of local nationalism and of Islam would doubtless have occurred even without the massive purges that have recently swept the Central Asian republics, especially the largest ones, Uzbekistan and Kazakhstan, but the purges have clearly lent them greater force. A dramatic example is the rioting that occurred in Alma-Ata in 1986 when Kazakh First Secretary Kunaev was replaced by the Russian Kolbin. The purges are seen as violating a kind of unwritten compact between Moscow and the Central Asians under which Moscow paid for their docility by tolerating high levels of corruption among the local elites, who in turn were indulgent to corrupt practices lower down the line, practices linked partly to traditional values and commitments.

The war in Afghanistan has thus been one among several factors currently tending to alienate the Central Asian peoples from the Soviet regime. It is obvious that the significance of the war has been quite different for them than for their Slavic fellow citizens, given not only their Islamic background but also, in the case of the Tajiks, Uzbeks, and Turkomans, a common ethnic identify with part of the population of Afghanistan. No romantic "white man's burden" for their lads dying at the hands of the Afghan freedom-fighters!

It is difficult to judge how strong the linkage is between antagonism to the Afghanistan war and the ethnic, religious, and sociopolitical grievances of Central Asians. There is certainly some direct evidence of such a linkage, especially in Tajikistan. Some time ago there were reports (see Rabiev 1987) of mullahs who took advantage of the tolerance afforded them by officials and teachers in rural areas to publicly oppose the presence of Soviet troops in Afghanistan, on the grounds that they were being used to turn the Afghans into nonbelievers. Even more dangerous forms of spillover have been alleged more recently. Vladimir Petkel, the (Russian) Chairman of the local KGB, told the Tajik Central Committee in December 1987 that radical Muslims and "enemy agents" infiltrated over the border had been responsible for the big upsurge in draft-dodging and desertions from the Soviet armed forces, and that part of the Islamic clergy were calling for a "holy war" against Soviet rule (*Kommunist Tadzhikistana* 1987).[5] Such claims may or may not be exaggerated, but the Soviet authorities would not be drawing public attention to the linkage unless it was causing them major concern.

What, then, would be the effect in Central Asia of the establishment of an anticommunist Islamic regime in Kabul? To offer a confident answer to this question one would need far more knowledge of the area than I possess. However, I would like to cite the opinion of the late Professor Alexandre Bennigsen, one of the leading authorities on Soviet Central Asia in the Western world. Speaking in an interview shortly before his death on June 3, 1988, Bennigsen (*Radio Liberty Research* 1988: 6) said that the effect on Muslim society in Central Asia of a complete defeat for the Soviet Union would be "colossal." He went on, "It would be demonstrated that Soviet might was not invincible and that resistance is possible. What are the Afghans for Central Asia? It is a small, wild and poor country. So then, if the Afghans could inflict [such] a military and political defeat, then that makes anything possible. And everyone in Central Asia knows that. I think that in Soviet Russia they know it too." Precisely for that reason, in Benningsen's view, the Soviet leadership would not risk a complete withdrawal that would lead to a Mujahideen takeover, but would keep some troops in Kabul and in parts of the North.

Benningsen's estimate of the likely political impact in Soviet Central Asia of the loss of Afghanistan to anti-Soviet forces must be taken very seriously. Again, the significance of this for the Soviet Union generally is likely to depend on the contingent circumstances. Taken in isolation, Moscow might well succeed in keeping the Central Asian population docile by a combination of political, economic, and coercive measures. Even then, serious disorders in Central Asia could provoke disturbances in the Soviet leadership. Should they occur simultaneously with nationalist outbreaks elsewhere in the Soviet Union, or with worker unrest in Russia proper provoked by continued economic grievances, the consequences could be incalculable.

At the beginning of this chapter it was argued that the withdrawal from Afghanistan is unlikely to have profound and persistent domestic political implications in the Soviet Union. However, it will certainly have some influence on a number of levels, and there are factors involved that, given a particularly unfavorable concatenation of circumstances, could have a major impact on the course of Soviet politics.

NOTES

1. Pamiat' leader Dmitri Vasiliev is reportedly hostile to Russian involvement, and the nationalist writer Aleksandr Prokhanov, who sent many a gung-ho report from the battle zones, now declares it to have been a "mistake" (*Literaturnaia Gazeta* 1988).

2. I am indebted to Roderic Pitty for drawing my attention to this article.

3. For example, I. M. Dynin's collection (1985), which had a print run of 100,000.

4. There is now a campaign to enforce better treatment of Afghanistan veterans by local officials, but how far this will alleviate the widespread bitterness remains to be seen (see Ragimova 1988; Belozerova 1988; Ignatiev 1988).

5. Petkel also said that tens of clandestine Islamic leaders had been brought to trial in 1986–87.

REFERENCES

Akmuradov, I. "V. I. Lenin o Neobkhodimosti Ideinoi Bor'by s Religiei." *Turkmenskaia Iskra*, April 17, 1988.
Alimov, A. "Biznes na Durmane." *Kommunist Tadzhikistana*, January 31, 1987.
Belozerova, L. "Vmesto Serdtsa-kamennyi Protez." *Pravda Ukrainy*, July 10, 1988.
Bogomolov, Oleg. "Kto Zhe Oshibalsia?" *Literaturnaia Gazeta*, March 16, 1988.
Breslauer, George W. "Ideology and Learning in Soviet Third World Policy." *World Politics* 39(1987): 429–448.
Dynin, I. M. *Zvezdy Podviga: Na Zemle Afganistana*. Moscow: Voennoe izdatel'stvo, 1985.
Fukuyama, Francis. "Soviet Strategy in the Third World." In Andrzej Korbonski and Francis Fukuyama, eds., *The Soviet Union and the Third World: The Last Three Decades*. Ithaca and London: Cornell University Press, 1987.
Hosner, Stephen T., and Thomas W. Wolfe. *Soviet Policy and Practice toward Third World Conflicts*. Lexington, Mass.: Lexington Books, 1983.
Hough, Jerry F. *The Struggle for the Third World: Soviet Debates and American Options*. Washington D.C.: Brookings Institution, 1986.
Ignatiev, R. "S Grifom 'Sekretno'. " *Izvestiia*, July 15, 1988.
Katz, Mark N. *The Third World in Soviet Military Thought*. Baltimore: Johns Hopkins University Press, 1982.
Kommunist Tadzhikistana, December 30, 1987.
Konovalov, Valery. "Pesni Veteranov Afganistana." *Radio Liberty Research* RS 50/88, June 6, 1988.
Literaturnaia Gazeta, February 17, 1988.
MacFarlane, S. Neil. *Superpower Rivalry and Third World Radicalism: The Idea of National Liberation*. London: Croom Helm, 1985.
Nahaylo, Bohdan. "Ukrainian Mother's Protest Attracts Numerous Letters on the Afghanistan Theme." *Radio Liberty Research* RL 188/87, May 18, 1987.
Papp, Daniel S. *Soviet Perceptions of the Developing World in the 1980s: The Ideological Basis*. Lexington, Mass.: Lexington Books, 1985.
Petrash, Iu. " 'Privychki' Ostoiutsia Navsegda?" *Sovetskaia Kirgiziia*, May 14, 1988.
Pravda, January 21, 1988.
Rabiev, V. "V Klass . . . s Koranom?" *Kommunist Tadzhikistana*, January 31, 1987.
Radio Liberty Research. "Soviet Veterans of the War in Afghanistan: A New Social Force?" RS 198/86, December 9, 1986.
Radio Liberty Research. "Pamiati A. Bennigsena (1913–1988)." RS 58/88, July 5, 1988.
Ragimova, I. "Pochet bez Uvazheniia." *Bakinskii Rabochii*, July 8, 1988.

Shuster, Savik. "Problema Afganiskikh Veteranov v Sovetskom Obschchestve." *Radio Liberty Research* RS 198/86, December 9, 1986.

Simoniia, N. "Chestno Vesti Nauchnuiu Diskussiiu." *Aziia i Afrika Segodnia* No. 6, June 6, 1988.

Tsagolov, K. M. "Afganistan—Predvaritel'nye Itogi." *Ogonek* No. 30, 1988.

Tsagolova, Laura. In *Sobesednik* No. 1, January 1987.

Valkenier, Elizabeth K. *The Soviet Union and the Third World: An Economic Bind.* New York: Praeger, 1983.

Wise, Sally. " 'A War Should Never Have Happened': Soviet Citizens Assess the War in Afghanistan." *Radio Liberty Research* RL 226/88, June 1, 1988.

Zimmerman, William. *Soviet Perspectives on International Relations.* Princeton, N.J.: Princeton University Press, 1969.

8

Self-Fulfilling Prophecies: Sanctions and Apartheid in South Africa

Martin Holland

Opposition to apartheid has united the international community in its abhorrence and condemnation of the internal politics of an independent state. Yet, while the South African regime remains a pariah, the ability of the international community to end effectively the practice of racial segregation and discrimination has been found wanting. At the forefront of the global response to apartheid has been the application of sanctions: In international society, sanctions provide one of the few foreign policy instrumental alternatives to military coercion (Braun and Weiland 1989: 35).

Those who advocate sanctions argue that political change in South Africa will only come from the detrimental impact that sanctions will inevitably have upon the republic's core economy. According to Southall, "Sanctions work, they will be incrementally yet irreversibly applied, and in the long run, they will play an important, perhaps critical, role in defeating apartheid and installing a majority rule regime in South Africa" (Southall 1988: 104). Consequently, to bring about the end of apartheid, the most effective sanctions possible have to be adopted. However, despite this prescriptive confidence, Southall has to concede a crucial qualification: "Precisely how critical and how effective they will be of course remains to be determined by events" (Southall 1988: 105).

The question of effectiveness is central to a meaningful analysis of the impact sanctions can have in achieving foreign policy objectives. Is it really the case that "sanctions do not work?" Or is it a case of a self-fulfilling prophecy that sanctions do not work where the clear intent, from the very beginning, is for them to be ineffectual?

This chapter discusses the characteristics of an appropriate framework for evaluating the effectiveness of sanctions for accomplishing a foreign policy goal. The case study of the European Community's (EC) use of sanctions to stem apartheid is used to illustrate the empirical and theoretical problems associated with such an examination.

ANALYTIC FRAMEWORK

A generic problem in political science concerns establishing analytic frameworks that are empirically operational. The creation of such necessary evaluating criteria to judge the selection, implementation, and effectiveness of sanctions as a foreign policy goal has proved contentious. It is questionable whether the impact of sanctions can be measured other than by the very crude and potentially misleading analysis of embargoed trade statistics. How can we establish the relationships, or test causal hypotheses, between sanctions and political elite behavior? Simply, how can we judge who is right: the proponents of sanctions or their critics who deny the relevance of sanctions in resolving domestic conflict? Consensus on the appropriate conceptual framework for studying sanctions remains elusive; for reasons of comprehensibility and simplicity, this analysis is confined to considering two rudimentary but complementary schemas used by Love (1988) and Hanlon and Omond (1987).

Sanctions as foreign policy instruments can take various forms, both negative and positive. Negative sanctions may include direct trade embargoes on export to and/or imports from a targeted country; diplomatic censure; cessation of bilateral cooperation in military, technological, or nuclear areas; financial prohibitions; disinvestment; and cultural and sporting boycotts. Positive sanctions can be implemented through aid programs to nongovernmental bodies, support for other states within a region, and the use of codes of practice in relation to human rights.

Consequently, contrary to speculative opinion, sanctions are a very flexible foreign policy tool. However, their success is determined by a specific set of factors. As Hanlon and Omond argue, "It is essential to understand the role of sanctions, to set realistic goals and to introduce sanctions in the most effective ways and to make sure sanctions work as intended" (Hanlon and Omond 1987: 194).

Five factors can be isolated for evaluating the success of sanctions: objectives, vulnerability, choice, scope, and implementation. (1) The goals that sanctions are intended to achieve have to be identified; it is important that these policy objectives not be set unrealistically high or be inappropriate for the application of sanctions. (2) The targeted country's vulnerability to sanctions (usually economic) has to be calculated. (3) The choice of sanctions has to be compatible with the stated policy objectives. (4) The scope or extent of implementation is vital, with success being directly correlated to the number of third countries adopting sanctions. (5) Most crucially, the success of sanctions as a foreign policy tool will depend on the effectiveness of implementation (Love 1988: 93–94). After presenting a brief historical overview of the European Community's policy of sanctions toward South Africa, this general framework is adopted to analyze the impact that Community sanctions have had on the practice of apartheid in South Africa.

CASE STUDY: SANCTIONS AND EUROPEAN POLITICAL COOPERATION

European Community policy toward South Africa has developed within the context of what is known as European Political Cooperation (EPC). EPC constitutes the joint foreign policy behavior of the member states of the Community. While there is no obligation under EPC for Community member states to implement a common foreign policy, agreement on consensus positions has increasingly come to typify the European Community's international relations (Holland 1988b: 415). Consultation, coordination, and achieving collective policy positions are the objectives of EPC. Included among the policy successes are the European Community's pronouncements on an Arab-Israeli initiative, the Conference on Security and Cooperation in Europe process, and responses to Iranian terrorism in the 1980s. The difficulty, however, is that in a Community of twelve independent foreign policy actors with diverse priorities in international relations, policy inertia, or one based on the lowest common denominator, can predominate.

The European Community's sanctions against South Africa have been chosen for this case study because the Community collectively represents South Africa's major trading partner and its leading investor, and has strong cultural and historical ties to the English- and Afrikaans-speaking peoples. Furthermore, with European integration accelerating toward the idea of a single market in 1992, a Community-wide approach to third country relations becomes imperative: After 1992, national sanctions on trade, for example, may contravene Community law. The Community has assumed the attributes of a dominant international actor.

For the purpose of this case study, it is useful to divide the European Community's policy into three distinct periods: the operation of positive sanctions from 1977–1984; the introduction of punitive sanctions in 1985–86; and the post-sanctions policy since 1987.

Positive Sanctions: 1977–84

The European Community's first experience of a collective foreign policy toward South Africa was the 1977 Code of Conduct. This remained the central feature of Community policy until the beginning of civil unrest in 1985 and the progressive introduction of security legislation by the South African government. This early example of collective EPC promulgated two policy objectives: economic liberation for the black states of southern

Africa, and the abolition of apartheid. The dominant presumption during this period was that continuation of normal trading relations and implementation of the code were the most likely mechanisms for achieving the Community's primary policy objective—the abolition of apartheid.

The tentative and still experimental nature of EPC at that time ensured that the Community's collective southern African policy was based on the lowest common denominator. During the 1977–1984 period, joint diplomatic *démarches* and the Code of Conduct were the only Community instruments used to promote change in South Africa: Sanctions or embargoes on normal third-country relations were not employed. The code was directed at European Community firms with subsidiaries operating in South Africa, and its provisions were designed to promote equitable labor relations and to nullify apartheid legislation with regard to employment.

From the Community perspective the code was uniformly applicable (on a voluntary basis) to all European Community firms operating in South Africa. Each national government produced annual reports on its application, with the Community presidency compiling periodic summaries. All member states were in agreement that the code was sufficient; none called for a more demonstrative policy.

At one level, the code is a unique example of European Community foreign policy instrument; at another, the code is typical of such Community instruments. As has been demonstrated elsewhere (Holland 1988a: 77–94), uniformity was missing, in all but a superficial sense, in the application of the code as a foreign policy instrument. Its impact on apartheid was minimal.

Punitive Sanctions: 1985–1986

In contrast to the 1977–1984 period of constructive dialogue, the events of 1985 led to a critical reappraisal of Community–South African relations which jeopardized the continuance of European Community foreign policy cooperation. In particular, the effectiveness and appropriateness of the code as the Community's only instrument designed to eradicate apartheid was questioned.

Within days of the South African government's introduction of the first state of emergency on July 22, 1985, the Community's policy unity was fractured by unilateral action: France recalled her ambassador from Pretoria, prohibited new investments in South Africa, and sponsored a UN resolution calling for comprehensive international sanctions. In an attempt to maintain a common policy, the subsequent Council of Ministers meeting on September 9 agreed on the following common restrictive measures:

—withdrawal of member states' military attachés to Pretoria;

—banning nuclear and military cooperation, and sales of European Community oil and sensitive technology;

—freezing of official contacts and international agreements in the sphere of security;

—an embargo on exports of arms and paramilitary equipment;

—discouraging all sporting and cultural events "except where these contribute to-wards the ending of apartheid" (Foreign Ministers 1985)

In addition, a series of "harmonized" positive sanctions were introduced. These joint agreements included the strengthening of the Code of Conduct; assistance programs for anti-apartheid organizations; further support for the Southern African Development and Coordination Conference (SADCC) states; and, an "intensification of contacts" with, and educational support for, the non-white community.

This coordination activity was more appearance than substance. As foreign policy instruments, the 1985 negative sanctions were ineffectual and largely symbolic, and the widely discredited code (in its revised form) continued to constitute the most developed aspect of EPC toward South Africa.

Against a background of continuing internal unrest in South Africa, the June 1986 European Council meeting in The Hague issued a communiqué in which the European Council reaffirmed the main goal of Community policy as "the total abolition of apartheid." Three months later, the European Community finally adopted the foreign policy instrument of punitive sanctions within the framework of EPC, while stressing the need for "more effective co-ordination of the positive measures being taken to assist the victims of apartheid" (Foreign Ministers 1986). Despite Danish, Dutch, and Irish demands, the full range of sanctions discussed at the June European Council meeting in The Hague was not adopted. The Community agreed within the framework of the European Coal and Steel Community (ECSC) to ban by the end of September the import of certain types of steel and iron. In October, the Council of Ministers introduced restrictions on new investments and Krugerrands: A council decision limited new European Community direct investments in South Africa and a European Community regulation prohibited the import of Krugerrands. In the cause of preserving collective policy, West German and Portuguese opposition to the proposed coal embargo was sufficient to forestall its introduction. The full Hague package would have affected 16.5 percent of South Africa's 1985 exports to the Community (1,559.8 million ECU); without coal, this fell to 3.5 percent (330.4 million ECU)—see Table 8.1.

Post-Sanctions Policy: 1987–89

Since 1987, there has been reduced pressure for extending sanctions. This may reflect a general acceptance that there needs to be an interval in which the effects of sanctions can be evaluated, or it may indicate that the collective reflex of EPC was in jeopardy, as suggested by the European Community's

Table 8.1
Main European Community Imports of South African Products, 1985

Item:	Total EC Value ECU (m)[1]	Belgium[2] %	West Germany %	France %	Italy %	UK %	Other Six %
Gold	1,743.3	0.0	5.7	0.1	93.0	0.0	1.8
Diamonds	1,730.6	99.7	0.1	0.1	0.0	0.0	0.1
Minerals	1,268.8	10.8	15.0	24.9	27.2	5.4	16.7
Coal	1,229.4	11.1	14.7	24.5	24.2	5.2	20.3
Iron & steel products[3]	612.7	4.0	30.0	9.7	9.9	13.6	32.8
	(188.3)	(5.5)	(19.6)	(1.6)	(5.0)	(20.8)	(47.2)
Metal Ores	518.1	7.8	9.9	9.0	13.7	50.1	9.5
Fruit/ Vegetables	384.9	6.0	22.7	14.9	1.8	47.9	6.7
Wool/ Animal hairs	355.8	4.7	19.1	18.7	23.3	26.9	7.3
Copper	304.4	25.9	51.7	1.7	13.5	4.7	2.5
Chemicals	259.7	1.7	27.7	57.1	0.4	3.6	9.5
Ferro-alloys	236.1	1.7	46.8	22.6	17.6	2.2	9.1
Krugerrands	142.0	30.9	68.9	0.0	0.0	0.0	0.2

Notes:
1. European Currency Unit, in millions.

2. Includes figures for Luxembourg.

3. Figures in parentheses indicate value/percent of iron and
   steel products covered by the ECSC decision of September 15.

Source: Holland (1988a: 56).

failure in early 1987 to agree on a "charter of political principles" for domestic reform in South Africa (de Bassompierre 1988: 105). In the short term, the adoption of a sanctions package served an end in itself. Where policy could go from this point seemed less clear-cut.

The nominal effect of European Community sanctions made them fairly easy for member countries to adopt in principle. As is the case in the application of most trade sanctions, there was a danger that trade in the targeted products would increase in the short term. This tendency was compounded when the European Community gave a three-month warning of its intention to invoke sanctions; only then would the adopted restrictions apply to new contracts. In general, these fears have proved groundless. As Tables 8.2 and 8.3 demonstrate, the import of Krugerrands has been halted and that of the embargoed iron and steel products significantly reduced. Of course, behind these statistics a variety of sins can be disguised—in particular, the continuation of imports through contracts signed prior to the introduction of the Community ban.

Seeking some form of policy development, and hoping to reinforce collective agreement, Community policy shifted from a direct South African to a regional focus. This heralded a break from past reactive EPC. Historically, the less emphasized thrust of the European Community's twin policy

Table 8.2
European Community Imports of Krugerrands, 1984–87

Value of Krugerrands Imported (ECU, in thousands)

Year	EC Total	West Germany	Belgium[2]	Netherlands	Denmark
1984[1]	189,225	135,130	51,503	2,316	276
1985	141,968	97,939	43,964	–	65
1986	90,570	71,987	18,583	–	–

Monthly average value:

	EC Total	West Germany	Belgium[2]	Netherlands	Denmark
1984[1]	15,769	11,261	4,292	193	23
1985	11,831	8,162	3,664	–	5
1986 (Jan–Sept)	8,763	6,708	2,055	–	–
(Oct)	3,344	3,343	1	–	–
(Nov)	7,731	7,914	17	–	–
(Dec)	177	–	–	–	–
1987 (Jan)	1,875	1,875	–	–	–
(Feb)	134	–	–	134	–
(Mar)	3	3	–	–	–
(Apr)	22	14	8	–	–

Notes:

1. Excludes Spain and Portugal.

2. Includes Luxembourg.

Source: Holland (1988b: 421).

had been the promotion of economic independence for southern Africa, principally through SADCC. An extension and more effective deployment of regional funds has become the major theme of European Community policy since the beginning of 1987 (Holland 1988c).

EVALUATING THE IMPACT OF EUROPEAN COMMUNITY SANCTIONS

Objectives

"The question is not about sanctions per se, but rather whether sanctions are appropriate against South Africa to end apartheid" (Hanlon and Omond 1987: 193). This quotation focuses attention on a central issue: Did the Community set itself achievable foreign policy objectives in its policy toward South Africa? As already noted, the European Community promul-

Table 8.3

European Community Imports of South African Iron and Steel Products Covered by the ECSC Decision Embargo, 1984–87

Value of Embargoed Iron and Steel Imports (ECU, in thousands)

	EC Total	UK	West Germany	Italy	Belgium[2]	Greece	Spain	Portugal
					Major Importers			
1984[1]	85,134	25,968	30,077	2,478	10,196	8,562	NA	NA
1985	188,304	39,261	36,843	9,535	10,395	27,997	20,886	29,275
1986	174,502	35,978	45,904	7,643	8,483	31,127	15,195	16,008

Monthly average value:

	EC Total	UK	West Germany	Italy	Belgium[2]	Greece	Spain	Portugal
1984[1]	7,094	2,164	2,506	206	850	713	NA	NA
1985	15,692	3,272	3,070	795	866	2,333	1,740	2,440
1986 (Jan–Sept)	15,682	3,260	4,222	720	747	2,535	1,410	1,466
(Oct)	17,065	3,104	2,483	594	428	6,711	2,036	624
(Nov)	8,451	529	3,232	389	1,081	637	42	1,653
(Dec)	7,602	3,250	1,625	173	249	1,043	468	521
1987 (Jan)	7,419	1,019	2,314	2	262	1,382	1,325	302
(Feb)	14,181	2,973	692	1,171	405	3,093	3,501	2,199
(Mar)	7,419	933	2,261	1,022	407	1,044	456	479
(Apr)	8,704	2,172	3,581	80	221	619	1,030	574
(May)	7,200	1,533	2,307	67	290	1,295	75	977
(Jun)	10,487	4,036	3,138	200	527	NA	503	1,403
(Jul)	13,284	3,240	4,191	4,131	NA	NA	567	782

Notes:

1. Excludes Spain and Portugal.

2. Includes Luxembourg.

Source: Holland (1988b: 422).

gated two broad objectives: economic independence for the southern African region and the abolition of apartheid within South Africa. The latter goal has tended to dominate, and in recent years a series of incremental and reactive demands have been repeatedly issued by the Community, calling for the following:

1. an end to the restrictions on the freedom of the press;

2. a dialogue with the genuine representatives of all South Africans, irrespective of race;

3. the unconditional release of all political prisoners, including Nelson Mandela;

4. lifting the bans on the ANC, PAC, and latterly the UDF;

5. an end to detention without trial;

6. the cessation of forced removals and relocations;

7. the dismantling of discriminatory legislation; and

8. an end to the State of Emergency (Holland 1988a: 95).

As indicated by the third renewal of the State of Emergency in June 1989, and by the fact that more political organizations were banned in 1988 than during the whole of the previous forty years of National party rule (including the ban on the multiracial United Democratic Front), none of these eight demands has produced a reformist response from the South African government. Moreover, not only have these demands gone unheeded, such a catalogue of conditions are of limited utility in evaluating the success of European Community policy toward the abolition of apartheid. European Community policy appears to oscillate between short-term demands and longer-term objectives. In the context of a consensus-oriented EPC process, it may be politically sufficient to advance a generalized nonracial outcome; however, to gauge the application of policy effectively, it is necessary to stipulate specific criteria that need to be achieved. By such a procedure the European Community's chosen foreign policy instruments can be accurately evaluated as mechanisms for realizing these concrete policy goals.

The first of Love's five criteria for evaluating the success of sanctions is only partially met in the European Community–South African case. Policy goals were defined as early as 1977, but these objectives were zero–sum in character, as well as unrealistically optimistic, and have met with little, if any, success. However, the application of sanctions to achieve both economic and social reform is an appropriate foreign policy tool provided that the sanctions chosen are ones capable of significant impact. It is to this question of vulnerability and the choice of sanctions that this chapter now turns.

Vulnerability

How vulnerable is South Africa to the imposition of punitive sanctions by the European Community and the West in general? This section assesses vulnerability in terms of trade, exposure to financial loans and overseas debt, and the levels of foreign liabilities and disinvestment.

South Africa's trading relationship with the European Community is substantial and arguably crucial, thereby constituting an avenue for effective sanctions. The South African economy is dependent on international trade and investment, with the most important commercial link being to the European Community rather than the United States or Japan. According to statistics released by the International Monetary Fund, in 1988 the value of imports and exports between South Africa and the United States totaled $3.1 billion, and between Japan and South Africa, $3.8 billion. In comparison, trade with the leading six European Community countries amounted

Table 8.4

Distribution of European Community–South African Imports and Exports, 1977–86

EC Imports from South Africa	1977 ECU[1]	%	1981 ECU[1]	%	1983 ECU[1]	%	1985 ECU[1]	%	1986 ECU[1]	%
UK	3154	47.5	1612	22.6	1480	23.0	1792	18.9	1319	16.9
West Germany	930	14.0	1226	17.2	1166	18.2	1359	14.4	1289	16.1
Italy	729	11.0	1549	21.7	1464	22.8	2424	25.6	1951	24.3
Belgium[2]	1244	18.8	1486	20.8	1343	20.9	2226	23.5	2235	27.9
France	431	6.5	886	12.4	645	10.0	825	8.7	480	6.0
Netherlands	107	1.6	193	2.7	116	1.8	237	2.5	220	2.7
Ireland	11	.2	9	.1	11	.2	18	.2	14	.2
Denmark	24	.4	154	2.1	154	2.4	207	2.2	102	1.2
Greece	–	–	19	.2	44	.7	57	.6	54	.7
Spain	–	–	–	–	–	–	248	2.6	262	3.3
Portugal	–	–	–	–	–	–	62	.7	61	.8
TOTAL	6630	100%	7134	100%	6423	100%	9456	100%	8021	100%

EC Exports to South Africa										
UK	889	31.7	2196	31.7	1901	32.6	1709	30.0	1258	26.9
West Germany	981	34.9	2451	35.4	2194	37.6	2246	39.5	1970	42.1
Italy	229	8.2	656	9.5	534	9.2	434	7.6	357	7.6
Belgium[2]	117	4.2	270	3.9	249	4.3	243	4.3	218	4.7
France	435	15.5	968	14.0	562	9.6	511	8.9	411	8.8
Netherlands	127	4.5	285	4.1	263	4.5	279	4.9	260	5.6
Ireland	9	.3	31	.4	45	.8	41	.7	41	.9
Denmark	20	.7	61	.9	74	1.3	77	1.4	54	1.1
Greece	–	–	6	.1	4	.1[3]	2	.1[3]	2	.1[3]
Spain	–	–	–	–	–	–	124	2.1	87	.9
Portugal	–	–	–	–	–	–	20	.4	16	.3
TOTAL	2807	100%	6924	100%	5826	100%	5688	100%	4674	100%

Notes:

1. European Currency Unit, in millions.

2. Includes figures for Luxembourg.

3. Less than .1%.

Source: Holland (1988a: 53).

to $13.3 billion ($4.9 billion with West Germany and $3.2 billion with the United Kingdom) (*Focus on South Africa* 1989: 12).

In 1986, the South African government ceased publishing detailed trade figures. Figures produced by the European Commission show that in 1985 South Africa purchased 41 percent of its total imports from the Community, with the European Community's corresponding share of South Africa's exports being 20 percent. As indicated in Table 8.4, within the twelve Community members, the bilateral trade has been dominated by the United Kingdom, West Germany, and, to a lesser extent, the Benelux countries and Italy. Despite a decline from its position of preeminence as a trading partner in the early 1980s, by 1989 the United Kingdom was still South Africa's third most valuable bilateral export market (behind Japan and West Germany). In comparison, West Germany has steadily increased its trade and by 1983 had replaced the United Kingdom as South Africa's most important bilateral European partner. In 1986, Germany supplied 42 percent of European Community exports to South Africa and took 16 percent of South Africa's imports to the Community.

During the peak of the sanctions debate (1985–87), there was an overall reduction in European Community–South African trade, reflecting the impact of the Community's trade restrictions and depreciation in the value of the rand, as well as a decline in trade in real terms. This period saw the most significant decline in trade between the European Community and South Africa. For example, between January and March 1985 the European Community imported South African goods to the value of 2,282 million ECU (European currency units); for the same period in 1987 imports amounted to 1,343 million ECU, a drop of 40 percent. Similarly, between January and March 1985 European Community exports to South Africa totalled 1,526 million ECU, falling to just 1,081 million ECU two years later (Holland 1988a: 55). There is evidence, however, that this trend was reversed in 1988. A comparison between the value of 1987 and 1988 bilateral trade showed that West Germany increased its trade by 33 percent, the United Kingdom by 26 percent, Italy by 19 percent, and France by 22 percent (*Focus on South Africa* 1989: 12).

There are three specific areas in which the South African market is vulnerable to a European Community export ban. First, in 1985 (the last year prior to the adoption of sanctions) machinery to the value of 1,558 million ECU was exported (corresponding to 27 percent of European Community– South African exports). Vehicles and parts were a second significant area, worth 677 million ECU in 1985. Third, in the same year the European Community exported electrical goods worth 712 million ECU. Cumulatively, these three categories represented just over half of the European Community's total value of 5,688 million ECU for exports to South Africa in 1985.

South Africa's major areas of vulnerability in terms of Community imports are shown in Table 8.1. Italy was the main importer of South African minerals (27 percent) and gold (93 percent). The United Kingdom took 27 percent of wool and animal hairs, 48 percent of fruit and vegetables, and 50 percent of South Africa's metal ores. West Germany was the major European Community buyer of iron and steel (30 percent), ferro-alloys (47 percent), copper (52 percent), and Krugerrands (69 percent). Belgium and Luxembourg were responsible for importing virtually all of the Community's supply of South African diamonds, and France imported 25 percent of the coal and 57 percent of South African chemical products.

Two broad dichotomies are apparent. First, 86.2 percent of South Africa's exports to the Community were raw materials. Second, except for one category, six of the twelve Community states collectively purchased more than four-fifths of the European Community's South African exports.

Either specific product embargoes, or concerted across-the-board action by the four major Community states, plus Belgium, could have a significant impact on South Africa's trading capacity.

A second area where South Africa displays commercial vulnerability is its exposure to European bank loans and overseas debt. The pressure from banks on South Africa to repay loans has proved, to date, a more formidable economic sanction than direct governmental embargoes on specific commodities. In 1985, it was estimated that out of a total foreign debt of $23.5 billion ($14.6 billion of which was short-term), $5.3 billion was with British banks, $2.0 billion with West German banks, and $2.5 billion with French banks. In September 1985, short-term loan repayment problems precipitated the fall of the rand, the closure of the Johannesburg stock exchange, and a six-month moratorium on the payment of interest of foreign loans. However, the subsequent Interim Debt Agreement between South Africa and her thirty-four foreign creditor banks signed in March 1987 eased this crisis, at least in the short term. In 1990, South Africa debt repayment was $1.8 billion; to fund this, a massive current account surplus of some 5 billion rands was required.

The third measure of vulnerability concerns the level of foreign investment (direct and indirect) in South Africa and the global confidence in the stability of the South African market. The Community's share of all direct and nondirect investment in South Africa in 1984 was estimated at just below 50 percent, over three-quarters of which was British. However, since the mid–1980s, commercial disinvestment has been intensifying, reflecting both reduced profit margins and political instability. South Africa was once one of the world's most attractive markets for investment; now rising inflation (which has been in double figures since 1984), industrial unrest, civil disturbances, and currency devaluation (from U.S. $0.93 to just $0.35 in July 1985) have persuaded many foreign companies that more stable and more profitable markets exist elsewhere.

Disinvestment, however, need not be tantamount to an economic sanction: The post–1985 trend has been for foreign companies to sell off their stakes in South African subsidiaries to local managers at suppressed market value without necessarily severing the economic link (Becker 1987). Through licensing agreements with third-country subsidiaries of the parent company, a continued supply of a product can be maintained. However, the employment practices of these new operations no longer fall under the scrutiny of their former parent companies' governing boards, so that the scope of the Code of Conduct for European Community firms is reduced.

By the end of 1988, 205 U.S. firms had withdrawn (compared with 114 from the rest of the world), leaving just 138 U.S. businesses with direct investment in South Africa and 440 non–U.S. companies, approximately half of which are British. One of the most celebrated European withdrawals was that of Barclays Bank in November 1986. While the anti-apartheid boycott of Barclays was a contributing factor, the dominant criterion for disinvestment was the substantial decline in the bank's South African profits. In the early 1980s, Barclays derived approximately 10 percent of its net profits from South Africa. This amount had slumped to 2.7 percent by 1985, with every expectation that the decline would continue.

The Community has acknowledged the potential power of these market-driven sanctions; in an answer to a European Parliament question, the Community responded: "The most effective action against the apartheid regime has been taken by the market itself. . . . Sanctions have prompted many industrialists and bankers to bestir themselves, and they are now beginning to divest in South Africa" (*EPC Bulletin* 1987: 85/221).

In summary, appropriate sanctions can inflict an economic crisis in South Africa, thereby, it is argued, producing radical political change. As one critic has concluded, "Maximum damage would be done by a package of partial sanctions, applied and effectively enforced by South Africa's major trade and investment partners, that combined embargoes on exports of capital goods and high technology products, as well as bans on new direct investment and bank loans" (Love 1988: 107). However, the sanctions imposed by the European Community and other western trade and investment partners have not sought to inflict "maximum damage" to promote the economic destabilization of South Africa.

Choice

Despite being a collective foreign policy actor operating within the limitations of EPC, the Community not only possesses the legal competence to impose economic sanctions, it has exercised this ability in the recent past. Under the Treaty of Rome, Article 113 was applied to invoke sanctions against both Iran and the Soviet Union and Article 223 to embargo arms sales to Iran in 1980 (Carter 1989: 227–228). Furthermore, in times of crisis, such as the Falklands War, Article 224 can form the basis for trade sanctions (Edwards 1984: 304). Clearly it is not an absence of legal competence that inhibits the use of sanctions against South Africa.

In order to succeed, sanctions must be selected according to their ability to affect the vulnerable sectors of the targeted state. The choice of sanctions, therefore, is paramount in dictating their likely success. To execute its policy objectives, the Community has chosen to use the following measures: a labor code; economic sanctions on trade, technology, and financial investment; military, cultural, and diplomatic sanctions; and positive aid for regional states and for the victims of apartheid (see Tables 8.5 and 8.6).

Labor Code. Between 1977 and 1984 the European Community adopted the positive sanction of the code as its foreign policy instrument designed to bring about the Community's stated objective of removing apartheid. This raised a fundamental question: Simply, could the chosen policy in-

Table 8.5

European Community Positive Sanctions, 1977–89

Positive Sanction	Applications Instrument	Level	Date of Adoption	Effect
1. Code of Conduct	EPC Statements	National	1977-85	partial normalization of labor relations between black workers and EC firms
2. regional aid	Lome III agreement	EC	1985-89	776 million ECU aid to offset effects of regional destabilization
	EPC Statement	EC	1986	110 million ECU for regional resources cooperation program
3. direct aid	EPC Statement	EC	1986	Annual budget of 20 million ECU to assist the disadvantaged population of South Africa

strument fulfill the stated policy aim? The code encouraged European Community firms to recognize, negotiate, and conclude agreements with black trade unions, and discouraged the use of the migrant labor system. It recommended a minimum wage at least 50 percent above "the minimum level needed to satisfy the basic needs of an employee and his family," promoted the principle of "equal pay for equal work," advocated fringe benefits and job advancement for black employees, and encouraged firms "to abolish any practice of segregation" (Department of Trade 1977).

What changes has the labor code achieved? There is general agreement among analysts in South Africa that the code has made a contribution to removing some of the labor abuses that existed in the mid–1970s. It acted as an example and catalyst for the development of various domestic codes, such as those produced by the Urban Foundation and the Employer's Consultative Committee of Labour Affairs. However, the overall effect of the European Community code remains marginal; at best it makes poverty more palatable for a few black people without doing anything to end apartheid. The code cannot abolish segregation, and, ironically, disinvestment has undermined the code's limited impact by reducing the number of black workers covered by its paternalistic provisions (Denton 1988: 11). Furthermore, critics (Ethical Investment Research and Information Service 1987; Holland 1989) of the code have argued that it merely deflected attention from those lobbying for total withdrawal from South Africa and the introduction of sanctions.

Economic Sanctions: Trade, Technology, and Finance. As for the negative

Table 8.6
European Community Negative Sanctions, 1977–89

Negative Sanction	Applications Instrument	Level	Date of Adoption	Effect
1. Economic trade: cessation of oil exports	EPC Statement	National	9/10/85[1]	curtailed crude oil exports
ban on imports of iron and steel	ECSC Decision	ECSA	9/15/86[2]	prohibited specific types of iron and steel imports
ban on imports of Krugerrands	Council Regulation	EC	9/15/86[3]	ended import of Krugerrands
2. Technology: prohibition on new collaboration in nuclear sector	EPC Statement	National	9/10/85	ended cooperation
ban on exports of security equipment	EPC Statement	National	9/10/85	ended cooperation
3. Financial: ban on new investments	Council Decision	National	9/10/85[3]	investments still maintained
4. Military: embargo on import/ export of arms;	EPC Statement	National	9/10/85	sanctions complied with, although a
no military cooperation;	EPC Statement	National	9/10/85	delay of up to two years in some cases
military attaches removed	EPC Statement	National	9/10/85	
5. Cultural: discourage cultural and scientific agreements;	EPC Statement	National	9/10/85	generally implemented though with some exceptions; no power
freezing of sports and security contacts	EPC Statement	National	9/15/85	to ensure compliance in every case
6. Diplomatic: temporary removal of ambassadors	EPC Statement	National	7/31/85	normal diplomatic relations resumed

Notes:

1. Implemented January 31, 1986.
2. Implemented September 27, 1986.
3. Implemented October 27, 1986.

sanctions adopted in 1985–86, given the structure of the South African economy, the European Community's choice of economic sanctions can hardly be said to have undermined the core of that country's economy. In terms of European Community–South African bilateral trade, the sanctions adopted in 1986 (regarding iron, steel, and Krugerrands) affected just 3.5 percent of trade; with the Community's blessing, the bulk of iron and steel exports have continued unimpeded. Similarly, Krugerrands were worth a mere 142 million ECU in 1986, compared with 1,743.3 million for gold,

1,730.6 million for diamonds and 1,229.4 million ECU for coal.

The other harmonized restrictions chosen suggested a higher concern with affectation, rather than with the effectiveness of the measures adopted. The embargo on oil exports is partial (excluding, for example, all refined petroleum) and is regularly violated. The technology sanctions were a response to the perception that collaboration with South Africa on security issues could help facilitate domestic repression. Similarly, the ban on new investments was seen as a minimal gesture to counter the anti-apartheid criticism of continued European investment in an apartheid-based labor market. However, as the section on implementation below shows, this sanction has been largely ineffectual.

Symbolic Sanctions: Military, Cultural, and Diplomatic. The military embargoes complemented the technology restrictions on security cooperation by prohibiting any trade in arms and paramilitary equipment, and ended the exchange of military attachés. These, in tandem with the cultural and sporting boycotts and the removal, albeit temporarily, of European Community ambassadors from Pretoria, all signaled the European Community's condemnation of the coercive action of the South Africa government. Such actions, however, remain in the realm of symbolic, rather than effective, sanctions.

Positive Sanctions. The choice of introducing positive sanctions was a reflection of both the internal divisions among the European Community states (between the pro- and anti-sanctioneers) and the recognition that the European Community's objectives were not just anti-apartheid, but included regional economic development. Aid for the SADCC states was intensified and a new program established to assist the disadvantaged population of South Africa.

In short, the compatibility between the European Community's policy objectives and its choice of appropriate sanctions is questionable. What impact these moderate measures were intended to have remains unclear. An initial evaluation of their effectiveness suggests that economically they have had a modest impact upon South Africa, though the longer-term consequences of disinvestment on capital formation may be significant.

Scope

The fourth criterion determining effectiveness concerns the extent of implementation. Within the context of EPC, this is an important condition. All European Community foreign policy commitments have to be by consensus; consequently, by definition, EPC must involve all twelve states, producing maximum participation.

The adoption of the Community's limited sanctions illustrates the power for consensus outcomes in EPC. Given the opposing views on sanctions held by the United Kingdom, West Germany, and Portugal on the one hand, and the remaining nine members on the other, there was a real danger that collective action would be impossible. The adopted policy solution seemed to promote the objective of intra–European Community unity, rather than that of abolishing apartheid. Sanctions were enacted (thereby satisfying the majority European Community view), but the mechanisms for adoption and the targets chosen meant that the impact would be marginal (even to the point of "proving" the anti-sanctions case that sanctions do not work), thereby satisfying the Anglo-German-Portuguese agenda. Policy consensus was the victor, sanctions coherence the loser.

Of course, the European Community's sanctions do not operate in a vacuum; the international application of sanctions (through the United Nations and the Commonwealth, and under the U.S. Comprehensive Anti-Apartheid Act) is, from a South African perspective, the crucial determinant. Even where the European Community can impose a comprehensive policy, any such sanctions, if taken alone, may not be sufficient.

Implementation

Irrespective of the choice of which sanctions to adopt, the most important factor remains how these measures are implemented. Effectiveness depends upon the procedures used for implementation, the ability to carry out such measures, and success in monitoring compliance.

The key to understanding implementation in a European Community context is the legal bias utilized. Under the Treaty of Rome, the hierarchy of European Community competences is, in descending order: Regulations, Directives, Decisions, recommendations, and opinions. Only a Regulation is "binding in its entirety" and directly applicable and directly effective in all member states, leaving no role or discretionary powers to the national parliaments. Decisions, in contrast, while directly binding, are rarely directly effective. Where Decisions are phrased in general rather than in precise language, their legal vagueness can undermine the applicability of the "directly binding" clause.

The authority for EPC action on South Africa drew on four types of competences—European Community Council Regulations and Decisions, ECSC Decisions, and EPC statements. These new instruments of collective policy were constrained by the form of competences chosen, which generally placed the responsibility for policy application at the national rather than Community level. Thus, only one measure was enacted through a Community Regulation—the European Community–wide ban on the import of Krugerrands—with a second through an ECSC Decision suspending certain iron and steel imports.[1] The remaining instruments used have all taken the weaker form of Community Decisions or EPC statements.

These limitations mean that, depending on the instrument chosen, opportunities are created for the member states to take differing interpretations of the measures adopted. The positive aspect for EPC was that unity for unity's sake was more easily achieved. The price paid, however, was that the limited policy instruments that were agreed upon were not implemented either simultaneously or comprehensively by all member states—in spite of an obligation to do so. Indeed, as the United Kingdom's breach of the new investments agreement in February 1990 indicated, such obligations as did exist rested on the convention of consensus rather than on legal imperative. The following analysis of sanctions on new investments and on gold, iron, and steel illustrates this tendency.

Three factors restrained the effect of the Community's measures restricting new investments in South Africa: the Community instrument chosen, the level of compulsion, and the definition of what constituted new investment (Holland 1988b: 418). In October 1986, the member states introduced the measures as a Council Decision, thereby impeding the possibility for harmonized national law being developed. As noted above, the Decision also created a foreign policy instrument that lacked legal compulsion or penalties for noncompliance. Article 1 of the Decision requires member states to "take the necessary measures to ensure that the new direct investments in the Republic of South Africa . . . are suspended." However, this requirement "may be compiled with *by the issue of guidance*," not legislation.

Defining "new investments" also inhibited implementation. Long-term shareholdings and loan capital were considered investments, but portfolio investments and the reinvestment of remittable earnings by South African subsidiaries of European Community companies were not, arguably rendering the entire measure inoperative. Furthermore, contracts concluded prior to October 27, 1986, and direct investment that maintained rather than increased existing links were exempt. The use of an investments ban as a policy instrument illustrated the difficulty of creating a new consensus within EPC that was tantamount to an effective sanction. Prime Minister Thatcher's breaking of the consensus in early 1990 merely served to underline this policy-making impediment.

Similarly, the application of the embargo on steel and iron was not a dramatic sanction concession. The effect of the embargo was marginal. By way of illustration, in 1985, European Community imports from South Africa totaled 9,456 million ECU, of which iron and steel imports amounted to 612.7 million ECU. The ECSC ban, however, affected only 188.3 million ECU worth of goods because ferro-alloys, iron ore, and a range of manufactured or semimanufactured products were excluded. Even the anti-sanctioneers found it possible to accept sanctions that were, at best, symbolic.

CONCLUSION

Have the European Community's sanctions been effective? If not, how, if at all, can they be made more effective? The Community's record in terms of the five criteria for effectiveness stipulated by Love is poor. Only one of the preconditions was clearly present. South Africa is dependent on trade with and investment by the European Community, and sanctions could have a significant economic impact. This economic vulnerability, however, has not been the primary focus of Community sanctions: The European Community consciously chose not to precipitate such an outcome. The objectives of Community policy, while desirable in themselves, were not ones that could be realized by the chosen sanctions. The sanctions were irritants, not direct challenges to the economic foundations of apartheid.

While the scope of the measures was superficially complete, among the twelve Community members there were dissension and marked differences in the expression of enthusiasm for sanctions. The dichotomy between the pro-sanctions majority and the minority anti-sanctioneers was sufficient to produce a series of collective policies that by their very implementation procedures and choice of targets seemed designed to be ineffectual. The sanctions package had more to do with domestic European Community bargaining processes and the centripetal tendency of EPC than with the design of a coherent policy dedicated to ending racial discrimination. It was hardly surprising, then, that during the 1980s the response of the South African government was to deride the European Community's impotence and moral duplicity and to reject foreign prescriptions and interference in the country's domestic affairs.

Despite the release of Nelson Mandela in early 1990 and the legalization of the ANC and other black opposition groups, Community sanctions seem to have been singularly unsuccessful in producing reforms. From 1977 to 1989 repeated, but vague, suggestions of "greying" the Group Areas legislation have been made; however, the cornerstone of apartheid—racial classification—continues unabated, and universal suffrage within a unitary state remains a chimera for the foreseeable future.

Paradoxically, Community policies in the area of labor relations may even be responsible for undermining the European Community's overall objectives. The revised Code of Conduct was designed to empower and promote black trade unions as a mechanism for democratic reform. This external "provocation" prompted the South African government to adopt a Labour Relations Amendment Act in September 1988. The act has restricted the legality of strikes, diluted the unions' collective bargaining rights, provided employers with a legal basis for suing unions for damages, and weakened security of employment and unemployment rights (Labour Research Department 1989: 21). Rather than erode apartheid, the code may have inadvertently been a catalyst for more draconian labor legislation designed to emasculate black trade unionism.

Only in an indirect sense has the policy of sanctions contributed to the weakening of the South African state. Anti-apartheid activity has contributed to the economic crisis facing South Africa. The political instability of the government resulted in the rand being further devalued by 21 percent between the end of 1987 and May 1989. From 1985 to 1988, there was a 25-billion-rand outflow of capital. The annual average inflation since 1977 has been 14.4 percent, fueled by high government expenditure (primarily in the defense and police budgets) and punitively high interest rates. Consequently, the economy has not grown in real terms since the early 1980s (Labor Research Department 1989: 2). Massive levels of black urban and rural unemployment, a demographic explosion in the black population, and a shrinking domestic capital base are the likely mechanisms for eroding apartheid, not any newfound sense of moral justice on the part of the South African government. Thus, while the direct impact of sanctions has been modest, their indirect contribution to the perceived economic insecurity of South Africa has been significant.

However, the rider that has to be appended to this interpretation is that in the short term, sanctions may constrain rather than promote the prospects for internal change; de Klerk, like Botha before him, cannot afford to be seen to comply with international pressures. The costs inflicted by such a perception would be further losses to the Conservative party and other far-right-wing groups in the South African political spectrum. This authoritarian paranoia was particularly evident in the weeks preceding the September 1989 elections for the tricameral parliament. Under its State of Emergency powers, the South African government ruthlessly suppressed even the most trivial anti-apartheid gestures of the newly formed Mass Democratic Movement. In doing so, it hoped to stem the tide of Afrikaner discontent, at least at the electoral level. Paradoxically, the release of Nelson Mandela may further limit de Klerk's options as he attempts to retain the National party's leadership of the white Afrikaner electorate.

The fundamental question raised in the introduction to this chapter was how to evaluate the effect of sanctions on political behavior. In considering this question, it is useful to consider the events of February 1990: Nelson Mandela was released, the bans imposed on political organizations such as the UDF and the ANC were removed, and "negotiations about negotiations" were raised between the government and the ANC. Can we now argue that sanctions have been effective? Mandela in his first speech upon his release from his long-term custody clearly saw a continuing role for sanctions. However, such direct positive correlations, though appealing in a normative sense, are questionable; such causal speculations are impossible to refute and, consequently, are unscientific and confined to the realm of opinion.

The most reliable answer we can offer is that sanctions can only have the possibility of being effective if that is the actual purpose for invoking them. Where they constitute symbolic gestures, no such expectation of effectiveness is justified.

NOTE

1. ECSC general Decisions are normally interpreted as having the equivalent authority of EC Regulations.

REFERENCES

Becker, Charles M. "Economic Sanctions against South Africa." *World Politics* 39(1987): 147–173.

Braun, Gerald, and H. Weiland. "Sanctions against South Africa: Placebo Politics?" In J. D. Brewer, ed., *Can South Africa Survive? Five Minutes to Midnight.* London: Macmillan, 1989.

Carter, Barry E. *International Economic Sanctions.* Cambridge: Cambridge University Press, 1989.

de Bassompierre, Guy. *Changing the Guard in Brussels.* New York: Praeger, 1988.

Denton, Geoffrey. "South and Southern Africa: Prospects for Ending Apartheid and Restoring Regional Stability." *Wilton Park Papers.* London: HMSO, no. 2, 1988.

Department of Trade (United Kingdom). *Code of Conduct for Companies with Interests in South Africa.* London: HMSO, Cmnd. 7233, 1977.

Edwards, Geoffrey. "Europe and the Falkland Islands Crisis 1982." *Journal of Common Market Studies* 22(1984): 295–313.

EPC Bulletin. Luxembourg: European Community, 1987.

Ethical Investment Research and Information Service. *EEC South African Code: The Reporting Practices of Selected United Kingdom Companies.* London: EIRIS, 1987.

European Council. *Thirty-Fourth European Council Meeting: Statement on South Africa.* The Hague: European Community, June 27, 1986.

Focus on South Africa. Johannesburg: South African Foundation, August 1989.

Foreign Ministers of the European Community. *Statement on South Africa.* Brussels: European Community, September 10, 1985.

———. *Statement on South Africa.* Brussels: European Community, September 15, 1986.

Hanlon, Joseph, and Roger Omond. *The Sanctions Handbook.* Harmondsworth, England: Penguin, 1987.

Holland, Martin. *The European Community and South Africa: European Political Co-operation under Strain.* London: Pinter, 1988a.

———. "The European Community and South Africa: In Search of a Policy for the 1990s." *International Affairs* 64(1988b): 415–30.

———. "The Other Side of Sanctions: Positive Initiatives for Southern Africa." *Journal of Modern African Studies* 26(1988c): 303–318.

———. "Disinvestment, Sanctions and the European Community's Code of Conduct in South Africa." *African Affairs* 88(1989): 529–547.

Labour Research Department. *South Africa: How British Business Profits from Apartheid.* London: LRD Publications, 1989.

Love, Janice. "The Potential Impact of Economic Sanctions against South Africa." *Journal of Modern African Studies* 26(1988): 91–111.

Southall, Roger. "Apartheid and the Case for Sanctions." *Journal of Commonwealth and Comparative Studies* 26(1988): 104–109.

Bibliography

Abramson, Paul R., John H. Aldrich, and David W. Rohde. *Change and Continuity in the 1980 Elections*. Washington, D.C.: Congressional Quarterly Press, 1983.

Aimer, Peter, and Jack Vowles. "Nuclear Free New Zealand and Rogernomics: The Survival of the Labour Government." Paper presented at the New Zealand Political Studies Conference, Wellington, New Zealand, 1989.

Akmuradov, I. "V. I. Lenin o Neobkhodimosti Ideinoi Bor'by s Religiei." *Turkmenskaia Iskra*, April 17, 1988.

Albinski, Henry. "The ANZUS Crisis: U.S. Policy Implications and Responses." In Jacob Bercovitch, ed., *ANZUS in Crisis: Alliance Management in International Affairs*. London: Macmillan, 1988.

Aldrich, John, John L. Sullivan, and Eugene Borgida. "Foreign Affairs and Issue Voting: Do Presidential Candidates 'Waltz Before a Blind Audience'?" *American Political Science Review* 83(1989): 123–142.

Alimov, A. "Biznes na Durmane." *Kommunist Tadzhikistana*, January 31, 1987.

Almond, Gabriel, and Sidney Verba. *The Civic Culture*. Boston: Little, Brown, 1965.

Arian, A., and M. Shamir. "The Primarily Political Functions of the Left-Right Continuum." *Comparative Politics* 15(1983): 139–158.

Arterton, F. Christopher. "The Impact of Watergate on Children's Attitudes toward Authority." *Political Science Quarterly* 89(1975): 269–288.

Arthur, Paul. *The People's Democracy: 1968–1973*. Belfast: Blackstaff Press, 1974.

Arthur, Paul, and Keith Jeffrey. *Northern Ireland since 1968*. Oxford: Basil Blackwell, 1988.

Azar, Edward E. *The Theory of Protracted Social Conflict and the Challenge of Transforming Conflict Situations*. Merriam Seminar Series on Research Frontiers. Vol. 20, bk. 2. Denver, Colo.: University of Denver Graduate School of International Studies, 1983.

Becker, Charles M. "Economic Sanctions against South Africa." *World Politics* 39(1987): 147–173.

Bell, Geoffrey. *The Protestants of Ulster.* London: Pluto Press, 1987.

Belozerova, L. "Vmesto Serdtsa-kamennyi Protez." *Pravda Ukrainy,* July 10, 1988.

Bercovitch, Jacob, ed. *ANZUS in Crisis: Alliance Management in International Affairs.* London: Macmillan, 1988.

Bew, Paul, and Henry Patterson. *The British State and the Ulster Crisis: From Wilson to Thatcher.* London: Verso, 1985.

Bogomolov, Oleg. "Kto Zhe Oshibalsia?" *Literaturnaia Gazeta,* March 16, 1988.

Bowen, Gordon L. "Presidential Action and Public Opinion about U.S. Nicaraguan Policy: Limits to the 'Rally 'Round the Flag' Syndrome." *P.S.* 12(1989): 793–799.

Box, George E. P., and Gwilym M. Jenkins. *Time Series Analysis: Forecasting and Control.* Rev. ed. San Francisco: Holden-Day, 1976.

Box, George E. P., and G. C. Tiao. "Intervention Analysis with Applications to Economic and Environmental Problems." *Journal of the American Statistical Association* 70(1975): 70–79.

Boyd, Andrew. *Brian Faulkner and the Crisis of Ulster Unionism.* Tralee, Ireland: Anvil Books, 1972.

Braun, Gerald, and H. Weiland. "Sanctions against South Africa: Placebo Politics?" In J. D. Brewer, ed., *Can South Africa Survive? Five Minutes to Midnight.* London: Macmillan, 1989.

Breslauer, George W. "Ideology and Learning in Soviet Third World Policy." *World Politics* 39(1987): 429–448.

Brody, Richard A. "International Crises: A Rallying Point for the President." *Public Opinion* 6(1984): 41–43.

Buckland, Patrick. *A History of Northern Ireland.* New York: Holmes and Meier, 1981.

Burnett, Alan. *The A–NZ–US Triangle.* Canberra: Strategic and Defence Studies Centre, Australian National University, 1988.

Burton, John W. "About Winning." *International Interactions* 12 (1985): 71–91.

Burton, Michael G., and John Higley. "Elite Settlements." *American Sociological Review* 52 (1987): 295–307.

Butler, David, and Donald Stokes. *Political Change in Britain.* New York: St. Martin's Press, 1969.

Callaghan, James. *A House Divided: The Dilemma of Northern Ireland.* London: William Collins Sons, 1973.

Campbell, Angus, Philip E. Converse, Warren E. Miller, and Donald Stokes. *The American Voter.* New York: Wiley, 1960.

Campbell, Donald T., and H. Laurence Ross. "The Connecticut Crackdown on Speeding." In Edward R. Tufte, ed., *The Quantitative Analysis of Social Problems.* Reading, Mass.: Addison-Wesley, 1970.

Carter, Barry E. *International Economic Sanctions.* Cambridge: Cambridge University Press, 1989.

Ceaser, James. "The Reagan Presidency and American Public Opinion." In Charles O. Jones, ed., *The Reagan Legacy: Promise and Performance.* Chatham, NJ: Chatham House, 1988.

Christchurch Press. Christchurch, New Zealand. December 18, 1984.

Citrin, Jack, and Donald Philip Green. "Presidential Leadership and the Resurgence of Trust in Government." *British Journal of Political Science* 16(1986): 431–453.

Clarke, Harold, William Mishler, and Paul Whiteley. "Recapturing the Falklands—Models of Conservative Popularity, 1979–1983." *British Journal of Political Science* 20(1990): 63–81.

Clarke, Harold, Marianne Stewart, and Gary Zuk. "Politics, Economics and Party Popularity in Britain, 1979–83." *Electoral Studies* 5(1986): 123–141.

Clements, Kevin. "New Zealand's Role in Promoting a Nuclear Free Pacific." *Journal of Peace Research* 25(1988): 395–410.

Clymer, Adam. "Perception of America's World Role Ten Years after Vietnam." Paper presented at the American Political Science Association Annual Meeting, New Orleans, Louisiana, 1985.

Contemporary Record. "Controversy: The Falklands Factor." Autumn 1987.

———. "The Falklands Factor: The Latest Blast." Winter 1988a.

———. "Controversy: The Falklands Factor." Spring 1988b.

Coser, Lewis. *The Functions of Social Conflict*. New York: Free Press, 1956.

Crewe, Ivor. "Is Britain's Two-Party System Really About to Crumble?" *Electoral Studies* 2(1982): 275–313.

———. "How to Win a Landslide Without Really Trying." In Austin Ranney, ed., *Britain at the Polls 1983*. Durham, N.C.: Duke University Press, 1985.

Dawson, Richard. *Public Opinion and Contemporary Disarray*. New York: Harper and Row, 1973.

de Bassompierre, Guy. *Changing the Guard in Brussels*. New York: Praeger, 1988.

Defence Committee of Enquiry. *Public Opinion Poll on Defence and Security: What New Zealanders Want*. Wellington: Government Printer, 1986.

The Defence Question: A Discussion Paper. Wellington: Government Printer, 1985.

De Fleur, Melvin L., and Sandra Ball-Rokeach. *Theories of Mass Communication*. New York: Longman, 1966.

Denton, Geoffrey. "South and Southern Africa: Prospects for Ending Apartheid and Restoring Regional Stability." *Wilton Park Papers*. London: HMSO, no. 2, 1988.

Department of Trade (United Kingdom). *Code of Conduct for Companies with Interests in South Africa*. London: HMSO, Cmnd. 7233, 1977.

Deutsch, Karl W. *Nationalism and Social Communication*. Cambridge, Mass.: MIT Press, 1953.

Deutsch, Richard, and Vivien Magowan. *Northern Ireland 1968–74: A Chronology of Events*. Vol. 3. Belfast: Blackstaff Press, 1975.

Devlin, Paddy. *The Fall of the N. I. Executive*. Belfast: Paddy Devlin, 1975.

Dillon, Martin, and Denis Lehane. *Political Murder in Northern Ireland*. Harmondsworth, England: Penguin, 1973.

Dunleavy, Patrick, and Christopher T. Husbands. *British Democracy at the Crossroads*. Boston and London: Allen and Unwin, 1985.

Dynin, I. M. *Zvezdy Podviga: Na Zemle Afganistana*. Moscow: Voennoe izdatel'stvo, 1985.

Easton, David, and Jack Dennis. *Children in the Political System*. New York: McGraw-Hill, 1969.

Economist. "How Britons Think." April 17, 1982a.

——. "We Like It so Far." April 24, 1982b.

——. "Satisfaction Peaks." May 8, 1982c.

——. "End of War." June 26, 1982d.

Edwards, Geoffrey. "Europe and the Falkland Islands Crisis 1982." *Journal of Common Market Studies* 22(1984): 295–313.

Eisenstadt, S. N. *Israel Society*. London: Weidenfeld and Nicolson, 1967.

Elms, Alan C. *Personality in Politics*. New York: Harcourt Brace Jovanovich, 1976.

EPC Bulletin. Luxembourg: European Community, 1987.

Epstein, Leon. *British Politics in the Suez Crisis*. Urbana, Ill.: Illinois University Press, 1964.

Ethical Investment Research and Information Service. *EEC South African Code: The Reporting Practices of Selected United Kingdom Companies*. London: EIRIS, 1987.

European Council. *Thirty-Fourth European Council Meeting: Statement on South Africa*. The Hague: European Community, June 27, 1986.

Farrell, Michael. *Northern Ireland: The Orange State*. London: Pluto Press, 1976.

Faulkner, Brian. *Memoirs of a Statesman*. London: Weidenfeld and Nicolson, 1978.

Feldman, Stanley. "Economic Self-Interest and Political Behavior." *American Journal of Political Science* 26(1982): 446–466.

Focus on South Africa. Johannesburg: South African Foundation, August 1989.

Foreign Affairs Group. *New Zealand and Australian Public Opinion on Nuclear Ships and ANZUS*. Report prepared for the Parliament of Australia. Canberra: Legislative Research Service, 1985.

Foreign Ministers of the European Community. *Statement on South Africa*. Brussels: European Community, September 10, 1985.

——. *Statement on South Africa*. Brussels, European Community, September 15, 1986.

Freedman, Lawrence. *Britain and the Falklands War*. New York and Oxford: Basil Blackwell, 1988.

Fukuyama, Francis. "Soviet Strategy in the Third World." In Andrzej Korbonski, and Francis Fukuyama, eds., *The Soviet Union and the Third World: The Last Three Decades*. Ithaca and London: Cornell University Press, 1987.

Gallup, George H. *The Gallup International Public Opinion Polls: Great Britain 1937–1975*. Vol. 1. New York: Random House, 1976.

Gallup Poll. *Gallup Opinion Index*. No. 180, 1980a.

——. *Gallup Opinion Index*. No. 182, 1980b.

——. *Gallup Opinion Index*. No. 183, 1980c.

——. *Gallup Report*. No. 218, 1983.

——. *Gallup Report*. No. 246, 1986.

——. "Public More Upbeat about State of Nation." December 25, 1988a.

——. *Gallup Report*. No. 274, 1988b.

——. *Gallup Report*. No. 277, 1988c.

Gilmour, Robert S., and Robert B. Lamb. *Political Alienation in Contemporary America*. New York: St. Martin's Press, 1975.

Greenstein, Fred. *The Hidden-Handed Presidency*. New York: Basic Books, 1982.

Grielsammer, A. *Les Communistes Israéliens*. Paris: Presses de la Fondation Nationale des Sciences Politiques, 1978.

Gutmann, E. "Political Parties and Groups: Stability and Change." In M. Lissak and E. Gutmann, eds., *The Israeli Political System* (in Hebrew). Tel-Aviv:

Am Oved., 1977.

Haddad, S., R. D. McLaurin, and E. A. Nakhleh. "Minorities in Containment: The Arabs of Israel." In R. D. McLaurin, ed., *The Political Role of Minority Groups in the Middle East*. New York: Praeger, 1979.

Hamill, Desmond. *Pig in the Middle: The Army in Northern Ireland 1969–1984*. London: Methuen, 1984.

Hanlon, Joseph, and Roger Omond. *The Sanctions Handbook*. Harmondsworth, England: Penguin, 1987.

Harris, Louis. *The Anguish of Change*. New York: Norton, 1973.

————. *The Harris Survey*. No. 22, 1983.

Harris Poll. No. 103, 1988.

————. No. 1, 1989a.

————. No. 4, 1989b.

Hastings, Max. *Ulster 1969: The Fight for Civil Rights in Northern Ireland*. London: Victor Gollancz, 1970.

Hastings, Max, and Simon Jenkins. *The Battle for the Falklands*. New York and London: Norton, 1983.

Hess, Robert, and Judith Torney. *The Development of Political Attitudes in Children*. Chicago: Aldine, 1967.

Hibbs, Douglas A., Jr. "On Analyzing the Effects of Policy Interventions: Box-Jenkins and Box-Tiao vs. Structural Equation Models." In David Heise, ed., *Sociological Methodology 1977*. San Francisco: Jossey-Bass, 1977.

Holland, Martin. *The European Community and South Africa: European Political Co-operation under Strain*. London: Pinter, 1988a.

————. "The European Community and South Africa: In Search of a Policy for the 1990s." *International Affairs* 64(1988b): 415–30.

————. "The Other Side of Sanctions: Positive Initiatives for Southern Africa." *Journal of Modern African Studies* 26(1988c): 303–318.

————. "Disinvestment, Sanctions and the European Community's Code of Conduct in South Africa." *African Affairs* 88(1989): 529–547.

Hosner, Stephen T., and Thomas W. Wolfe. *Soviet Policy and Practice toward Third World Conflicts*. Lexington, Mass.: Lexington Books, 1983.

Hough, Jerry F. *The Struggle for the Third World: Soviet Debates and American Options*. Washington, D.C.: Brookings Institution, 1986.

Ichilov, O. "Citizenship Orientations of Two Israeli Minority Groups: Israeli-Arab and Eastern-Jewish Youth." Tel-Aviv University (unpublished), 1983.

Ichilov, O., and N. Nave. "The Good Citizen as Viewed by Israeli Adolescents." *Comparative Politics* 13(1981): 361–376.

Ignatiev, R. "S Grifom 'Sekretno'. " *Izvestiia*, July 15, 1988.

Inglehart, Ronald. "The Silent Revolution in Europe: Intergenerational Change in Post-Industrial Societies." *American Political Science Review* 65(1971): 991–1017.

————. "Post-materialism in an Environment of Insecurity." *American Political Science Review* 75(1981): 880–900.

————. "The Renaissance of Political Culture." *American Political Science Review* 82(1988): 1203–1230.

Jaros, Dean, Herbert Hirsch, and Frederick J. Fleron, Jr. "The Malevolent Leader: Political Socialization in an American Subculture." *American Political Science*

Review 62(1968): 564–575.

Katz, Elihu. "The Two-Step Flow of Communication: An Up-to-Date Report on an Hypothesis." *Public Opinion Quarterly* 21(1957): 61–78.

Katz, Mark N. *The Third World in Soviet Military Thought.* Baltimore, Md.: Johns Hopkins University Press, 1982.

Kelley, Stanley. *Interpreting Elections.* Princton, N.J.: Princeton University Press, 1983.

Kernell, Samuel. "Explaining Presidential Popularity." *American Political Science Review* 72(1978): 506–522.

———. *Going Public: New Strategies of Presidential Leadership.* Washington, D.C.: Congressional Quarterly Press, 1986.

Key, V. O. *Public Opinion and American Democracy.* New York: Knopf, 1961.

Kiewiet, Roderick D. *Macroeconomics and Macropolitics.* Chicago: University of Chicago Press, 1983.

Kommunist Tadzhikistana, December 30, 1987.

Konovalov, Valery. "Pesni Veteranov Afganistana." *Radio Liberty Research* RS 50/88, June 6, 1988.

Kriesberg, Louis. *Social Conflicts.* 2nd ed. Englewood Cliffs, N.J.: Prentice-Hall, 1973.

Labour Research Department. *South Africa: How British Business Profits from Apartheid.* London: LRD Publications, 1989.

Lamare, James W. "Party Identification and Voting Behaviour in New Zealand." *Political Science* 36(1984): 1–9.

———. "International Conflict: ANZUS and New Zealand Public Opinion." *Journal of Conflict Resolution* 31(1987a): 420–437.

———. "International Conflict and Opinion Change in New Zealand." *Public Opinion Quarterly* 51 (1987b): 392–399.

———. "Gender and Public Opinion: Defense and Nuclear Issues in New Zealand." *Journal of Peace Research* 26(1989): 285–296.

Landau, J. M. *The Arabs in Israel: A Political Study.* London: Oxford University Press, 1969.

Lane, Robert E. "The Politics of Consensus in an Age of Affluence." *American Political Science Review* 59(1965): 874–895.

———. *Political Thinking and Consciousness.* Chicago: Markham, 1969.

Lange, David. "New Zealand Foreign Policy: The Nuclear Issue and Great Power–Small State Relations." The George Herbert Walker, Jr., Lecture, Yale University, 1989.

Lasswell, Harold D. "Conflict and Leadership: The Process of Decision and the Nature of Authority." In Anthony de Reuck and Julie Knight, eds., *Conflict and Society.* London: J. and A. Churchill, 1966.

Lawrence, D. "Procedural Norms and Tolerance: A Reassessment." *American Political Science Review* 70(1976): 80–100.

Lee, Jack. "Rally 'Round the Flag: Foreign Policy Events and Presidential Popularity." *Presidential Studies Quarterly* 7(1977): 252–255.

Levine, R. A., and D. T. Campbell. *Ethnocentrism: Theories of Conflict, Ethnic Attitudes, and Group Behavior.* New York: Wiley, 1972.

Levy, Jack, and Lily Vakili. "External Scapegoating by Authoritarian Regimes: Argentina in the Falklands/Malvinas Case." Paper presented at the Annual

Meeting of the American Political Science Association, Atlanta, Georgia, 1989.

Lewin, Kurt. *Resolving Social Conflicts.* New York: Harper and Row, 1948.

Lindblom, Charles. "The Science of Muddling Through." *Public Administration Review* 19(1959): 79–88.

Lipset, Seymour M. "Feeling Better: Measuring the Nation's Confidence." *Public Opinion* 6(1983): 6–9, 56–58.

Lipset, Seymour M., and William Schneider. *The Confidence Gap.* New York: Free Press, 1983.

Literaturnaia Gazeta, February 17, 1988.

Love, Janice. "The Potential Impact of Economic Sanctions against South Africa." *Journal of Modern African Studies* 26(1988): 91–111.

Lustick, I. *Arabs in The Jewish State: Israel's Control of a National Minority.* Austin: University of Texas Press, 1980.

MacFarlane, S. Neil. *Superpower Rivalry and Third World Radicalism: The Idea of National Liberation.* London: Croom Helm, 1985.

Maddox, William S., and Roger Handberg. "Presidential Affect and Chauvinism among Children." *American Journal of Political Science* 23(1979): 426–433.

Maudling, Reginald. *Memoirs.* London: Sidgwick and Jackson, 1978.

McCleary, Richard, and Richard A. Hay, Jr. *Applied Time Series Analysis.* Beverly Hills, Calif., and London: Sage, 1980.

McClosky, Herbert. "Consensus and Ideology in American Politics." *American Political Science Review* 58(1964): 561–382.

McMillan, Stuart. *Neither Confirm nor Deny.* Wellington: Allen and Unwin, 1985.

Miller, Arthur H. "Political Issues and Trust in Government, 1964–1970." *American Political Science Review* 68(1974): 951–972.

Mishler, William, Marilyn Hoskin, and Roy Fitzgerald. "British Parties in the Balance: A Time Series Analysis of Long-Term Trends in Labour and Conservative Support." *British Journal of Political Science* 19(1989): 211–236.

Monroe, Kirsten. *Presidential Popularity and the Economy.* New York: Praeger, 1984.

Moon, J. Donald. "The Logic of Political Inquiry: A Synthesis of Opposed Perspectives." In Fred I. Greenstein and Nelson W. Polsby, eds., *Handbook of Political Science.* Vol. 1. Reading, Mass.: Addison-Wesley, 1975.

Morgan, Michael. "How the British Created the Provos." *Fortnight* 275(1989): 12–13.

Mueller, John. *War, Presidents and Public Opinion.* New York: Wiley, 1973.

Nahaylo, Bohdan. "Ukrainian Mother's Protest Attracts Numerous Letters on the Afghanistan Theme." *Radio Liberty Research* RL 188/87, May 18, 1987.

Newhouse, John. "Profiles: Margaret Thatcher." *The New Yorker*, February 10, 1986.

New Zealand Herald. March 30, 1983.

———. March 22, 1985a.

———. April 3, 1985b.

New Zealand Times. September 23, 1984.

NOP Market Research, Ltd. "Public Opinion in Northern Ireland." NOP/7513, London: NOP Market Research, 1974.

Norpoth, Helmut. "Economics, Politics and the Cycle of Presidential Popularity." *Political Behavior* 6(1984): 253–273.

———. "The Falklands War and Government Popularity in Britain: Rally without Consequence or Surge without Decline?" *Electoral Studies* 6(1987a): 3–16.

———. "Guns and Butter and Government Popularity in Britain." *American Political Science Review* 81(1987b): 949–959.

North, Robert C. "International Conflict and Integration: Problems of Research." In M. Sherif, ed., *Intergroup Group Relations and Leadership*. New York: Wiley, 1962.

Olson, Mancur. *The Logic of Collective Action*. Cambridge, Mass.: Harvard University Press, 1971.

O'Neill, Terence. *The Autobiography of Terence O'Neill*. London: Rupert Hart-Davis, 1972.

Ostrom, Charles W., and Dennis M. Simon. "Promise and Performance: A Dynamic Model of Presidential Popularity." *American Political Science Review* 79(1985): 334–358.

———. "The Man in the Teflon Suit: The Environmental Connection, Political Drama, and Popular Support in the Reagan Presidency." *Public Opinion Quarterly* 53(1989): 353–387.

Papp, Daniel S. *Soviet Perceptions of the Developing World in the 1980's: The Ideological Basis*. Lexington, Mass.: Lexington Books, 1985.

Peres, Y. "Modernization and Nationalism in the Identity of the Israeli Arab." *Middle East Journal* 24(1970): 479–492.

———. "Ethnic Relations in Israel." *American Journal of Sociology* 76(1971): 1021–1047.

Peres, Y., and N. Yuval-Davis. "Some Observations on the National Identity of the Israeli Arab." *Human Relations* 22(1969): 219–233.

Petrash, Iu. " 'Privychki' Ostoiutsia Navsegda?" *Sovetskaia Kirgiziia*, May 14, 1988.

Pravda, January 21, 1988.

Prothro, James W., and C. W. Grigg. "Fundamental Principles of Democracy: Bases of Agreement and Disagreement." *Journal of Politics* 22 (1960): 276–294.

Rabiev, V. "V Klass . . . s Koranom?" *Kommunist Tadzhikistana*, January 31, 1987.

Radio Liberty Research. "Soviet Veterans of the War in Afghanistan: A New Social Force?" RS 198/86, December 9, 1986.

———. "Pamiati A. Bennigsena (1913–1988)." RS 58/88, July 5, 1988.

Ragimova, I. "Pochet bez Uvazheniia." *Bakinskii Rabochii*, July 8, 1988.

Reagan, Ronald. Farewell Address to the Nation. 1989.

Rees, Merlyn. *Northern Ireland: A Personal Perspective*. London: Methuen, 1985.

Reese, Trevor. *Australia, New Zealand and the United States*. London: Oxford University Press, 1969.

Rejai, Mostafa. "Theory and Research in the Study of Revolutionary Personnel." In Ted Robert Gurr, ed., *The Handbook of Political Conflict*. New York: Free Press, 1980.

Rekhess, E. *The Israeli Arabs since 1967: The Issue of Identity* (in Hebrew). Sekirot No. 1 Tel Aviv: Shiloah Center, Tel Aviv University, 1976.

Rodgers, Harrell, and Edgar Lewis. "Student Attitudes toward Mr. Nixon: The Consequences of Negative Attitudes toward a President for Political System Support." *American Politics Quarterly* 3(1975): 423–436.

Roll, Charles W., and Albert H. Cantril. *Polls: Their Use and Misuse in Politics*. New York: Basic Books, 1972.

Rootes, C. A. "On the Social Structural Sources of Political Conflict: An Approach from the Sociology of Knowledge." In Louis Kriesberg, ed., *Research in Social Movements, Conflicts and Change.* Vol. 5, Greenwich, Conn.: JAI Press, 1983.

Sanders, David, Hugh Ward, David Marsh, and Tony Fletcher. "Government Popularity and the Falklands War: A Reassessment." *British Journal of Political Science* 17(1987): 281–313.

Schnall, D. *Radical Dissent in Contemporary Israeli Politics: Cracks in the Wall.* New York: Praeger, 1979.

Shamir, Michal, and John L. Sullivan. "Political Tolerance and Intolerance in Israel." Final Report to the United States–Israel Binational Science Foundation, 2297/80, 1982.

———. "The Political Context of Tolerance: The United States and Israel." *American Political Science Review* 77 (1983): 911–928.

Shapiro, Robert Y., and Benjamin I. Page. "Foreign Policy and the Rational Public." *Journal of Conflict Resolution* 32(1988): 211–247.

Shapiro, Y. *The Formative Years of the Israeli Labor Party: The Organization of Power, 1914–1930.* Beverly Hills, Calif.: Sage, 1976.

———. *Israeli Democracy* (in Hebrew). Ramat-Gan, Israel: Massada, 1977.

Shefter, Martin. "Political Parties, Political Mobilization, and Political Demobilization." In Thomas Ferguson and Joel Rogers, eds., *The Political Economy.* Armonk, N.Y.: M. E. Sharpe, 1984.

Shuster, Savik. "Problema Afganiskikh Veteranov v Sovetskom Obschchestve." *Radio Liberty Research* RS 198/86, December 9, 1986.

Sigel, Roberta S., and Marilyn Brookes. "Becoming Critical about Politics." In Richard G. Niemi and Associates, ed., *The Politics of Future Citizens.* San Francisco: Jossey-Bass, 1974.

Simoniia, N. "Chestno Vesti Nauchnuiu Diskussiiu." *Aziia i Afrika Segodnia* No. 6, June 6, 1988.

Simpson, Alan. "Hamilton Electoral Surveys—1987." Paper presented at the New Zealand Political Studies Conference, Wellington, New Zealand, 1989.

Smooha, S. *Israel: Pluralism and Conflict.* Berkeley, Calif.: University of California Press, 1978.

———. *The Orientation and Politicization of the Arab Minority in Israel.* Monographs on the Middle East, 2. Haifa: Jewish-Arab Center, University of Haifa, 1980.

———. "Minority Responses in a Plural Society: A Typology of the Arabs in Israel." *Sociology and Social Research* 67(1983): 436–456.

Smooha, S., and D. Peretz. "The Arabs in Israel." *Journal of Conflict Resolution* 26 (1982): 451–484.

Snyder, Jack. "International Leverage on Soviet Domestic Change." *World Politics* 62(1989): 1–30.

Southall, Roger. "Apartheid and the Case for Sanctions." *Journal of Commonwealth and Comparative Studies* 26(1988): 104–109.

Soviet News. February 2, 1990.

Statistical Abstract of Israel 1983. No. 34. Jerusalem: Central Bureau of Statistics, 1983.

Stein, Arthur A. "Conflict and Cohesion." *Journal of Conflict Resolution* 20(1976): 143–172.

Stouffer, Samuel. *Communism, Conformity, and Civil Liberties*. New York: Double-
    day, 1955.
Strachan, David. "A Party Transformed: Organisational Change in the New Zea-
    land Labour Party." In Hyam Gold, ed., *New Zealand Politics in Perspective*.
    Wellington: Longman Paul, 1985.
Sullivan, John L., G. E. Marcus, S. Feldman, and J. Piereson. "The Sources of
    Political Tolerance: A Multivariate Analysis." *American Political Science Re-
    view* 74(1981): 92–106.
Sullivan, John L., J. Piereson, and G. E. Marcus. "An Alternative Conceptualization
    of Political Tolerance." *American Political Science Review* 73(1979): 781–794.
———. *Political Tolerance and American Democracy*. Chicago: University of Chicago
    Press, 1982.
Sullivan, John L., Michal Shamir, Nigel Roberts, and Patrick Walsh. "Political
    Intolerance and the Structure of Mass Attitudes: A Study of the United States,
    Israel, and New Zealand." *Comparative Political Studies* 17(1984): 319–344.
Sullivan, John L., Michal Shamir, Patrick Walsh, and Nigel Roberts. *Political Tol-
    erance in Context: Support for Unpopular Minorities in Israel, New Zealand, and
    the United States*. Boulder, Colo.: Westview Press, 1985.
Sumner, W. G. *Folkways*. New York: Ginn, 1906.
Sunday Times of London Insight Team. *War in the Falklands*. New York and London:
    Harper and Row, 1982.
Tessler, M. A. "Israel's Arabs and the Palestinian Problem." *Middle East Journal*
    31(1977): 313–329.
Theroux, Paul. *The Kingdom by the Sea*. New York: Washington Square Press, 1984.
Tsagolov, K. M. "Afganistan—Predvaritel'nye Itogi." *Ogonek* No. 30, 1988.
Tsagolova, Laura. In *Sobesednik* No. 1, January 1987.
Tsemah, M. "The Attitudes of the Jewish Majority in Israel Towards the Arab
    Minority" (in Hebrew). Research Report. Jerusalem: Van Leer Foundation,
    1980.
Valkenier, Elizabeth K. *The Soviet Union and the Third World: An Economic Bind*.
    New York: Praeger, 1983.
White, Barry. *John Hume: Statesman of the Troubles*. Belfast: Blackstaff Press, 1984.
Wilson, J. V. "New Zealand's Participation in International Organisations." In
    T. C. Larkin, ed., *New Zealand's External Relations*. Wellington: New Zealand
    Institute of Public Administration, 1962.
Wise, Sally. " 'A War Should Never Have Happened': Soviet Citizens Assess the
    War in Afghanistan." *Radio Liberty Research* RL 226/88, June 1, 1988.
Worcester, Robert. "Comment." *Electoral Studies* 2(1982): 84.
Worcester, Robert, and Simon Jenkins. "Britain Rallies 'Round the Prime Minister."
    Public Opinion 5(1982): 53–55.
Yankelovich, Daniel, and Larry Kaagen. "Assertive America." *Foreign Affairs*
    59(1981): 696–713.
Yuval-Davis, N. "Mazpen: The Israeli Socialist Organization" (in Hebrew with
    English abstract). Papers in Sociology. Jerusalem: Eliezer Kaplan School
    Economics and Social Sciences, Hebrew University, 1977.
Zimmerman, William. *Soviet Perspectives on International Relations*. Princeton, N.J.:
    Princeton University Press, 1969.

Index

ABOUT THE CONTRIBUTORS

JAMES W. LAMARE is Senior Lecturer and Head of the Department of Political Science, University of Canterbury, Christchurch, New Zealand. His most recent articles have appeared in the *Journal of Conflict Resolution*, the *Public Opinion Quarterly*, the *Journal of Peace Research*, and *Political Psychology* (with Thomas W. Milburn). He is also the author of *What Rules America?*

GAVAN DUFFY is Assistant Professor of Political Science at Syracuse University.

NATHALIE FRENSLEY is a doctoral candidate in government at the University of Texas at Austin.

MARTIN HOLLAND is Senior Lecturer in Political Science at the University of Canterbury.

W. KEITH JACKSON is Professor of Political Science at the University of Canterbury.

HELMUT NORPOTH is Professor of Political Science at the State University of New York, Stony Brook.

T. H. RIGBY is Professor of Political Science at the Research School of the Social Sciences, Australian National University.

MICHAL SHAMIR is Associate Professor of Political Science at Tel Aviv University.

JOHN L. SULLIVAN is Professor of Political Science at the University of Minnesota.